High-Frequency Trading

The Race to Zero Latency

William Johnson

Published by HiTeX Press

For permissions and other inquiries, write to:
P.O. Box 3132, Framingham, MA 01701, USA

Contents

Preface

Welcome to a journey through one of the most electrifying, complex, and innovative domains in modern finance: High-Frequency Trading (HFT). Picture this—you're in a sophisticated trading room, where milliseconds make the difference between colossal gains and devastating losses. Here, algorithms, not humans, execute trades in the blink of an eye, leveraging cutting-edge technology to outperform the competition. As someone who seeks to understand the intricacies of stock trading and investment, you are about to delve into the compelling world of HFT, where the pace is relentless, and the rewards are extraordinary.

High-Frequency Trading is not merely a buzzword; it is a symbiosis of finance and technology, transforming market landscapes globally. This book, "High-Frequency Trading: The Race to Zero Latency," illuminates the pulse-pounding arena of HFT, unraveling its complexities in an accessible yet thorough manner. Whether you are an aspiring trader, a finance student, or a seasoned professional, the insights and knowledge captured within these pages will arm you with a profound understanding of the field's core principles and evolving dynamics.

The core message of this book is straightforward: mastering HFT requires a blend of financial acumen, technological prowess, and relentless innovation. But it is not just about making money at lightning speed; it is about understanding market microstructures, optimizing algorithms, managing risks, and navigating a stringent regulatory landscape. This book provides a comprehensive exploration of these essential topics, structured to elevate your grasp of both theoretical concepts and practical implementations.

Imagine yourself equipped with the knowledge to dissect market microstructures and develop sophisticated trading algorithms. Envision understanding the technological underpinnings that empower HFT, from reducing latency to leveraging machine learning for predictive analytics. Consider the confidence you will gain from grasping effective risk management strategies and staying compliant with regulatory standards. The potential to transform your trading strategies and decision-making processes is immense.

Starting with a concise introduction to HFT, the book unfolds to cover market microstructures, algorithm design, latency, risk management, and regulation—each chapter meticulously crafted to build your knowledge step by step. Real-world applications and ethical considerations are not sidelined but instead are addressed with earnest insight and detailed case studies. This ensures that your learning is not confined to theoretical frameworks but is grounded in practical understanding and real-world relevance.

As you turn these pages, you will explore vivid examples and illustrative scenarios that bring the dry statistics to life. Visualize strategies such as arbitrage and market making in action, and understand how they operate in the split-second world of HFT. Appreciate the rigorous backtesting and simulations that hone these strategies before they ever reach the live markets. Each segment of the book is designed to keep you engaged and motivated, with a clear emphasis on practical application and skill development.

Finally, this exploration would not be complete without addressing the ethical considerations intrinsic to high-speed trading. HFT, with its rapid pace and significant impact, has raised questions about market fairness and investor protection. This book does not shy away from these debates but rather facilitates a balanced discourse to help you form an informed perspective.

Dive in, challenge yourself, and engage with the material. This book promises to be more than just a guide—it is a gateway to mastering the electrifying world of High-Frequency Trading. Equip yourself with knowledge, sharpen your analytical skills, and prepare to thrive in a domain where milliseconds matter and innovation is king. Welcome to "High-Frequency Trading: The Race to Zero Latency." Let's begin this fascinating journey together.

Chapter 1

Introduction to High-Frequency Trading

High-Frequency Trading (HFT) is a sophisticated mechanism in financial markets where trading desks utilize highly advanced algorithms and high-speed communications networks to execute large volumes of orders at rapid speeds. This chapter delves into the fundamental concepts and historical development of HFT, identifying the key players and basic terminology critical for understanding this domain. It explains HFT's role within financial markets, outlining the benefits and criticisms associated with these high-speed transactions. Additionally, it offers a glimpse into the operational dynamics of an HFT professional's daily routine, providing a well-rounded introduction to this transformative aspect of modern trading.

1.1 Definition and Scope of High-Frequency Trading

High-Frequency Trading (HFT) represents a segment of electronic trading characterized by extremely high speeds and large volumes of trade execution. At its core, HFT relies on sophisticated algorithms and state-of-the-art technological infrastructures to execute orders in fractions of a second, often capitalizing on minor price discrepancies that exist for just milliseconds.

To understand the full scope and impact of HFT in today's financial markets, it is essential to start with a precise definition and then delve into its operational mechanics, implications, and distinctive features.

Definition of High-Frequency Trading: High-Frequency Trading can be defined as a method of trading that utilizes complex algorithms to analyze multiple markets and high-speed data feeds. It allows traders to execute orders based on market conditions in time frames significantly shorter than traditional trading. HFT typically involves the following characteristics:

- *Ultra-Low Latency:* The time delays, known as latency, are measured in microseconds or nanoseconds. Firms often invest heavily in reducing latency to gain a competitive edge.

- *Algorithm-Driven Decision Making:* Decisions to buy or sell are made by algorithms, eliminating the slow, manual processes.

- *High Order Volumes:* A considerable number of orders are executed within short periods, even though many may be canceled almost immediately after submission.

- *Short Holding Periods:* Positions are typically held for very short durations, from milliseconds to a few minutes. The strategies don't rely on long-term market trends but on transient opportunities.

These attributes make HFT distinct from traditional trading forms, which usually involve higher latency, longer holding times, and manual intervention.

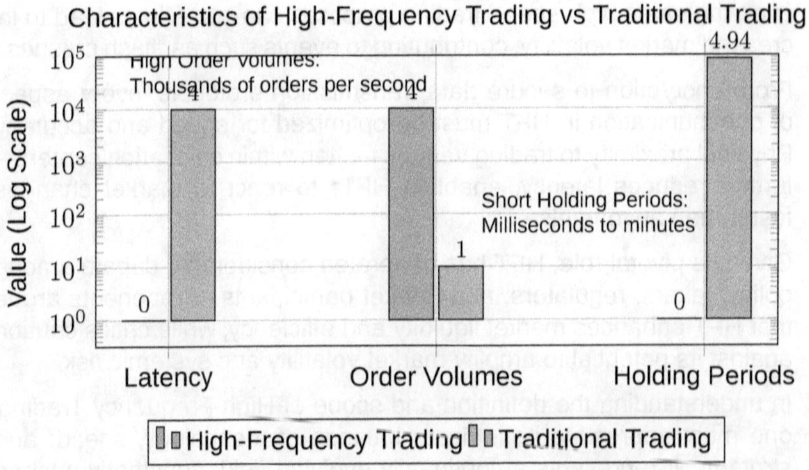

Scope of High-Frequency Trading: The scope of HFT extends to various aspects of the financial markets, influencing liquidity, market behavior, and the structure of trading platforms.

Market Making: HFT firms often act as market makers, providing liquidity to the markets. They place thousands of buy and sell orders to capture small spreads, facilitating smoother and faster transactions for other market participants.

Arbitrage: One of the most common HFT strategies is arbitrage, exploiting small price differentials in different markets. This could include statistical arbitrage, index arbitrage, or cross-asset arbitrage. By quickly identifying and reacting to these inefficiencies, HFTs ensure that prices across markets remain aligned.

Algorithmic Implementation Shortfall: This strategy seeks to minimize the execution cost of large orders. Algorithms break down large orders into smaller parts, executing them across different times and venues to avoid significant impact on the market price.

Liquidity Detection: Some HFT firms use algorithms to detect large orders from other traders. The algorithms might identify patterns in the order book that indicate a large trade is being executed. This information may be used to front-run the order or position themselves advantageously.

Impact on Market Dynamics: The ultra-rapid execution of trades by HFT firms contributes to high market liquidity and tighter bid-ask spreads, which can be beneficial for all market participants. However, the same high-speed trading practices can sometimes lead to increased market volatility, contributing to events such as "flash crashes."

From encryption to secure data transmission protocols, every aspect of communication in HFT must be optimized for speed and accuracy. Physical proximity to trading venues—often within colocation centers—further reduces latency, enabling HFTs to react to market changes faster than anyone else.

Given its pivotal role, HFT has generated considerable debate among policymakers, regulators, and market participants. Proponents argue that HFT enhances market liquidity and efficiency, while critics caution against its potential to amplify market volatility and systemic risk.

In understanding the definition and scope of High-Frequency Trading, one must appreciate its intricate balance of technology, speed, and strategy. It represents a continually evolving field, constantly pushed by advancements in computing power and connectivity. Whether HFT serves as a stabilizing force or a disruptive influence depends largely on its application and the regulatory frameworks governing its use.

1.2 Historical Development of HFT

High-Frequency Trading (HFT) as we know it today is the culmination of numerous technological advancements and regulatory changes that have occurred over several decades. Its development is deeply intertwined with the evolution of financial markets, computer technology, and telecommunications infrastructure. To fully appreciate the scope of HFT, one must trace its roots back to the pivotal moments and innovations that shaped its emergence in the financial trading landscape.

The inception of HFT can be traced back to the 1970s, when the advent of electronic trading systems began revolutionizing the way financial markets operated. Prior to this, trading was primarily conducted through physical exchanges, where traders would manually execute orders in an open outcry environment. This method was inherently slow and prone to human error. The introduction of electronic systems, such as the New York Stock Exchange's (NYSE) Designated Order Turnaround (DOT) system, marked the beginning of a move towards automation. The DOT system allowed for orders to be sent electronically to the exchange floor, significantly speeding up the execution process.

The 1980s and 1990s saw further advancements with the development of computer networking and software technology. The establishment of the NASDAQ in 1971, as the world's first electronic stock market, played a crucial role in this transformation. NASDAQ's automated trading system enabled the processing of transactions more efficiently than traditional exchange-based systems. During this period, trading firms began to leverage algorithmic strategies to facilitate market making, arbitrage, and other trading activities, laying the groundwork for what would eventually become HFT.

A significant milestone in the historical development of HFT occurred in 1998 when the Securities and Exchange Commission (SEC) in the United States authorized the use of electronic communication networks (ECNs) for trade execution. ECNs created a platform for matching buy and sell orders outside of traditional stock exchanges, enhancing the speed and efficiency of trading. This regulatory change dramatically increased the capacity for high-speed transactions and provided the technological infrastructure necessary for HFT to thrive.

The early 2000s marked the beginning of explosive growth in HFT. This period was characterized by rapid advancements in computer processing power, the proliferation of high-speed internet, and the implementation of sophisticated trading algorithms. The introduction of co-location services, where trading firms could place their servers in close proximity to exchange data centers, further reduced latency and facilitated the rise of HFT. By minimizing the time it took to send and receive data, co-location provided HFT firms with a significant competitive advantage, allowing them to execute trades in fractions of a second.

Amidst these technological innovations, the regulatory environment continued to evolve, often reacting to the growing prevalence of HFT. The SEC's Regulation National Market System (Reg NMS), implemented in 2007, aimed to modernize the national market system and ensure fair competition among all types of trading venues. Reg NMS introduced rules that affected how orders were routed and executed, which inadvertently spurred further growth in HFT as firms sought to capitalize on new arbitrage opportunities created by the regulation.

The financial crisis of 2008 and the subsequent market turbulence highlighted both the potential benefits and risks associated with HFT. On one hand, HFT was credited with providing liquidity and narrowing bid-ask spreads, which are generally seen as positive for the efficiency of financial markets. On the other hand, critics argued that HFT contributed to volatility and systemic risk, exemplified by events such as the Flash Crash of May 6, 2010. During the Flash Crash, major U.S.

stock indices experienced a rapid and severe decline before recovering just as quickly, with HFT activities being scrutinized in the aftermath.

Post-2010, HFT has continued to evolve, driven by ongoing technological innovation and regulatory adjustments. Advances in machine learning and artificial intelligence have increasingly been integrated into trading algorithms, enabling more complex decision-making processes that can adapt to market conditions in real time. At the same time, global regulators have introduced measures to address the potential risks posed by HFT, including enhanced market surveillance and circuit breakers designed to prevent disorderly trading conditions.

The development of HFT is a testament to the dynamic interplay between technology, regulation, and market forces. It represents a significant shift towards automation and speed in financial trading, reshaping the landscape in profound ways. As we move forward, HFT will undoubtedly continue to be influenced by new advancements in technology and evolving regulatory frameworks, making it an ever-interesting area of finance to observe and study.

1.3 Key Players in the HFT Ecosystem

Understanding the high-frequency trading (HFT) ecosystem necessitates a deep dive into the entities that shape this sophisticated and fast-paced domain. The HFT landscape is not only occupied by the trading firms that execute rapid transactions but also supported and influenced by various crucial players. These include exchanges and trading venues, technology providers, regulatory bodies, and institutional investors. Each of these entities plays a pivotal role in the seamless operation and evolution of high-frequency trading, forming an interconnected web that drives the ecosystem forward.

- **1. High-Frequency Trading Firms**

  At the core of the HFT ecosystem are the trading firms themselves. These entities design and deploy advanced algorithms to capitalize on market inefficiencies and small price discrepancies, executing trades at lightning speed. Leading HFT firms, such as Citadel Securities, Virtu Financial, and Tower Research Capital, invest significantly in technology, data analysis, and infrastructure to maintain their competitive edge. These firms employ quant researchers, data scientists, and software engineers to continually refine their trading strategies. The hallmark of successful HFT firms lies in their ability to manage latency—optimizing the time it takes for their trades to be executed in the market.

- **2. Exchanges and Trading Venues**

  Exchanges such as the New York Stock Exchange (NYSE), NASDAQ, and various other global trading venues play a critical role in the HFT ecosystem. These platforms provide the necessary infrastructure for trade execution, offering services that facilitate the rapid matching of buy and sell orders. With the rise of HFT, many exchanges have developed co-location services, allowing HFT firms to place their servers in close physical proximity to the exchange's matching engines. This significantly reduces latency, giving HFT firms an advantage in executing trades milliseconds faster than their competitors. Moreover, exchanges often provide low-latency data feeds, which are crucial for the real-time decision-making processes of HFT algorithms.

- **3. Technology Providers**

  The technological backbone of HFT is fortified by an array of specialized technology providers. These companies supply the hardware, software, and network solutions that enable HFT firms to operate at high speeds and efficiency. Notable technology providers include firms like Intel, known for their high-performance processors, and Cisco, which specializes in low-latency networking solutions. Additionally, firms like FPGA vendors and custom chip designers create hardware tailored to the unique needs of HFT operations. These technology providers continually innovate to push the boundaries of speed and reliability, ensuring that HFT firms maintain their competitive edge.

- **4. Data Providers**

  Real-time market data is the lifeblood of HFT strategies. Data providers such as Bloomberg, Thomson Reuters, and smaller specialized firms offer a vast array of market data services, from historical data to real-time feeds. Accurate and timely data is crucial for HFT algorithms to make informed trading decisions. Besides, data analytics and machine learning tools provided by these entities help HFT firms to analyze market trends, forecast movements, and backtest their strategies. These services are often coupled with high-speed data delivery systems, ensuring that firms receive the most current information available.

- **5. Regulatory Bodies**

  Regulatory bodies, including the Securities and Exchange Commission (SEC) in the United States, the Financial Conduct Authority (FCA) in the United Kingdom, and other global regulators, play an essential role in overseeing the activities within the HFT ecosystem. These agencies establish rules and guidelines to ensure market integrity, transparency, and fairness. They monitor HFT activities to prevent manipulative practices such as spoofing and layering. In recent years, regulations such as the European Union's Markets in Financial Instruments Directive II (MiFID II) have introduced stringent requirements for HFT firms, including enhanced reporting obligations and the implementation of robust risk controls.

- **6. Institutional Investors**

  While not directly involved in the execution of high-frequency trades, institutional investors such as mutual funds, pension funds, and hedge funds interact with the HFT ecosystem in various ways. These investors often rely on the liquidity provided by HFT firms to enter and exit large positions without significantly impacting market prices. Moreover, some institutional investors collaborate with HFT firms, leveraging their technology and expertise to enhance their own trading strategies. The relationship between HFT firms and institutional investors is symbiotic, as the presence of large institutional orders can drive market dynamics that HFT algorithms seek to exploit.

- **7. Academics and Researchers**

  The academic community also plays a noteworthy role in the evolution of HFT. Researchers and academics contribute to the ecosystem through studies that analyze market microstructure, algorithmic strategies, and the economic impacts of HFT. Their findings often lead to innovations and improvements in trading algorithms and risk management practices. Additionally, academic conferences, journals, and industry partnerships facilitate the exchange of ideas and advancements, fostering a collaborative environment that propels the HFT industry forward.

In understanding the key players within the HFT ecosystem, it becomes clear that high-frequency trading is the result of a complex interplay between various entities. Each player contributes to the ecosystem's functionality and evolution, driving the continuous advancement of this cutting-edge field. As HFT continues to develop, the roles and interactions of these players will undoubtedly evolve, reflecting the dynamic nature of financial markets.

1.4 Basic Concepts and Terminology

High-Frequency Trading (HFT) operates on a bedrock of fundamental concepts and specialized terminology that are essential for both novice and experienced traders to grasp fully. Understanding these basics is crucial for navigating the intricacies of HFT, as they underpin all subsequent strategies and methodologies discussed in this book.

At its core, HFT relies on advanced algorithms and high-speed communications to execute a large number of orders within extremely short time frames. The primary objective is to capitalize on minute price discrepancies that exist for fleeting moments in the market. Below, we dissect the primary concepts and terminology that form the backbone of HFT.

Latency: Latency refers to the time delay between the initiation of an order and its execution. In HFT, even microseconds can make a substantial difference, making minimization of latency a top priority. Various factors contribute to latency, including the speed of data transmission, processing time of algorithms, and execution speed of trades. A typical formula to calculate latency is:

$$Latency = \frac{Distance}{Speed} + Processing\ Time$$

Here, *Distance* refers to the geographical distance between trading servers, and *Speed* is the velocity at which data travels, often close to the speed of light in fiber-optic networks. *Processing Time* includes all computational delays.

Order Book: An order book is an electronic list of buy and sell orders for a specific security, organized by price level. HFT algorithms often interact directly with order books to determine the best bid and ask prices quickly.

small

$$Order\ Book = \begin{cases} Buy\ Orders & \{\{Price_1, Quantity_1\}, \{Price_2, Quantity_2\}, \ldots\} \\ Sell\ Orders & \{\{Price_1, Quantity_1\}, \{Price_2, Quantity_2\}, \ldots\} \end{cases}$$

Market Making: Market making involves providing liquidity to the market by continuously quoting both buy and sell prices for a particular security. Market makers profit from the bid-ask spread, the difference between the buying (bid) price and the selling (ask) price.

$$Profit = \sum_{i=1}^{n} (Ask\ Price_i - Bid\ Price_i) \times Quantity_i$$

Arbitrage: Arbitrage is the practice of exploiting price differences of the same asset in different markets to generate profit. In HFT, algorithms are designed to detect these discrepancies within milliseconds and execute trades to lock in risk-free returns.

$$\text{Arbitrage Profit} = \text{Price}_{Market\ A} - \text{Price}_{Market\ B}$$

Colocation: Colocation involves placing trading servers in close proximity to the exchange's servers to reduce latency. By minimizing the physical distance that data must travel, HFT firms can ensure quicker order execution.

Spoofing and Layering: These are tactics sometimes used by unscrupulous traders to manipulate market prices. Spoofing involves placing large orders with the intention of canceling them before execution, creating a false impression of demand or supply. Layering is a form of spoofing where multiple orders are placed at different price levels to create a misleading impression of market depth.

Liquidity: Liquidity refers to the ease with which an asset can be bought or sold in the market without affecting its price. High liquidity is essential for efficient HFT operations, as it allows for rapid entry and exit from positions.

Spread: The spread is the difference between the highest bid price and the lowest ask price. In HFT, smaller spreads are preferred as they reduce transaction costs.

$$Spread = Ask\ Price - Bid\ Price$$

Tick Size: Tick size is the minimum price movement of a trading instrument. Smaller tick sizes can increase the granularity of price movements, which can be advantageous for HFT strategies as they allow for finer price discrimination.

Slippage: Slippage occurs when an order is executed at a different price than expected because of market movement during the delay between placing an order and its execution. Minimizing slippage is critical in high-frequency environments where rapid price changes are common.

Integrating these concepts, one must develop a strong foundation in both the theoretical and practical aspects of HFT. By mastering the terminology and the mechanics underlying each of these key areas, readers can better comprehend subsequent advanced strategies and techniques. As we move forward, keep these fundamental principles in mind, as they will continually serve as the underpinnings of successful high-frequency trading strategies.

1.5 The Role of HFT in Financial Markets

High-Frequency Trading (HFT) plays a pivotal role in modern financial markets, acting as both a facilitator and innovator in the trading ecosystem. By leveraging advanced algorithms and high-speed communications networks, HFT firms execute large volumes of orders with unparalleled speed and precision. This section explores the multifaceted roles that HFT occupies within financial markets, illustrating how it enhances liquidity, improves price discovery, and influences market efficiency.

HFT firms significantly contribute to market liquidity, which is the ability to quickly buy or sell assets without causing a drastic change in their price. Liquidity is essential for ensuring that markets operate smoothly, allowing participants to enter and exit positions with minimal price impact. HFT market makers quote bid and ask prices continuously, providing liquidity that benefits all market participants. By doing so, they reduce the bid-ask spread, which is the difference between the buying and selling prices, thereby lowering the transaction costs for investors.

Another critical role of HFT in financial markets is in price discovery, the process through which the market determines the fair value of an asset. HFT firms utilize sophisticated algorithms to analyze vast amounts of market data in real-time, identifying price discrepancies and arbitrage opportunities across different trading venues. This rapid action helps align prices more closely with the underlying value of the securities, facilitating efficient markets where prices reflect all available information. The constant buying and selling by HFTs ensure that any new information is quickly incorporated into asset prices, enhancing the overall efficiency and transparency of the markets.

Market efficiency, defined as the degree to which prices fully reflect all available information, is another area where HFT has a profound impact. Efficient markets enable more informed decision-making by investors, thus fostering a level playing field. High-frequency traders contribute to market efficiency by exploiting even the smallest inefficiencies and price anomalies. Their presence ensures that any arbitrage opportunities are short-lived, as HFTs swiftly execute trades that correct pricing discrepancies. This continuous activity helps uphold the principles of the Efficient Market Hypothesis (EMH), which posits that asset prices are a reliable measure of intrinsic value.

Moreover, HFT can enhance market stability through the rapid provision of liquidity during times of market stress. During periods of high volatility, such as financial crises or unexpected geopolitical events, traditional market makers may withdraw from the market, leading to increased spreads and reduced liquidity. HFT firms, equipped with automated trading strategies, can step in to fill this liquidity void, providing stability and continuity in trading. For instance, during the Flash Crash of May 2010, while some HFT firms exacerbated the initial volatility, others provided crucial liquidity that helped markets recover swiftly. This duality underscores the nuanced role of HFT in stabilizing and sometimes destabilizing market conditions.

However, it is essential to acknowledge the complexities and potential drawbacks associated with HFT. The speed and volume of HFT transactions can contribute to market fragmentation, where orders are dispersed across multiple trading venues. This dispersion can complicate the process of matching buyers and sellers, leading to a less transparent marketplace. Additionally, the aggressive strategies employed by some HFT firms, such as latency arbitrage and quote stuffing, can create an environment of heightened volatility and uncertainty. These practices may undermine the perceived fairness of the market, raising concerns about the equitable treatment of all market participants.

Despite these criticisms, it is undeniable that HFT plays an integral role in the functioning of contemporary financial markets. The technological advancements and methodological innovations driven by HFT have pushed the boundaries of trading efficiency and market dynamics. HFT firms' contributions to liquidity, price discovery, and market efficiency have redefined the landscape of financial trading, making it more competitive and, arguably, more resilient to shocks.

By appreciating the dual-edged nature of HFT, traders, regulators, and market participants can better navigate the complex interplay of high-speed trading within the broader financial ecosystem. Understanding HFT's vital contributions, alongside its potential risks, equips us to foster a more robust and inclusive market environment. As technology and market practices evolve, HFT will undoubtedly continue to shape the future of financial markets, driving innovation and efficiency while challenging stakeholders to address its inherent complexities.

1.6 Benefits and Criticisms of High-Frequency Trading

As High-Frequency Trading (HFT) cements its position in the financial markets, it attracts both advocates and detractors. Understanding the multifaceted benefits and criticisms of HFT is crucial for grasping its complex impact. Unlike traditional trading, HFT leverages speed and technology to operate on a scale that can transform market dynamics.

One of the principal benefits of HFT is the enhancement of market liquidity. By placing large numbers of buy and sell orders at rapid speeds, HFT firms create a more fluid market environment. This brisk activity reduces bid-ask spreads, facilitating better price discovery. For instance, when HFT algorithms execute trades within milliseconds, they help to accurately reflect the latest information in market prices, thereby tightening spreads and reducing trading costs for all participants.

Another significant advantage of HFT is improved market efficiency. High-frequency traders utilize algorithms to arbitrage discrepancies across various exchanges and asset classes. An HFT firm might recognize a momentary divergence in the price of a stock between two exchanges and act swiftly to exploit this inefficiency. By doing so, they help to quickly eliminate arbitrage opportunities, nudging the market towards a more efficient equilibrium. Over time, such activities contribute to more stable and fairer market conditions.

Despite these benefits, the criticisms aimed at HFT are robust and manifold. A leading concern is the potential for market manipulation. Some contend that HFT firms may engage in practices like quote stuffing, where thousands of orders are rapidly submitted and then canceled, to mislead other traders. This artificial market movement can create a false sense of supply or demand, potentially manipulating prices in a beneficial direction for the HFT firm.

Additionally, critics argue that HFT exacerbates market volatility. The flash crash of May 6, 2010, for example, underscored the potential destabilizing influence of algorithmic trading. On that day, the market plummeted nearly 1,000 points in a matter of minutes, a move partially attributed to the massive selling pressure from HFT algorithms operating on auto-pilot. This incident highlighted the risks associated with the sheer speed and volume of trades executed by HFT systems, which can amplify market movements and lead to rapid and unanticipated price swings.

Another point of criticism is the unfair advantage that HFT firms may hold over traditional traders and long-term investors. The technology and infrastructure required for HFT are prohibitively expensive, often necessitating colocated servers and ultra-low latency communication networks. This technological edge affords HFT firms milliseconds of advantage in receiving and acting on market information, setting a playing field that tilts significantly in their favor. As a result, critics argue that this creates a market environment where only the technologically empowered can thrive, potentially undermining the principles of fair and equitable trading.

Furthermore, there are concerns regarding the ethical dimensions of HFT practices. Some traditional market participants feel that HFT's focus on exploiting minute, short-term price inefficiencies stands contrary to the notion of investing based on fundamental economic indicators and long-term value creation. This chasm between HFT tactics and traditional investment strategies fuels ongoing debates about the role and morality of HFT in modern financial markets.

While HFT brings a multitude of efficiency and liquidity benefits, it is also fraught with systemic risks and ethical dilemmas that warrant careful consideration. The dialogue between supporters and critics of HFT sheds light on a landscape characterized by rapid evolution and complex interplay of technology and finance. This ever-evolving discourse is vital in shaping regulatory frameworks and market practices that will determine the future trajectory of HFT.

1.7 A Day in the Life of a High-Frequency Trader

High-Frequency Trading (HFT) professionals operate in a realm where microseconds can determine the difference between significant gains and losses. Their days are meticulously structured yet extremely dynamic, woven with precision, rapid decision-making, and constant monitoring. This section explores the routine of an HFT trader, emphasizing the intricate balance between technology, strategy, and execution that defines their professional lives.

HFT traders typically start their day long before the markets open. Around 5:00 AM, their routines often begin with a thorough review of overnight market activities and global economic news that might influence the day's trading strategies. Major stock exchanges in Europe and Asia have already seen some activity by this time, providing clues about potential market directions.

Before the opening bell, an HFT trader engages in several preparatory tasks. Reviewing the performance of algorithms used in previous trading sessions is critical. This task involves analyzing performance metrics, such as execution speed, latency, and profitability. Any anomalies or underperformance are flagged for further evaluation. This period is also used to calibrate existing algorithms and develop new strategies based on overnight market data and upcoming economic releases.

At around 8:30 AM, the team assembles for a daily briefing. This meeting is crucial for synchronizing efforts across different trading desks and aligning strategies with broader market expectations. Topics discussed include overnight market developments, anticipated economic reports, and any technical issues encountered in the previous day's trading. Collaboration is essential, even in a highly automated environment, as human judgment often complements algorithmic execution.

As the market opening approaches, typically at 9:30 AM, the atmosphere intensifies. Each trader monitors their multiple screens displaying various real-time data feeds, including market depth, price movements, and news alerts. Once the market opens, the high-frequency trading algorithms start executing trades at lightning speed. The role of the trader shifts to monitoring these algorithms to ensure they operate as intended. Any deviation from expected behavior warrants immediate attention, as even minor discrepancies can result in significant financial losses.

Throughout the trading session, HFT traders continually engage in overseeing key performance indicators like trade execution speed, latency, fill rates, and slippage. They leverage sophisticated software to identify and rectify issues instantaneously. Often, they employ real-time analytics to adjust strategies dynamically, responding to minute fluctuations in the market.

To maintain optimal system performance, close collaboration with IT and system engineers is necessary. Periodic system checks and latency tests are conducted to ensure that the infrastructure supports the high-speed demands of HFT. Additionally, traders work on enhancing algorithms by integrating the latest machine learning techniques and statistical models.

Meal breaks are brief and usually coincide with periods of lower market activity. However, even during these downtimes, traders remain vigilant. They often use such intervals to delve into deeper data analysis, seeking patterns or anomalies that could inform future trades.

As the market draws to a close at 4:00 PM, traders prepare for a rapid end-of-day analysis. It's a time to review the day's performance, evaluating both the wins and the setbacks. A post-market briefing is typically conducted to assess the day's activities. This session includes a detailed examination of trade logs, algorithm performance reports, and a discussion on market conditions encountered during the day.

Post-market hours (4:30 PM and beyond) are dedicated to detailed analysis and strategy refinement. HFT traders scrutinize extensive performance data, identifying areas for improvement in their algorithms. This period is also when longer-term strategic initiatives are developed, often focusing on new algorithmic models, market opportunities, and technological advancements.

Despite the market's closure, the work doesn't halt entirely. The global nature of financial markets requires some HFT professionals to actively monitor other international financial centers. Continuous education and staying updated with the latest financial news, regulatory changes, and technological innovations are integral to an HFT trader's professional development.

The life of an HFT trader is a perpetual cycle of analyze, execute, monitor, and adjust. It demands a blend of technical proficiency, analytical acuity, and an unwavering focus on precision. While technology and automation play pivotal roles, the human element—expertise, intuition, and decision-making—remains indispensable in navigating the fast-paced world of high-frequency trading.

Their ability to seamlessly integrate technology with strategy underscores the transformative impact of HFT on modern financial markets, setting the stage for continuous evolution in trading methodologies.

Chapter 2

Market Microstructure and HFT Strategies

This chapter explores the internal workings of financial markets, known as market microstructure, and its significance to High-Frequency Trading (HFT) strategies. It provides a detailed examination of order types, exchange mechanics, and the dynamic nature of limit order books. The chapter addresses key HFT strategies including arbitrage, market making, and momentum trading, and delves into the use of statistical arbitrage and pair trading. It also covers the role of liquidity provision and the importance of order flow analysis and prediction, offering a comprehensive understanding of how HFT firms exploit market microstructure for profit.

2.1 Introduction to Market Microstructure

Market microstructure is the study of the processes and mechanisms through which securities are traded, encompassing the intricate details of how orders are handled, matched, and executed on various trading platforms. A profound understanding of market microstructure is essential for any trader, particularly those involved in High-Frequency Trading (HFT), as it directly influences trading strategies and their efficacy.

At its core, market microstructure investigates the ways in which the trading environment impacts price formation, liquidity, and transaction costs. This field examines the specificities of how buyers and sellers interact, the role of different market participants, and the technology that underpins the trading infrastructure. By dissecting these elements, traders can gain insights into the behavior of order flows, the functionality of different order types, and the implications for short-term price movements.

One of the fundamental components of market microstructure is the understanding of several types of market participants and their roles. Market participants generally include market makers, arbitrageurs, institutional investors, and retail traders. Each participant operates with distinct objectives and strategies, which collectively shape the market dynamics. Market makers, for instance, provide liquidity by continuously quoting buy and sell prices, profiting from the bid-ask spread. Arbitrageurs exploit price discrepancies across different markets or instruments, ensuring price efficiency through their trades.

Trading platforms, or exchanges, are another critical aspect of market microstructure. Exchanges can be physical or electronic and are where the aggregation of buy and sell orders occurs. These platforms are responsible for order matching, trade execution, and often the dissemination of market data. The evolution from traditional open outcry systems to sophisticated electronic exchanges has significantly altered the landscape, vastly increasing the speed and efficiency of trades—a foundational element for HFT.

Order types and their handling are central to the effective functioning of financial markets. Basic order types include market orders, limit orders, and stop orders, each with distinct instructions and implications for execution. A market order aims for immediate execution at the best available price, while a limit order sets a specific price threshold. A stop order, often used for risk management, triggers a market or limit order once a specified price is reached. Alongside these basic types, there are numerous advanced order types tailored to meet specific needs and strategic objectives.

The advent of electronic trading has also introduced the concept of smart order routing. Algorithms are employed to optimally route orders to various venues to achieve the best execution in terms of price, speed, and reliability. This technological advancement minimizes market impact and enables HFT strategies to capitalize on transient price inefficiencies across multiple trading venues.

Another significant concept in market microstructure is the limit order book, which is a real-time record of all outstanding limit orders in the market. It maps out the supply and demand for a security at various price levels, providing a transparent view of where potential trades may occur. The dynamics of the limit order book, such as the depth and spread, are indicative of the market's liquidity and volatility.

Market microstructure also delves into the process of price formation and discovery. Price formation involves the mechanisms and interactions through which transaction prices are determined. This is heavily influenced by the flow of orders, the depth of the market, and the actions of informed traders versus liquidity traders. Price discovery, on the other hand, is the process by which the market assimilates new information and adjusts prices accordingly. Effective price discovery is vital for market efficiency, ensuring that prices reflect the true underlying value of securities.

In the realm of HFT, a detailed comprehension of market microstructure is paramount. The rapid and constant influx of orders characteristic of HFT necessitates a robust understanding of how different factors influence execution quality and opportunities for arbitrage. HFT strategies often rely on algorithmically dissecting the microstructural features to identify and exploit fleeting inefficiencies.

Thus, a comprehensive grasp of market microstructure provides traders with the insights necessary to navigate the complexities of modern financial markets, optimizing their strategies in an ever-evolving trading landscape.

2.2 Order Types and Exchange Mechanics

Understanding the various order types and the mechanics of exchanges is fundamental for anyone engaged in high-frequency trading. Financial markets offer a myriad of order types, each serving specific purposes, and the functionality of exchanges ensures that these orders are matched efficiently. Mastery of these elements is crucial for exploiting market microstructure.

The most common order type is the *market order*, which instructs the broker to execute a trade immediately at the best available current price. Market orders prioritize speed and certainty of execution over price. This type is especially relevant in high-frequency trading where rapid execution is paramount. However, the risk of market orders is slippage, where the executed price may significantly differ from the expected one due to rapid market movements.

In contrast, a *limit order* specifies a particular price at which the trader is willing to buy or sell a security. A buy limit order is executed at the limit price or lower, while a sell limit order is executed at the limit price or higher. Limit orders provide control over the entry or exit price but do not guarantee execution if the market price doesn't reach the limit. They contribute significantly to the liquidity of the market, populating the limit order book and influencing price formation and discovery.

A *stop order*, often referred to as a stop-loss order, combines elements of market and limit orders. It becomes a market order once a specified stop price is reached. This order type is critical for risk management, automatically exiting a position to limit potential losses. High-frequency traders might use stop orders to protect their strategies from adverse price movements without constant manual monitoring.

Furthermore, exchanges offer more sophisticated order types designed to cater to advanced trading strategies. A prominent example is the *immediate-or-cancel (IOC) order*, which mandates that any portion not immediately executed is canceled. Similarly, a *fill-or-kill (FOK) order* requires the entire order to be executed immediately or not at all, with no partial fills allowed. These order types are particularly utilized in high-frequency trading to precisely control order execution without leaving residual orders exposed in the market.

Exchanges also employ *hidden orders*, which are not visible to other market participants in the limit order book. These orders help large traders execute substantial positions without revealing their intentions to the market, thus mitigating the impact on price. However, the presence of hidden orders introduces complexity to the trading environment, where HFT algorithms must infer potential hidden liquidity when assessing market depth.

Understanding the mechanics of exchanges is equally important. Modern exchanges operate on sophisticated electronic trading platforms, where the matching engine plays a central role. The matching engine is responsible for matching buy and sell orders based on a set of rules and priorities. Typically, exchanges use a price-time priority, prioritizing orders with better prices and those placed earlier. This system ensures that the order book remains orderly and efficient, crucial for high-frequency trading.

High-frequency traders must account for various exchange mechanisms such as *maker-taker pricing*, where liquidity providers (makers) receive rebates, and liquidity takers (takers) pay fees. This pricing model incentivizes the provision of liquidity and influences the strategies traders deploy. For instance, a market-making strategy benefits from maker rebates, while aggressive strategies might incur higher costs due to taker fees.

Moreover, *latency* is a critical consideration in high-frequency trading. Exchanges strive to minimize latency, the delay between the initiation and execution of an order, through advanced infrastructure and co-location services. Co-location allows traders to place their servers close to the exchange's matching engine, reducing latency and providing a vital edge in executing orders quicker than competitors.

Arbitrage opportunities, market manipulation, and regulatory compliance are also integral components of exchange mechanics. Exchanges constantly evolve to enhance fairness and transparency while countering manipulative tactics like spoofing and layering. For high-frequency traders, this necessitates continuous adaptation and refinement of strategies to maintain an edge within the regulatory framework.

Engaging with these order types and understanding the intricate mechanics of exchanges empowers traders to implement refined strategies, efficiently manage risk, and capture opportunities in the microsecond fabric of modern financial markets. The optimal use of these tools and insights into exchange operations provides a solid foundation for the subsequent exploration of complex HFT strategies and market phenomena.

2.3 Limit Order Books and Their Dynamics

The limit order book (LOB) is a fundamental element within the architecture of modern electronic financial markets. It plays a crucial role in the price discovery process and provides a transparent view of the supply and demand for a given security. The LOB aggregates all buy and sell orders for a security, organized by price levels. Orders that specify a price are called limit orders, and they populate this book until they are executed, canceled, or modified. Understanding the dynamics of the LOB is essential for high-frequency traders who leverage this information to develop and refine trading strategies.

At its core, the LOB is a data structure maintained by trading exchanges. It consists of lists of buy orders, known as bids, and sell orders, termed asks or offers. Each list is sorted by price and time priority, with the highest bids and lowest asks given precedence. Traders submit their orders to the exchange, where they either enter the LOB if they are limit orders, or they execute against existing orders if they are market orders.

Mathematically, let $P_{\text{bid},i}$ and $P_{\text{ask},j}$ represent the ith highest bid price and the jth lowest ask price, respectively. The quantities available at these levels are $Q_{\text{bid},i}$ and $Q_{\text{ask},j}$, which correspond to the volume of securities traders are willing to buy or sell at those prices. The top of the book, or the best bid and best ask, are denoted as $P_{\text{bid},1}$ and $P_{\text{ask},1}$, and they are crucial indicators of the current market sentiment and immediate trading decision points.

$$\text{Top of the Book:} \quad P_{\text{bid},1} \quad \& \quad P_{\text{ask},1}$$

$$\text{Market Spread:} \quad \Delta P = P_{\text{ask},1} - P_{\text{bid},1}$$

The difference between the best ask and the best bid, known as the bid-ask spread or market spread, represents the cost of immediacy for traders. A narrow spread often indicates high liquidity and lower transaction costs, while a wider spread might suggest lower liquidity and higher costs.

The dynamics of the LOB are governed by a continuous stream of order flow. This flow consists of new limit orders, which add liquidity to the market; market orders, which consume liquidity; and cancellations or modifications of existing limit orders, which alter the available liquidity. High-frequency traders (HFTs) monitor these order flows meticulously to gain insights into short-term market movements and potential price changes.

One of the primary models used to study the dynamics of limit order books is the queuing model, where limit orders at each price level are treated as customers queuing for execution. The rate at which buy and sell orders arrive, λ_{buy} and λ_{sell}, respectively, and the rate at which they are executed, μ_{buy} and μ_{sell}, drive the shape and evolution of the LOB.

$$N_{\text{bid}}(t) = N_{\text{bid}}(t-1) + \lambda_{\text{buy}} - \mu_{\text{buy}}$$

$$N_{\text{ask}}(t) = N_{\text{ask}}(t-1) + \lambda_{\text{sell}} - \mu_{\text{sell}}$$

Where $N_{\text{bid}}(t)$ and $N_{\text{ask}}(t)$ denote the number of buy and sell orders in the book at time t, respectively.

Moreover, the statistical properties of LOB changes, such as order arrival and cancellation rates, help HFTs to construct predictive models. By employing statistical techniques and machine learning algorithms, traders can forecast immediate future states of the LOB and devise strategies that capitalize on anticipated short-term imbalances between supply and demand.

Impactful events within the LOB, such as large orders or sudden market movements, can cause significant perturbations. These events often result in rapid changes in the bid-ask spread, depth of the book, and liquidity conditions. HFT strategies like market making mitigate risks arising from such events by continuously adjusting quotes to reflect real-time market conditions.

Visualizing the LOB over time provides deeper insights into its dynamics. A heatmap of the LOB displays the evolution of bid and ask prices and volumes, often revealing patterns that are non-trivial to detect otherwise. These visual tools are invaluable for traders to recognize the ongoing interaction between market participants and the resultant market microstructure.

Real-world application of LOB analysis entails sophisticated tools and frameworks like the following Python code snippet utilizing the Pandas library for a snapshot analysis of the LOB:

```
import pandas as pd

# Load order book data
order_book = pd.read_csv('order_book_data.csv')

# Extract relevant columns
bids = order_book[['bid_price', 'bid_volume']]
asks = order_book[['ask_price', 'ask_volume']]

# Analyze top of the book
best_bid = bids.iloc[0]
best_ask = asks.iloc[0]
market_spread = best_ask['ask_price'] - best_bid['bid_price']

print(f"Best Bid: {best_bid['bid_price']} Volume: {best_bid['bid_volume']}")
print(f"Best Ask: {best_ask['ask_price']} Volume: {best_ask['ask_volume']}")
print(f"Market Spread: {market_spread}")
```

Through precise analysis and continuous monitoring of the limit order book, high-frequency traders can gain a substantial edge in the market. Their ability to quickly interpret and act on LOB dynamics fosters an environment where even minute informational advantages can translate into significant profit margins. Hence, mastery over the mechanics and intricacies of the LOB remains a cornerstone of effective high-frequency trading strategies.

2.4 Price Formation and Discovery

The process of price formation and discovery plays a central role in financial markets, particularly in the context of high-frequency trading (HFT). Understanding these mechanisms is crucial for designing effective HFT strategies that can capitalize on minuscule price differences and market inefficiencies. This section delves into the intricate dynamics underlying how prices are determined and discovered in the marketplace, emphasizing the importance of market microstructure elements and the interplay between supply and demand forces.

Price formation refers to the process by which the price of a security is established in the market. At its core, this involves the interaction of buyers and sellers through their respective orders, where the agreement on price leads to the execution of trades. The fundamental building blocks of price formation include the limit order book (LOB), the types of orders submitted by traders, and the rules of the trading venue.

The limit order book is a dynamic, real-time repository of all outstanding buy and sell orders for a given security. It consists of limit orders, which specify the maximum price a buyer is willing to pay or the minimum price a seller is willing to accept. The highest price in the buy orders is known as the bid price, while the lowest price in the sell orders is called the ask price. The difference between the bid and ask prices is referred to as the bid-ask spread. The LOB's structure and activity are crucial in understanding price formation, as it continuously evolves based on order placement, cancellation, and execution.

Price discovery refers to the process by which the market determines the fair value of a security. This involves the aggregation of information from all market participants and the translation of this collective information into market prices. High-frequency traders play a pivotal role in this process by quickly reacting to new information and adjusting their orders to capitalize on perceived discrepancies between the current market price and the expected future price.

One of the key elements in price discovery is the concept of informational efficiency. In an informationally efficient market, prices fully reflect all available information. High-frequency traders contribute to this efficiency by using advanced algorithms to rapidly process and react to news, economic indicators, and other relevant data. These algorithms can detect patterns and correlations that might be invisible to the human eye, thus ensuring that prices adjust swiftly to new information.

The interaction between large institutional orders and high-frequency trading activity is another essential aspect of price formation and discovery. Institutional trades often involve significant volumes that can influence market prices. High-frequency traders, with their ability to execute trades at lightning speed, can either facilitate these large orders by providing liquidity or exploit the temporary imbalances they create. This interplay between different market participants highlights the complex and dynamic nature of price formation.

Consider the following simplified example to illustrate the mechanics of price formation and discovery:

Suppose a large institutional investor decides to buy a substantial number of shares of a particular stock. The investor enters a market order, which is designed to execute immediately at the best available prices. The market order sweeps through the LOB, consuming the existing sell orders starting from the lowest ask price and moving upward. As these sell orders are executed, the price of the stock rises, reflecting the increased demand.

High-frequency traders, constantly monitoring the LOB, detect the sudden spike in buy activity. They may respond by placing new sell orders slightly below the current ask price to capitalize on the elevated demand or by adjusting their positions in correlated securities. The rapid adjustments by HFTs help stabilize the price, ensuring that it converges towards its new equilibrium level.

In addition to direct market interactions, external factors such as news announcements, macroeconomic data releases, and geopolitical events significantly influence price formation and discovery. High-frequency trading algorithms are programmed to scan and interpret these external signals in real-time. For instance, a positive earnings report for a company can trigger buy signals across HFT systems, leading to immediate order placements that drive the stock price upwards.

Mathematically, the process of price formation and discovery can be modeled using various techniques, including supply and demand curves, econometric models, and stochastic processes. One such model is the Efficient Market Hypothesis (EMH), which posits that asset prices fully reflect all available information. While the EMH provides a theoretical foundation, real-world deviations from this hypothesis are exploited by high-frequency strategies to derive profits.

$$P_t = P_{t-1} + \epsilon_t$$

In the above equation, P_t represents the price of a security at time t, and ϵ_t denotes a random shock or news impact at time t. The model suggests that price changes are a result of new information arriving randomly. High-frequency traders aim to predict and react to these random shocks with minimal latency.

To summarize, the processes of price formation and discovery are integral to understanding market dynamics and the role of high-frequency trading within them. By dissecting these processes, one gains insights into the mechanisms that drive market efficiency and the opportunities that arise from temporary price dislocations. The ability to swiftly interpret and act upon relevant information, coupled with the continuous interaction within the limit order book, underscores the sophisticated and competitive nature of modern financial markets.

2.5 Key HFT Strategies: Arbitrage, Market Making, and Momentum

High-Frequency Trading (HFT) strategies are designed to capitalize on the rapid and complex nature of modern financial markets. Among the most prominent strategies employed by HFT firms are arbitrage, market making, and momentum trading. Each of these strategies leverages specific characteristics of market microstructure to generate profits through high-speed transactions and precise timing.

Arbitrage involves exploiting price discrepancies of the same or similar financial instruments across different markets or related instruments within the same market. This strategy hinges on the notion of market efficiency — theoretically, prices of identical assets should converge to the same value. However, due to temporal and spatial inefficiencies, brief windows of opportunity arise, allowing traders to buy low in one market and sell high in another, locking in the price differential as profit. Mathematically, consider asset A traded on two different exchanges, with prices P_1 and P_2. An arbitrage opportunity exists if $|P_1 - P_2| > C$, where C represents the cost of transaction. To capitalize on this, traders employ algorithms that continuously monitor various markets and execute trades within milliseconds when such discrepancies are detected.

Market making is characterized by providing liquidity to the markets by continuously posting buy (bid) and sell (ask) orders for a range of securities. Market makers profit from the bid-ask spread, the difference between the price at which they are willing to buy and the price at which they are willing to sell. The role of a market maker is crucial as it enhances market liquidity and stability. The strategy is essentially to "make a market" in certain securities, providing quotes that other market participants can trade against. A market maker's algorithm calculates the optimal bid B and ask A prices by assessing the current market conditions, order flow, and inventory levels. The objective is to capture the spread $S = A - B$, ensuring the smallest possible inventory risk and adverse selection:

$$\text{Profit} = \sum(A_i - B_i) * V_i$$

where A_i and B_i are the ask and bid prices respectively for the i-th trade, and V_i represents the trade volume.

Momentum trading in the context of HFT leverages the short-term trends in the market prices, operating under the assumption that price momentum from past periods will persist into the future, at least in the very short term. This strategy relies on sophisticated algorithms that detect patterns and trends in asset prices, using them to predict future movements. One common approach is to employ moving averages or regression models to signal entry and exit points. For instance, a simple moving average crossover strategy might buy the asset when the short-term moving average surpasses the long-term moving average, and sell when the opposite occurs. The momentum-based HFT models heavily rely on speed and accuracy, exploiting the brief continuation of trends before they revert:

$$\text{Signal} = \sum_{i=1}^{n} \alpha_i P_{t-i}$$

where P_{t-i} represents historical prices and α_i are weights assigned based on the model used.

The implementation of these strategies demands not only a deep understanding of market microstructure but also advanced technological infrastructure. Speed is paramount; therefore, HFT firms invest in cutting-edge technologies, such as low-latency networks and powerful computing systems, to ensure their algorithms can act faster than the competition.

Understanding these strategies is essential for comprehending how HFT firms generate profits and influence the broader market ecosystem.

High-frequency traders act as the catalysts, ensuring price efficiency and liquidity, despite the sheer competitiveness of their operations.

2.6 Statistical Arbitrage and Pair Trading

Statistical arbitrage, commonly referred to as StatArb, is a cornerstone strategy in the domain of high-frequency trading (HFT). It encompasses a range of quantitative methods for achieving market-neutral positions and exploiting inefficiencies across various asset prices. Key to this approach is its reliance on statistical and econometric techniques to model and predict price movements, thereby allowing traders to capitalize on short-term deviations from an established equilibrium.

A popular subset of statistical arbitrage is pair trading. This strategy involves identifying two historically correlated securities and establishing positions that benefit from their relative movements. When the price relationship diverges beyond a certain threshold, the strategy anticipates a reversion to the mean, presenting an opportunity for profit.

To illustrate these concepts more concretely, let's delve deeper into the mechanics and mathematical foundations of pair trading.

The first step in pair trading is to identify two securities that exhibit a stable historical correlation. This can be achieved using statistical tests such as the cointegration test, which examines whether a linear combination of two non-stationary time series is itself stationary. If such a combination exists, the series are said to be cointegrated, implying a mean-reverting relationship.

Given two price series $P_A(t)$ and $P_B(t)$, the cointegrating relationship can be expressed as:

$$P_A(t) = \alpha + \beta P_B(t) + u(t) \tag{2.1}$$

where α and β are coefficients, and $u(t)$ is the residual term, ideally exhibiting mean-reversion properties. The next task is to estimate the parameters α and β using regression analysis or more sophisticated econometric techniques.

Once the pair is identified and parameters estimated, the strategy involves monitoring the spread, defined as:

$$S(t) = P_A(t) - \beta P_B(t) - \alpha \tag{2.2}$$

When $S(t)$ deviates significantly from zero (or another long-term mean value), positions are taken assuming this deviation is temporary and will eventually revert. For instance, if $S(t)$ is significantly positive, implying $P_A(t)$ is overpriced relative to $P_B(t)$, one would short P_A and go long P_B. Conversely, if $S(t)$ is significantly negative, the strategy would entail going long P_A and shorting P_B.

The execution of this strategy in a high-frequency trading environment hinges on rapid computation and precise timing. Algorithmic systems continuously scan the market for opportunities, execute trades when preset criteria are met, and manage positions dynamically to mitigate risk.

A practical example can further elucidate these concepts. Consider two stocks, X and Y, with a historical price relationship indicative of cointegration. Suppose through rigorous backtesting, the spread $S(t)$ typically ranges within a band of -2 to 2. The trading algorithm is set to establish positions when the spread exceeds these bounds.

$$\text{If } S(t) > 2 \quad \text{short X, long Y} \tag{2.3}$$

$$\text{If } S(t) < -2 \quad \text{long X, short Y} \tag{2.4}$$

The algorithm monitors the real-time spread and executes trades, anticipating a convergence back to the mean. Risk management protocols, such as stop-loss orders, are essential to limit potential losses if the spread fails to revert as expected.

Beyond pair trading, statistical arbitrage encompasses a broader spectrum of strategies, including multi-asset arbitrage, market-neutral portfolios, and convergence trades in derivatives markets. Central to these approaches is the reliance on advanced statistical models, machine learning techniques, and comprehensive backtesting to ensure robustness and profitability.

In catering to varying market conditions, traders often adjust their models and parameters dynamically. For instance, during periods of heightened volatility, the thresholds for trade initiation might be expanded to accommodate larger deviations from the mean, thereby reducing the likelihood of premature or false signals.

Sophisticated software infrastructure and computational resources are indispensable in modern StatArb operations. High-frequency trading firms invest heavily in low-latency networks and parallel computing to enhance the speed and accuracy of their trading algorithms.

In essence, statistical arbitrage and pair trading illustrate the profound impact of quantitative analysis on trading strategies. By systematically exploiting statistical anomalies, traders can achieve consistent returns while maintaining market neutrality, thereby hedging against broader market risks.

2.7 Liquidity Provision and Market Making

Liquidity provision and market making are critical functions within the realm of High-Frequency Trading (HFT). These activities ensure smoother market operation by enabling the continuous availability of buy and sell orders, thereby reducing spreads and improving price stability. Market makers play an instrumental role in maintaining liquidity in both tranquil and volatile market conditions, and their operations are often underpinned by sophisticated algorithmic strategies.

Market making involves quoting both buy (bid) and sell (ask) prices for a given financial instrument, with the intention of profiting from the bid-ask spread. The spread compensates the market maker for the risk taken by holding inventory and providing liquidity. In high-frequency environments, this process is automated and relies heavily on advanced technology to adjust bids and asks dynamically based on a myriad of factors.

One of the essential concepts in market making is the bid-ask spread, which can be expressed as:

$$\text{Spread} = \text{Ask Price} - \text{Bid Price}$$

Market makers earn the spread for each round-trip trade they complete. However, maintaining profitability requires a deep understanding of market conditions, inventory risk, and the costs associated with order execution.

To operate effectively, market makers leverage order flow information, which provides insights into buying and selling pressure. By analyzing order flow, market makers can better predict short-term price movements and adjust their quotes accordingly. For instance, an unexpected surge in buy orders might prompt a market maker to raise their ask price, anticipating further price increases.

A mathematical description of market making strategies often involves the use of stochastic models. One such model is the Avellaneda-

Stoikov model, which dynamically adjusts bid and ask quotes to balance the trade-off between profitability and inventory risk. The model can be formulated as follows:

$$q_t = q_0 - \int_0^t (N_s^b - N_s^a)\, ds,$$
$$S_t = S_0 + \sigma B_t,$$

where q_t represents the inventory position at time t, N_s^b and N_s^a denote the number of buy and sell market orders, S_t is the mid-price, σ is the volatility, and B_t is a Brownian motion representing price changes.

Computing optimal bid (p_b) and ask (p_a) prices involves solving the Hamilton-Jacobi-Bellman (HJB) equation, often set up to maximize an objective function that balances expected profit and risk. The adjusted quotes can be defined as:

$$p_b = S_t - \frac{\Gamma \sigma^2 T}{k} + \frac{q_t \theta \Gamma}{k},$$
$$p_a = S_t + \frac{\Gamma \sigma^2 T}{k} - \frac{q_t \theta \Gamma}{k},$$

where Γ denotes risk aversion, k is a parameter indicating the market's liquidity, θ is the intensity of trading, and T is the remaining time of the trading horizon.

In volatility-heavy environments, managing inventory risk becomes paramount. Market makers must ensure that their holdings remain balanced to avoid significant losses due to adverse price movements. One approach to managing this risk involves setting inventory limits, beyond which the trading algorithm either halts trading or implements hedging strategies.

Furthermore, latency plays a crucial role in competitive market making. The ability to quickly process market data, update quotes, and execute trades can significantly impact a firm's profitability. High-frequency market makers continuously invest in reducing latency through technological upgrades, such as co-locating servers near exchange data centers and utilizing faster communication protocols.

Algorithmic market making also requires stringent compliance with regulatory frameworks. Market makers must adhere to rules imposed by exchanges and regulators, such as maintaining minimum levels of liquidity and providing quotes for a specified duration. Regulatory oversight aims to ensure that market makers contribute positively to market stability and transparency.

In the context of global financial markets, market making strategies are tailored to the unique characteristics of different asset classes, including equities, fixed income, commodities, and currencies. Each asset class presents distinct challenges and opportunities, necessitating bespoke algorithms and risk management approaches.

By systematically providing liquidity and reducing price volatility, market makers enhance the overall efficiency of financial markets. Their presence ensures that traders can execute large orders without causing significant market disruptions, thereby fostering a more stable and predictable trading environment.

2.8 Order Flow Analysis and Prediction

Order flow analysis and prediction stand as pivotal elements in the landscape of High-Frequency Trading (HFT), offering traders substantial insights into market movements and enabling the formulation of preemptive trading strategies. This section delves into the intricacies of order flow, discussing its characterization, analytical techniques, and the predictive models that are often employed by HFT firms.

Order flow essentially refers to the influx and pattern of buy and sell orders in the market. It can be bifurcated into two primary categories: aggressive orders and passive orders. Aggressive orders demand immediate execution, often utilizing market orders, whereas passive orders aim for favorable prices, typically employing limit orders. Understanding the nature and impact of these orders is crucial for traders who seek to exploit microstructure inefficiencies.

One effective approach to analyzing order flow is through the examination of order book dynamics. The limit order book (LOB) displays outstanding limit orders at various price levels, providing a transparent view of market liquidity and the potential supply and demand equilibrium. By closely monitoring the LOB, traders can identify patterns such as order book imbalances, where there is a significant discrepancy between the volume of buy and sell orders, often suggesting impending price movements.

Mathematically, the order flow imbalance OFI can be quantified using the following formula:

$$OFI = \Delta S - \Delta D \tag{2.5}$$

where ΔS represents the change in sell orders and ΔD represents the change in buy orders over a given period. A positive OFI indicates an excess of buying pressure, likely driving prices upward, and vice versa.

Advanced statistical techniques are also employed to dissect order flow. One such method involves the use of Markov chains to model order arrivals and their transitions between states. This stochastic approach allows traders to estimate the probabilities of subsequent order events based on current market conditions, thereby refining their predictive power.

$$P(X_{t+1} = j \mid X_t = i) = p_{ij} \tag{2.6}$$

In the above equation, $P(X_{t+1} = j \mid X_t = i)$ represents the probability of transitioning from state i to state j at time $t+1$, with p_{ij} being the transition probability.

Machine learning models have revolutionized order flow prediction. Utilizing algorithms such as Support Vector Machines (SVMs), Random Forests, and Deep Learning, traders can construct predictive models that learn from historical data and order patterns. These models identify subtle and complex relationships within the data, providing enhanced accuracy in forecasting future order flows.

For example, a typical machine learning pipeline for order flow prediction might involve the following steps:

- **Feature Extraction**: Derive relevant features from raw order book data, such as mid-price changes, order arrival rates, and LOB depth.
- **Data Preprocessing**: Normalize and clean the data to ensure consistency and remove anomalies.
- **Model Training**: Train the predictive model using a portion of the historical data, optimizing parameters through cross-validation techniques.
- **Model Prediction**: Apply the trained model to new data, generating predictions on future order flows and actionable trading signals.

The performance of these models can be evaluated using metrics like precision, recall, and the area under the receiver operating characteristic (ROC) curve. High-performing models offer critical advantages in high-frequency environments, where milliseconds can make a significant difference.

Moreover, sentiment analysis has emerged as a complementary tool in order flow prediction. By analyzing news articles, social media, and other textual data for market sentiment, traders can gain additional foresight into market movements. Sentiment scores can be integrated with traditional order flow analysis to create more robust predictive frameworks.

In conclusion, mastering order flow analysis and prediction is essential for HFT practitioners. By leveraging sophisticated mathematical models, statistical techniques, and machine learning algorithms, traders can gain a strategic edge in anticipating market dynamics, thereby optimizing their trading performance. This confluence of quantitative analysis and technological innovation underscores the relentless pursuit of efficiency in the fast-paced world of high-frequency trading.

Chapter 3

Technological Foundations of HFT

This chapter examines the technological underpinnings essential for High-Frequency Trading (HFT). It covers the computational and networking requirements necessary for HFT operations, including hardware components like CPUs, GPUs, and FPGAs. The discussion extends to low-latency communication protocols, data storage and management solutions, and techniques for measuring and optimizing latency. The chapter also contrasts cloud computing with on-premises solutions and introduces emerging technologies that are shaping the future of HFT. These insights provide a thorough grounding in the technology driving this high-speed trading phenomenon.

3.1 Computational Requirements for HFT

High-Frequency Trading (HFT) is characterized by an intense reliance on computational resources to execute trades within microseconds. The computational requirements for HFT go beyond mere processing power; they encompass a combination of speed, efficiency, and scalability tailored to the unique demands of high-speed financial markets.

At the heart of HFT operations lies the need for specialized hardware and optimized software configurations. The cornerstone of these configurations includes Central Processing Units (CPUs), Graphics Processing Units (GPUs), and Field Programmable Gate Arrays (FPGAs), each playing distinct roles within the trading ecosystem.

CPUs: These are the workhorses of HFT computations, responsible for executing trading algorithms with precision. Modern HFT systems frequently employ multi-core CPUs to parallelize tasks and enhance throughput. A crucial aspect of CPU selection is the balance between clock speed and core count. While higher clock speeds allow for the execution of individual threads with minimal latency, multi-core architectures enable the parallel processing of multiple algorithms or data streams, enhancing overall system efficiency.

Mathematically, the throughput capabilities of a CPU can be modeled as:

$$T = C \times f \times N,$$

where T is the total throughput, C is the average number of instructions per cycle, f is the clock frequency, and N is the number of cores. This relationship underscores the importance of both clock speed and core count in the CPU's performance for HFT applications.

GPUs: Originally designed for rendering graphics, GPUs have found a critical role in HFT due to their ability to perform parallel processing across thousands of small cores. GPUs are particularly effective for data-intensive tasks such as risk modeling, backtesting strategies, and processing large data sets. They leverage parallelism to accelerate computations that would otherwise be bottlenecked on traditional CPU architectures.

The computational power of a GPU is quantified by the number of floating-point operations per second (FLOPS) it can execute:

$$P_{\text{GPU}} = C_{\text{GPU}} \times f_{\text{GPU}} \times N_{\text{GPU}},$$

where P_{GPU} denotes the performance, C_{GPU} the FLOPS per cycle per core, f_{GPU} the clock frequency, and N_{GPU} the number of cores. The massively parallel nature of GPUs allows for the efficient execution of complex calculations essential for predictive analytics and algorithm optimization.

FPGAs: Field Programmable Gate Arrays offer the unique advantage of customizability. Unlike CPUs and GPUs, FPGAs can be reconfigured to adapt to specific algorithmic requirements, enabling hardware-level acceleration of critical trading functions. These devices excel in deterministic low-latency tasks, making them ideal for executing order entry strategies and managing high-frequency data feeds.

The performance of an FPGA can be characterized by its ability to perform parallel operations with minimal latency:

$$P_{\text{FPGA}} = f_{\text{FPGA}} \times \text{LUTs},$$

where P_{FPGA} represents the performance, f_{FPGA} is the operating frequency, and LUTs are the number of look-up tables employed in the FPGA's configuration. The reconfigurable nature of FPGAs allows for bespoke optimizations that can be tuned to specific market conditions and trading strategies.

Beyond hardware, the software stacks running on these systems are meticulously optimized to reduce latency and maximize throughput. Key aspects include operating system tweaks, optimized network stacks, and specialized trading platforms capable of handling high volumes of transactions with minimal overhead.

Operating System and Kernel Tuning: To meet the demands of HFT, operating systems are often stripped of unnecessary services and features that could introduce latency. Real-time operating systems (RTOS) and customized Linux kernels are popular choices due to their ability to prioritize critical processes and offer fine-grained control over system resources.

Network Stack Optimization: Efficient network communication is vital for HFT. Low-latency transport protocols and kernel bypass techniques are employed to minimize the time taken for data packets to traverse the network stack. InfiniBand and RDMA (Remote Direct Memory Access) are frequently utilized to enhance data transfer speeds and reduce latency.

Trading Platforms: Custom-built trading platforms are engineered to process trades at unprecedented speeds. These platforms integrate directly with exchange APIs, often employing direct market access (DMA) to reduce the number of intermediaries and, consequently, the latency.

In summary, the computational requirements for HFT are multifaceted, demanding a harmonious blend of cutting-edge hardware and finely tuned software. The relentless pursuit of speed and efficiency drives continual advancements in both areas, enabling traders to capitalize on fleeting market opportunities with precision and agility.

3.2 Networking Basics for Financial Markets

In the realm of High-Frequency Trading (HFT), network performance is critical. Effective HFT strategies depend on the ability to receive, process, and respond to market data faster than competitors. This requires a deep understanding of networking fundamentals tailored to financial markets.

At the heart of networking basics is the concept of latency. Latency refers to the time delay from when a data packet is sent from one point to when it is received at another point. In the context of financial markets, even microseconds can make a significant difference in competitive advantage. Therefore, optimizing every aspect of network performance is essential.

Data Transmission Fundamentals:

Financial market data is transmitted over networks using a variety of protocols. These protocols determine how data is structured and managed during transmission. The two primary types of protocols pertinent to financial markets are:

- **Transmission Control Protocol (TCP):** TCP is known for its reliability. It ensures data integrity by correcting errors and reordering out-of-sequence packets. While reliability is critical, the added steps to ensure data integrity introduce latency, making TCP less suitable for HFT environments where speed is paramount.

- **User Datagram Protocol (UDP):** Contrarily, UDP sacrifices some reliability for speed. It is a connectionless protocol that sends packets without waiting for acknowledgments, reducing latency. In HFT, UDP is frequently used for multicast data distributions, such as market data feeds, where speed is more critical than error-correction.

Network Topologies:

The physical layout of a network, or its topology, greatly impacts latency and data throughput. In financial markets, three common topologies are utilized:

- **Point-to-Point Network (P2P):** This topology creates a direct link between two endpoints without any intermediaries, minimizing the number of hops and ensuring the lowest possible latency. It is ideal for connecting trading firms to exchanges or between two key trading hubs.

- **Star Topology:** In a star topology, all data routes through a central hub, which simplifies network management and improves redundancy. It is commonly used within data centers to connect various servers to a central switch.

- **Mesh Topology:** This topology connects each node to multiple other nodes, providing multiple paths for data transmission. While this design improves fault tolerance and redundancy, it can also introduce additional hops that increase latency, and therefore it is less common in HFT environments.

Low-Latency Network Components:

Several specialized network components are integral to achieving and maintaining low-latency.

- **Switches:** Low-latency switches are designed to handle large volumes of data packets with minimal delay. Market-leading options emphasize reduced port-to-port latency, with some achieving latencies as low as sub-microseconds. Functionality such as cut-through switching, where a switch starts forwarding a packet before it is fully received, further reduces latency.

- **Network Interface Cards (NICs):** NICs are another key element in reducing network latency. Advanced NICs, often equipped with features like kernel bypass technologies, allow applications to communicate directly with the NIC hardware, skipping layers of the operating system and reducing processing time.

- **Fiber Optic Cables:** High-speed fiber optic cables are preferred for their ability to transmit data over long distances with minimal signal degradation. In HFT, dark fiber, which refers to privately-owned, non-shared fiber optic cables, is often used to connect directly to financial exchanges, offering the dual benefits of low-latency and enhanced security.

Synchronization and Time Protocols:

Precision in timekeeping is crucial for HFT. Accurate time synchronization across network components ensures ordered execution of transactions and proper sequence of timestamps on trades. Key protocols and tools include:

- **Network Time Protocol (NTP):** While widely used, NTP typically offers millisecond accuracy, which is insufficient for high-frequency trading. However, it is still used for less latency-sensitive applications within the network.
- **Precision Time Protocol (PTP):** Also known as IEEE 1588, PTP can achieve synchronization accuracy within nanoseconds. It is often employed in financial trading networks to ensure that all systems and devices are synchronized to a precise global time source, such as GPS.
- **Hardware Timestamping:** Techniques like hardware timestamping take timestamping out of the software stack and into the hardware NICs, ensuring packets are marked with a time as they pass through the network interface. This minimizes the variance and potential delays introduced by software processes.

Network Monitoring and Diagnostics:

High-performing networks necessitate continuous monitoring and diagnostics to identify bottlenecks and inefficiencies. Tools and techniques include:

- **Packet Capture:** Tools like Wireshark analyze traffic and diagnose issues at the packet level. By capturing packets, network administrators can diagnose latency issues, packet loss, and other performance impediments.
- **Latency Monitoring Solutions:** Specialized software monitors network paths and logs latency data, helping identify slow points and optimize route management. Solutions often employ visual dashboards to provide real-time insights into network performance.
- **Synthetic Transactions:** By injecting synthetic transactions into the network, administrators can test and measure latency under controlled conditions. This practice helps in understanding how the network handles transactions during peak trading periods.

Understanding and optimizing networking basics lays a critical foundation for any robust HFT system. With the right combination of low-latency protocols, topologies, specialized components, and rigorous synchronization, financial firms can achieve the speed and reliability required to compete in milliseconds-competitive trading environments. Being adept in network fundamentals will not only improve trading performance but also enhance the operational resilience of trading infrastructures.

3.3 Hardware: CPUs, GPUs, and FPGAs

High-Frequency Trading (HFT) relies heavily on cutting-edge hardware to achieve the lowest possible latencies and the highest computational speeds. This section delves into the critical roles that CPUs, GPUs, and FPGAs play in the technological framework of HFT, highlighting their unique advantages and the distinct functions they serve within trading systems.

Central Processing Units (CPUs)

CPUs form the core of many HFT systems due to their versatility and ability to handle a variety of tasks. Modern CPUs are designed with multiple cores, each capable of executing multiple threads simultaneously, allowing for parallel processing of trading algorithms and data feeds.

CPUs are particularly advantageous for tasks that require high single-threaded performance, such as order execution and decision-making logic. Their general-purpose nature enables them to handle a diverse set of operations, from mathematical computations to data parsing and network communication.

$$\text{Throughput} = \frac{\text{Number of instructions}}{\text{CPU Clock Cycle Time}}$$

The performance of a CPU in an HFT setup can be quantified by its throughput, which is determined by both the number of instructions it can execute per cycle and its clock speed. Enhancements such as larger caches and advanced branch prediction algorithms further optimize CPU performance, reducing latency and boosting execution speed.

Graphics Processing Units (GPUs)

GPUs, originally designed for rendering graphics, have evolved to become powerful tools for parallel processing tasks. The architecture of a GPU, with its thousands of smaller and energy-efficient cores, allows it to handle massive amounts of data simultaneously. This makes GPUs particularly well-suited for tasks such as risk modeling, complex numerical simulations, and machine learning algorithms that are integral to sophisticated HFT strategies.

$$\text{Compute Capability} = \text{Number of CUDA cores} \times \text{Clock Speed}$$

The compute capability of a GPU can be described by its number of CUDA cores and their clock speeds. GPU architectures, such as NVIDIA's CUDA and AMD's ROCm, provide the necessary frameworks for developers to harness this computing power effectively. For HFT applications, GPUs excel in scenarios where large datasets need to be processed rapidly, such as in real-time market data analysis or training predictive models.

Field-Programmable Gate Arrays (FPGAs)

FPGAs offer a unique advantage in HFT due to their customizability and extremely low latencies. Unlike CPUs and GPUs, which have fixed instruction sets and architectures, FPGAs can be reprogrammed to perform specific tasks with optimized hardware configurations. This flexibility allows for the creation of highly specialized processors tailored to specific trading algorithms and execution strategies.

FPGAs excel in tasks that demand ultra-low latency, such as high-frequency tick-by-tick data analysis and ultra-fast order routing. By designing custom data paths and control logic, FPGAs can process and respond to trading signals in nanoseconds. This performance is critical in scenarios where even microsecond delays can result in significant financial losses or missed opportunities.

$$\text{Latency Reduction} = f(\text{Custom Circuit Design, Pipeline Efficiency})$$

The ability to implement pipeline parallelism and custom circuit designs directly in hardware allows FPGAs to provide unparalleled latency reductions. These devices can be integrated into HFT systems to perform specific, time-critical tasks with minimal delay, complementing the more general-purpose CPUs and highly parallel GPUs.

Choosing the Right Hardware

Selecting the appropriate hardware configuration for an HFT system depends on the specific requirements and constraints of the trading strategy. CPUs are essential for their robust and versatile processing capabilities, particularly in the execution of trading decisions and handling of network communications. GPUs contribute significant computational power for data-intensive operations and machine learning tasks. FPGAs offer the lowest possible latencies for time-critical processes, providing a significant edge in highly competitive trading environments.

Considerations such as power consumption, heat dissipation, and the cost of development and maintenance should also influence hardware choices. It is often beneficial to create a hybrid architecture that leverages the strengths of CPUs, GPUs, and FPGAs to create an optimal HFT system that meets the demands of speed, flexibility, and processing power.

The interplay between these hardware components forms the backbone of modern HFT systems, enabling the rapid and efficient execution of complex trading strategies. By understanding the unique attributes and optimal use cases for CPUs, GPUs, and FPGAs, traders can design systems that maximize performance and minimize latency, ensuring a competitive advantage in the high-speed world of HFT.

3.4 Low-Latency Communication Protocols

In the realm of High-Frequency Trading (HFT), the efficiency and speed of data transmission are pivotal. Low-latency communication protocols are designed to minimize the delay between the sending and receiving of data, thus ensuring that trades are executed in fractions of a second. This section delves into the intricacies of these protocols and their crucial role in the technological ecosystem of HFT.

At the core of low-latency communication is the need to bypass traditional bottlenecks that impede data flow. Legacy protocols such as TCP/IP, while reliable, introduce latencies due to their overhead in ensuring data integrity and handling congestion. For HFT operations, every microsecond counts, and thus more streamlined protocols are employed.

One such protocol is the User Datagram Protocol (UDP). Unlike TCP,

UDP is connectionless and does not guarantee delivery, order, or error-checking, which significantly reduces its latency. By eliminating the need for acknowledgments and retransmissions, UDP facilitates ultra-fast data transmission. However, the trade-off is that it requires robust error-handling mechanisms built into the application layer to account for potential packet loss or out-of-order delivery.

An advanced variant of UDP utilized in financial markets is UDP Multicast. This technique allows a single data packet to be sent to multiple recipients simultaneously, rather than sending individual packets to each recipient. This multicast capability is particularly advantageous in market data dissemination, where the same data must be broadcasted to multiple trading systems concurrently, thereby reducing network load and enhancing synchronization across trading platforms.

Low-latency communication also heavily relies on the Financial Information eXchange (FIX) protocol, specifically its optimized versions such as FIX/FAST (FIX Adapted for STreaming). FIX is a standardized protocol for the electronic communication of trade-related messages. FIX/FAST enhances this by employing a combination of data compression techniques and binary encoding to reduce the message size and parsing time, facilitating faster data exchange.

Another critical protocol in HFT is the use of Remote Direct Memory Access (RDMA). RDMA allows data to be transferred directly from the memory of one computer to another with minimal CPU involvement, bypassing the kernel and providing low-latency, high-throughput communication. This direct memory access cuts down the number of context switches and copying operations typically involved in network communication, markedly reducing latency.

To exemplify the impact of optimized communication protocols, consider the deployment of Infiniband technology, which leverages RDMA. Infiniband networks offer higher throughput and lower latency compared to traditional Ethernet, as they are specifically architected for high-performance computing environments. By facilitating rapid data transfer with low overhead, Infiniband greatly enhances the performance of HFT systems.

Market participants have also increasingly adopted Message Queuing Telemetry Transport (MQTT) for its lightweight nature. While originally designed for constrained environments, MQTT's low bandwidth requirements and minimal latency make it suitable for the high-speed demands of financial trading.

In addition to choosing the right communication protocol, the physical placement of trading infrastructure—known as colocation—plays a critical role. By colocating servers close to the exchange's matching engine, firms can significantly reduce the physical distance data must travel, thereby cutting down on transmission delays.

On a software level, kernel bypass techniques such as TCP Direct and Solarflare OpenOnload allow applications to directly interface with network hardware. By bypassing the traditional network stack, these techniques further minimize latency and are widely implemented in HFT.

Achieving low latency extends beyond merely choosing the right protocol but involves a comprehensive optimization strategy. This includes fine-tuning network interface cards (NICs), employing precision time protocols (PTP) for clock synchronization, and rigorously monitoring network performance.

Ultimately, low-latency communication protocols are a linchpin in the operational excellence of HFT. Each micro-optimization, whether at the level of the protocol or the underlying hardware, contributes to the competitive edge of executing trades at the speed of light.

Through the integration of these sophisticated protocols and technologies, firms engaging in HFT can ensure that they remain at the forefront of market efficiency, capitalizing on fleeting trading opportunities that slower counterparts might miss. By continuing to innovate in communication protocols, the field of high-frequency trading will persist in its quest to shave off precious microseconds, maintaining a relentless pursuit of zero latency.

3.5 Data Storage and Management

In the rapid and intricate world of High-Frequency Trading (HFT), efficient data storage and management play a crucial role in ensuring that trading algorithms operate with the necessary speed and precision. The sheer volume of market data, along with the need for real-time analysis and decision-making, necessitates advanced storage solutions and rigorous data management practices. This section delves into the critical elements of data storage and management that underpin successful HFT operations.

A cornerstone of effective data management in HFT is the ability to handle vast quantities of data at exceptionally high speeds. Market participants must record every tick, trade, and quotational update to construct accurate order books and perform comprehensive backtesting of algorithms. The primary types of data involved include historical data for backtesting, real-time data for live trading, and metadata for logging and audit trails.

It is essential to choose the appropriate storage technologies to manage these different data types efficiently. Traditional relational databases can be insufficient due to their limitations in handling high-frequency updates and large-scale data retrievals. In contrast, columnar databases such as Apache Kudu and distributed databases like Apache Cassandra have gained popularity for their ability to manage sizable datasets with low-latency read and write operations.

Furthermore, innovative storage solutions like NewSQL databases offer the transactional consistency of SQL databases while also providing the horizontal scalability found in NoSQL systems. These databases facilitate real-time data ingestion and high-speed querying, which are pivotal in the high-frequency trading environment.

$$\text{Latency} = \left(\frac{\text{Data Ingestion Time} + \text{Query Execution Time}}{\text{Total Number of Transactions}} \right) \tag{3.1}$$

Optimizing this latency equation is essential for maintaining a competitive edge in HFT. The use of in-memory databases (IMDBs), such as Redis and MemSQL, further enhances performance by storing data directly in RAM rather than on disk, thereby significantly reducing access times.

For storage redundancy and fault tolerance, HFT firms often utilize distributed file systems like Apache Hadoop's HDFS or cloud-based solutions such as Amazon S3. These systems provide the necessary scalability and resilience, ensuring that data loss or corruption does not disrupt trading activities.

Data management is not just about storage but also about the speedy retrieval and processing of data. Advanced indexing techniques, such as inverted indexing or the use of B-trees and hash maps, are instrumental in accelerating query performance. Proper indexing reduces the time complexity of search operations, which is critical for real-time trading decisions.

Additionally, data compression techniques can vastly improve storage efficiency and retrieval speed. Algorithms such as LZ77, BZIP2, and

Snappy compress data to reduce storage space requirements while allowing rapid decompression for analysis and trading purposes.

Incorporating data management frameworks can streamline the entire data handling process. Frameworks like Apache Kafka for real-time data streaming and Apache Flink for stateful stream processing ensure that data flows seamlessly from source to storage to analysis, all in real-time. Integration with these frameworks allows traders to build robust pipelines that can process high-velocity market data and trigger trading algorithms without delay.

Security is another paramount concern in HFT data management. Implementing robust encryption protocols for data at rest and in transit, alongside stringent access control measures, protects sensitive trading data from unauthorized access and breaches.

In conclusion, investing in sophisticated data storage and management strategies is crucial for the success of HFT operations. By leveraging cutting-edge technologies and best practices, traders can ensure that they are well-positioned to process vast amounts of financial data with the speed and accuracy required to thrive in the highly competitive realm of high-frequency trading.

3.6 Latency Measurement and Optimization Techniques

In the world of High-Frequency Trading (HFT), latency, defined as the delay between the initiation and execution of a trade, is critically important. Even microsecond delays can result in significant financial impact, making the measurement and optimization of latency an indispensable aspect of HFT operations.

Understanding latency begins with its precise measurement. This process involves several aspects, including hardware monitoring, software profiling, and network latency measurement. Instruments such as latency probes, network time protocol (NTP) servers, and high-resolution timers are often employed to gather accurate data. The goal is to identify and quantify all sources of latency within the trading system, from the time a trading signal is generated to when the order is finalized on the exchange.

Let's first explore the tools and methodologies for measuring latency in an HFT environment.

Accurate latency measurement is foundational to optimization. Various tools and techniques are employed, each serving a distinct purpose:

- **Chronographic Profiling:** This technique involves timestamping events at various stages within the trading system. Tools like Chrony or in-house developed scripts can provide microsecond-level accuracy, allowing traders to analyze the time taken by each component.

- **Network Time Protocol (NTP):** NTP is crucial for synchronizing clocks across various components of the trading network. Proper configuration ensures accurate time-stamping and helps in comparing latency across geographically dispersed servers.

- **Latency Probes:** Latency probes are specialized hardware tools used to measure network latency with high precision. These devices capture packet timings and analyze data transfer delays, offering granular insights into network performance.

Software profiling complements hardware measurements by providing insights into the internal delays within the trading algorithms and systems:

- **Application Performance Monitoring (APM):** Tools such as New Relic and Dynatrace help in monitoring the real-time performance of software applications, identifying bottlenecks, and providing diagnostics.

- **Code Optimization:** Profiling tools like Perf for Linux and VTune for Intel processors allow developers to identify and optimize specific sections of the code that contribute to higher latency.

- **Micro-benchmarks:** Conducting micro-benchmarks on different algorithmic components helps in isolating and understanding the impact of each piece of code on overall latency.

Network latency can often be the most significant component of overall system latency:

- **Network Analyzers:** Tools such as Wireshark and tcpdump are essential for capturing and analyzing packet transfers. They help in identifying delays and pinpointing where latency is introduced.

- **Ping and Traceroute:** Simple yet effective, these tools can offer initial insights into the time taken for packets to travel from one node to another and the paths they take.

- **Latency Measurement Devices:** In more sophisticated setups, specialized devices that measure the one-way delay (OWD) between trading servers and exchanges are utilized. These devices provide microsecond accuracies and help in aligning trading strategies accordingly.

With a detailed understanding of latency measurement, we proceed to optimization techniques. Optimization spans both software and hardware realms, aiming to minimize delays at every step of the trading process.

Effective optimization requires both a systemic and a component-based approach:

- **Algorithmic Efficiency:** Ensuring that trading algorithms are efficiently coded and executed is critical. This can involve:
  - Reducing computational complexity.
  - Optimizing for parallel processing if using CPUs or GPUs.
  - Minimizing inter-process communication delays.

- **Hardware Acceleration:** Utilizing hardware-specific optimizations, such as:
  - Employing Field-Programmable Gate Arrays (FPGAs) to handle high-frequency tasks like order book management and signal processing.
  - Using multi-threading and vectorization capabilities of modern CPUs to speed up computation.

- **Network Optimization:** Reducing network latency through:
  - Direct market access (DMA) to bypass brokers and reduce order routing time.
  - Leveraging ultra-low latency network protocols such as Remote Direct Memory Access (RDMA) that allow direct memory access from one machine to another without involving either one's operating system.

    - Geographical optimization, including co-locating trading servers near exchange data centers to reduce physical distance and hence the time taken for data transmission.

- **Data Storage and Retrieval:** Techniques to expedite data handling include:
    - Utilizing in-memory data structures and databases for ultra-fast data retrieval.
    - Implementing efficient data caching mechanisms to reduce access time to frequently used data.

In addition to these methods, continuous monitoring and iterative improvements are imperative. HFT firms must maintain a cycle of measurement, analysis, and optimization. Real-time monitoring systems need to be robust, generating alerts for deviations in latency profiles and triggering automated adjustments where feasible.

Perfecting latency optimization is an ongoing challenge requiring relentless attention to detail and advanced technological implementations. The ability to measure and optimize latency effectively translates directly to competitive advantage in HFT, offering quicker trade executions and potentially higher profitability.

3.7 Cloud Computing vs. On-Premises Solutions

As the demands of High-Frequency Trading (HFT) continue to escalate, the choice between cloud computing and on-premises solutions becomes increasingly significant. This section delves into the nuances of both approaches, equipping traders and firms with the knowledge needed to make informed decisions based on their specific needs and constraints.

HFT operations rely heavily on rapid processing and minimal latency. Traditionally, firms have preferred on-premises solutions for the perceived control and performance they offer. However, advancements in cloud technology have made cloud computing a viable contender. Each approach has its unique set of advantages and challenges, which we will explore in detail.

On-premises solutions involve procuring, maintaining, and operating hardware and infrastructure within the firm's own facilities. This setup provides unparalleled control over the physical and virtual environments, crucial for minimizing latency and optimizing performance. High-performance computing resources such as state-of-the-art servers, networking hardware, and specialized devices like Field Programmable Gate Arrays (FPGAs) can be tailored specifically to the firm's requirements.

The advantages of on-premises solutions are numerous:

- **Latency Control:** Firms have direct control over their network configurations and hardware, enabling fine-tuning for minimal latency.
- **Security:** Physical and data security can be tightly managed with dedicated infrastructure, reducing the risks associated with multi-tenancy inherent in cloud environments.
- **Customization:** Proprietary algorithms and trading strategies can be implemented on highly customized hardware and software stacks, optimized specifically for the firm's needs.
- **Predictability:** Performance metrics are more predictable since the infrastructure is static and under the firm's direct management.

Despite these benefits, on-premises solutions come with significant drawbacks:

- **Cost:** The capital expenditure (CapEx) required for purchasing, operating, and maintaining high-end servers and networking equipment is substantial. Depreciation of these assets also impacts financials.
- **Scalability:** Scaling up operations involves additional hardware investments and potentially significant lead time for procurement and setup, limiting flexibility.
- **Maintenance:** Ongoing hardware and software maintenance can be resource-intensive, requiring specialized IT staff and infrastructure management practices.

Cloud computing, on the other hand, offers an alternative model characterized by flexibility and reduced upfront capital investment. Major cloud service providers like Amazon Web Services (AWS), Microsoft

Azure, and Google Cloud Platform (GCP) offer extensive infrastructure and services that can be scaled dynamically based on demand.

Key benefits of cloud computing include:

- **Scalability:** Resources can be scaled up or down quickly to meet the fluctuating demands of trading operations, often within minutes.
- **Cost Efficiency:** Transitioning to an operational expenditure (OpEx) model shifts financial burden, with firms paying only for what they use, thus avoiding large upfront investments.
- **Agility:** Rapid provisioning enables firms to deploy new services and expand into new markets swiftly.
- **Maintenance-Free:** The cloud provider manages infrastructure maintenance, allowing firms to focus more on their core competencies and less on IT overhead.

However, cloud computing also poses challenges:

- **Latency:** Despite advances, network latency to and from cloud data centers can still be higher compared to on-premises setups, potentially impacting trade execution speeds.
- **Security Concerns:** Data security and compliance risks are heightened in multi-tenant environments. Careful selection of providers and adherence to stringent security practices are necessary.
- **Vendor Lock-In:** Dependency on a specific cloud vendor's ecosystem can make future migrations costly and complex. Strategic planning and consideration of cross-platform compatibility are crucial.

Evaluating these factors, firms must align their choice with strategic goals and operational realities. An emerging trend serving as a middle ground is the hybrid model, combining on-premises and cloud infrastructure to leverage the strengths of both. Firms may choose to run latency-sensitive components on-premises while leveraging the cloud for non-critical operations, backups, and scaling needs. This hybrid approach provides a balanced framework, optimizing both performance and flexibility.

Technological advancements continue to evolve, and the gap between cloud and on-premises solutions in terms of HFT viability is narrowing. Conducting thorough latency, cost, and security assessments, alongside considering future needs and growth trajectories, will guide firms in making an optimal choice.

In the fast-paced environment of HFT, revisiting these options periodically ensures that infrastructure aligns dynamically with market conditions and technological advancements, enabling sustained competitive edge.

3.8 Emerging Technologies in HFT

As the landscape of High-Frequency Trading (HFT) evolves, staying ahead requires not only mastering current technologies but also anticipating future advancements. Emerging technologies offer opportunities for significant breakthroughs in speed, efficiency, and accuracy, each of which can provide a competitive edge. Here, we delve into some of these critical advancements and how they promise to shape the future of HFT.

One of the most promising developments is the integration of Artificial Intelligence (AI) and Machine Learning (ML) within trading algorithms. Unlike traditional algorithms that rely heavily on predefined rules, AI and ML allow for adaptive learning from vast amounts of historical and real-time market data. These systems optimize trading strategies by learning patterns and making real-time decisions, potentially offering superior predictive capabilities.

$$\text{Profit} = \sum_{i=1}^{n} (P_i - C_i) \cdot S_i$$

In recent years, Quantum Computing has emerged as a frontier technology with immense transformative potential for HFT. Quantum computers operate on the principles of quantum mechanics, enabling them to process and analyze data at speeds far surpassing classical computers. Specifically, their ability to perform complex calculations in parallel could significantly enhance the optimization of trading algorithms and risk management strategies. Although currently in its nascent stage, the implications for HFT are profound, promising unprecedented improvements in computational power and execution speed.

Deploying technologies like Blockchain can further advance the reliability and transparency of transactions in HFT. Blockchain's decentralized ledger technology ensures a tamper-proof and transparent record of trades and settlements. This can not only enhance security but also reduce counterparty risk and the need for intermediaries, leading to faster and more reliable trade settlements. For HFT firms, integrating blockchain into their infrastructure could streamline operations and mitigate risks associated with complex trading environments.

The Internet of Things (IoT) is another emerging technology that has the potential to revolutionize HFT. IoT devices collect and transmit data in real time, providing traders with an unprecedented level of market insight. For instance, sensors in the physical world can capture data related to economic indicators, commodities supply chains, or environmental conditions, all of which can be used to make more informed trading decisions. Leveraging real-time insights from IoT can significantly enhance the responsiveness and accuracy of HFT strategies.

Edge Computing is transforming data processing by bringing computation and data storage closer to data sources. This proximity reduces the latency associated with data transfer, which is crucial for HFT operations that depend on ultra-low latency. By processing data at the edge of the network rather than in centralized data centers, HFT firms can achieve faster execution times and more efficient data handling. This approach is particularly advantageous in scenarios requiring rapid decision-making and real-time analytics.

Furthermore, advancements in 5G technology are set to revolutionize the speed and reliability of data transmission in HFT. The enhanced bandwidth and reduced latency provided by 5G networks can significantly improve the performance of communication protocols used in HFT. This means faster access to market data, quicker order execution, and more efficient use of high-frequency trading algorithms. As this technology becomes more widespread, it will likely become a vital component of the HFT infrastructure.

Finally, developments in neuromorphic computing, which mimics the neural structure of the human brain, are paving the way for innovative computational approaches in HFT. Neuromorphic chips process information in a highly parallel manner, much like human brains, offering significant advantages in processing speed and efficiency. For HFT, this means potentially faster and more adaptive algorithms capable of handling complex and unpredictable market conditions.

The integration of these emerging technologies into HFT infrastructures is not without challenges. Regulatory considerations, infrastructure costs, and the need for specialized expertise are significant hurdles. However, the potential benefits in terms of speed, efficiency, and strategic advantage make them worthwhile investments for forward-thinking HFT firms. As these technologies mature, they will undoubtedly redefine the contours of high-frequency trading, setting new benchmarks for what is achievable in this dynamic and competitive field.

Chapter 4

Algorithm Design and Optimization

This chapter focuses on the principles of designing and optimizing algorithms for High-Frequency Trading (HFT). It covers the foundational building blocks of HFT algorithms and outlines the development process, emphasizing speed and efficiency. The discussion includes optimization techniques, error handling, fault tolerance, and the critical practice of backtesting. Additionally, the chapter addresses parameter tuning, sensitivity analysis, and the metrics used for evaluating algorithm performance. These insights are crucial for developing robust, high-performing trading algorithms.

4.1 Introduction to Algorithm Design

The world of High-Frequency Trading (HFT) relies heavily on the design and implementation of sophisticated algorithms that can execute trades at sub-millisecond speeds. These algorithms are the heartbeat of HFT, driving the rapid decision-making processes that capitalize on fleeting market opportunities. Understanding the intricacies of algorithm design is fundamental for any trader or developer aspiring to succeed in this competitive landscape.

At its core, algorithm design in HFT involves creating a set of well-defined rules and instructions that a computer can execute to achieve specific trading objectives. The primary goals are to maximize efficiency, minimize latency, and ensure robustness under varying market conditions. This section will introduce the essential aspects of algorithm design, addressing both the theoretical foundations and practical considerations.

A high-frequency trading algorithm typically consists of several key components, including market data handlers, signal generation modules, trade execution engines, and risk management protocols. Each of these components must work in harmony to deliver optimal performance. Below, we delve into the primary aspects of designing these components, starting with market data handlers.

Market data handlers are responsible for processing vast amounts of real-time data from various exchanges. They need to parse and interpret data with minimal latency, ensuring that the algorithm always has an up-to-date view of the market. Efficient data handling involves techniques such as sampling, filtering, and normalization of tick data. Furthermore, it requires sophisticated data structures that allow for rapid access and manipulation of incoming information. The design of these handlers influences the overall responsiveness and speed of the entire algorithm. For instance, using lock-free queues and memory-efficient data structures can significantly reduce processing delays.

Once the market data is properly handled, the next critical component is the signal generation module. This module analyzes the processed data to identify trading signals or opportunities. The complexity of signal generation can vary widely, ranging from simple threshold-based strategies to advanced machine learning models. Regardless of the approach, the design must prioritize both speed and accuracy. Optimization techniques such as feature selection and dimensionality reduction can help streamline the data inputs, while ensuring that the model remains responsive during real-time trading.

The trade execution engine is another vital piece of the algorithm. It translates trading signals into actionable orders and ensures that these orders are executed swiftly and accurately on the desired exchange. The execution engine must optimize order placement to reduce slippage and market impact, employing techniques like smart order routing and order slicing. The engine's design should account for different order types and execution strategies, making it adaptable to various market scenarios.

Risk management protocols underpin the entire algorithmic framework, safeguarding against potential losses and ensuring compliance with regulatory requirements. Effective risk management involves setting appropriate position limits, developing stop-loss mechanisms, and continuously monitoring market exposure. Designing robust risk management protocols requires a thorough understanding of the trading strategy's risk profile and incorporating real-time analytics to pre-empt and mitigate unforeseen risks. Stress testing and scenario analysis are crucial to validate the effectiveness of these protocols under extreme market conditions.

The design process is iterative and necessitates continuous refinement through rigorous testing and validation. Backtesting, a method of evaluating the algorithm's performance on historical data, is an invaluable part of this process. It helps identify potential flaws and optimization opportunities before the algorithm goes live. Sensitivity analysis further enhances robustness by assessing how the algorithm responds to variations in input parameters and market conditions.

In essence, designing an HFT algorithm is akin to building a high-speed race car: every component must be meticulously engineered for performance and reliability. The interplay between data processing, signal generation, trade execution, and risk management creates a complex but fascinating ecosystem. Mastery in designing these algorithms equips traders with a powerful tool to navigate and excel in the high-stakes arena of high-frequency trading, where speed and precision are paramount.

4.2 Basic Building Blocks of HFT Algorithms

High-Frequency Trading (HFT) algorithms are intricate systems that necessitate a profound understanding of both market dynamics and advanced computational techniques. At their core, these algorithms are designed to execute a large number of orders at extremely high speeds, capitalizing on the smallest price discrepancies. Understanding the basic building blocks is imperative for developing robust and efficient HFT algorithms. Let's delve into the key components that constitute the foundation of these systems.

1. Data Acquisition and Preprocessing

The first essential element of HFT algorithms is data acquisition. Trading decisions are heavily reliant on real-time market data, including price quotes, trade volumes, and order book depth. This data is streamed from various exchanges and needs to be captured with minimal latency.

$$S_{price}(t_i) = \text{stock price at time } t_i$$

The captured raw data often contains noise and inaccuracies. Preprocessing steps such as filtering, normalization, and synchronization are crucial to ensure that the data fed into the algorithm is accurate and reliable. For instance, missing data points can be handled through interpolation, while outliers might be adjusted or discarded based on predetermined criteria.

2. Signal Generation

Once the data is clean and ready, the next step is signal generation. This involves the detection of trading signals based on predefined criteria or patterns, often derived from technical indicators, statistical models, or machine learning techniques. Commonly used indicators in HFT include moving averages, Bollinger Bands, and Relative Strength Index (RSI).

$$MA(t, n) = \frac{1}{n} \sum_{i=0}^{n-1} P(t - i)$$

Signal generation can also employ more sophisticated approaches such as machine learning models that predict short-term price movements based on historical data and additional features.

3. Strategy Execution

After identifying a trading signal, the algorithm must decide on the strategy to employ. Strategy execution involves selecting the type of orders to place, the timing, and the size of each order. The common strategies in HFT include market making, arbitrage, and statistical arbitrage.

In market making, the algorithm places buy and sell limit orders in an attempt to profit from the bid-ask spread. Arbitrage strategies exploit price discrepancies between correlated instruments or across different markets. Statistical arbitrage involves complex mathematical models to identify and capitalize on mean reversion or other statistical relationships.

$$\text{Arbitrage Opportunity} = P_A(t) - P_B(t) - \text{Transaction Cost}$$

4. Risk Management

Risk management is a critical component that ensures the stability and longevity of an HFT algorithm. It involves setting parameters and constraints to mitigate potential losses and exposure to unfavorable market conditions. Key aspects include stop-loss limits, position sizing, and portfolio diversification.

Stop-loss orders automatically close positions that reach a pre-defined loss level, thereby limiting further losses. Position sizing rules determine the amount of capital allocated to each trade based on risk tolerance and market conditions.

$$\text{Position Size} = \frac{\text{Account Equity} \times \text{Risk Per Trade}}{\text{Stop-Loss Distance}}$$

5. Latency Optimization

Latency is the time delay between the occurrence of a market event and the corresponding reaction of the trading algorithm. In HFT, minimizing latency is paramount as even microseconds can differentiate between a profitable trade and a missed opportunity.

Latency optimization encompasses hardware improvements like using faster processors, proximity hosting (co-locating servers near exchange data centers), and efficient coding practices to minimize the algorithm's computational overhead.

6. Regulatory Compliance

Finally, regulatory compliance is an often-overlooked but vital element of HFT algorithms. Regulations such as the Markets in Financial Instruments Directive (MiFID II) in Europe or the Securities and Exchange Commission (SEC) rules in the United States govern trading practices and impose specific requirements. Ensuring that algorithms adhere to these regulations helps avoid legal repercussions and maintain market integrity.

Compliance includes maintaining audit trails, implementing pre-trade risk controls, and adhering to market abuse laws. Regular audits and updates to the algorithm code can assist in maintaining regulatory adherence.

Developing a high-frequency trading algorithm involves the seamless integration of these building blocks. Each component must be meticulously crafted and continuously optimized to achieve the desired performance and reliability. By understanding and effectively combining these elements, traders can build sophisticated HFT systems capable of thriving in the competitive world of high-speed trading.

4.3 Algorithm Development Process

Developing a high-frequency trading (HFT) algorithm is akin to constructing a finely tuned machine. Each component must work in harmony to achieve optimal performance and reliability. This section outlines the systematic process of developing an HFT algorithm, encompassing the conceptualization phase to the final implementation stage. A structured approach is critical, ensuring each element of the algorithm is meticulously designed and rigorously tested to handle the demands of live trading environments.

To begin with, the development process can be broken down into several key stages: conceptualization, data acquisition, model design, implementation, testing, and deployment. Each stage builds upon the prior, creating a robust pipeline for algorithm creation.

Conceptualization

At the heart of any successful HFT algorithm lies a sound trading strategy. Conceptualization involves defining the strategy based on market hypotheses, statistical models, and trading logic. During this phase, it is essential to identify market inefficiencies that the algorithm aims to exploit. Common strategies may include arbitrage, mean reversion, or momentum-based trading.

To formalize this, one might start by implementing a simplified mathematical expression of the trading logic. For instance, an arbitrage strategy could be expressed as:

$$\text{Profit} = P_{\text{market A}} - P_{\text{market B}} - \text{Transaction Costs}$$

where $P_{\text{market A}}$ and $P_{\text{market B}}$ represent the prices in two different markets. The initial hypothesis should align with the potential to generate consistent returns without relying on large market movements.

Data Acquisition

The lifeblood of any HFT algorithm is high-quality data. Accurate, low-latency market data is crucial. During this stage, developers must decide on the type of data required—historical, real-time, or both. Historical data is paramount for backtesting and validating the algorithm's performance over different market conditions.

Obtaining this data typically involves partnerships with data vendors or using APIs provided by exchanges. The acquired data must be meticulously cleaned and preprocessed, as any noise or inaccuracies can significantly impact the algorithm's decisions. An example of preprocessing involves handling missing values, removing duplicates, and aligning timestamps for time series data.

Model Design

With a clear strategy and cleaned dataset at hand, the next step involves designing the trading model. This includes selecting appropriate statistical methods and machine learning techniques, which may range from simple moving averages to complex predictive models.

For instance, a moving average crossover strategy can be outlined where the algorithm generates buy or sell signals based on the crossover of short-term and long-term moving averages:

$$\text{Signal} = \begin{cases} 1 & \text{if } MA_{\text{short}} > MA_{\text{long}} \\ -1 & \text{if } MA_{\text{short}} < MA_{\text{long}} \end{cases}$$

Here, MA_{short} and MA_{long} represent the short-term and long-term moving averages, respectively. The choice of parameters (e.g., window lengths for the moving averages) is crucial for ensuring the model aligns with the strategy's intent.

Implementation

The designed model must now be translated into code, a critical step as the efficiency of the code directly impacts the performance of the HFT algorithm. Programming languages like C++, Python, and Java are commonly used, each offering distinct advantages in terms of speed and flexibility.

During implementation, careful attention should be paid to optimizing the algorithm to minimize latency. This involves efficient data structures, multithreading, and low-level system optimizations. Below is a pseudocode snippet for a simple moving average crossover strategy illustrating the logic flow:

```
# Pseudocode for Moving Average Crossover Strategy
initialize short_term_window
initialize long_term_window

for each tick in market_data:
    update short_term_moving_average
    update long_term_moving_average

    if short_term_moving_average > long_term_moving_average:
        execute buy_order
    elif short_term_moving_average < long_term_moving_average:
        execute sell_order
```

Fault tolerance mechanisms must be incorporated to handle unexpected scenarios such as network failures, data feed disruptions, or software bugs.

Testing

Testing is perhaps the most iterative and critical phase of the development process. It involves both backtesting and forward testing to validate the effectiveness of the trading strategy under historical and real-time conditions.

Backtesting runs the algorithm over historical data and helps identify potential issues and refine the trading logic. Essential metrics to evaluate during backtesting include Sharpe ratio, drawdown, and maximum adverse excursion. An example backtesting result visualization, comparing the algorithm's returns against a benchmark index, can be depicted using a basic line chart.

Forward testing, on the other hand, deploys the algorithm in a paper trading setup to simulate live trading without financial risk. This showcases how the algorithm performs under current market conditions and assesses its robustness.

Deployment

Once testing confirms that the algorithm performs as expected, the final step is deployment in a live trading environment. This requires integration with brokerage APIs or trading platforms, ensuring that the infrastructure can handle the demands of live trading. Ongoing monitoring is critical to swiftly address any issues that may arise and to continuously refine the algorithm based on market feedback.

By following a structured development process, traders and developers can systematically build and refine high-frequency trading algorithms that are both robust and efficient, capable of thriving in the dynamic landscape of the financial markets.

4.4 Optimization Techniques for Speed and Efficiency

Developing high-frequency trading (HFT) algorithms necessitates a rigorous focus on speed and efficiency. Given the hyper-competitive nature of the market, even microseconds can spell the difference between profit and loss. Optimizing algorithms is therefore a paramount concern for HFT practitioners. This section delves into various optimization techniques designed to enhance the speed and efficiency of trading algorithms.

One fundamental aspect of optimizing HFT algorithms is minimizing latency. Latency, the delay between the initiation of an action and its corresponding result, can significantly affect trading performance. The components of latency include network latency, processing latency, and data feed latency. Each of these must be minimized to achieve optimal algorithm performance.

Network latency can be reduced by optimizing the physical and logical network paths between the trading algorithms and the exchanges. Techniques to achieve this include colocating servers in data centers near exchange servers, employing faster network technologies (such as fiber optics), and optimizing network configurations to reduce hops and improve data throughput. Furthermore, reducing packet size and avoiding network congestion can also contribute to minimizing network latency.

Processing latency, the time taken by the algorithm to process incoming data and make trading decisions, is another critical factor. Optimizing processing latency typically involves enhancing both software and hardware components. At the software level, this can mean using high-performance, low-level programming languages such as C++ or Rust, which provide greater control over memory allocation and processor instructions than higher-level languages like Python. Code profiling tools can be invaluable in identifying bottlenecks and optimizing critical code sections.

At the hardware level, utilizing multi-core processors and parallel processing techniques can significantly reduce processing times. Techniques such as data pipelining and branch prediction can also help to expedite processing. Furthermore, leveraging specialized hardware like Field-Programmable Gate Arrays (FPGAs) and Graphics Processing Units (GPUs) can provide substantial speed improvements. FP-

GAs, for example, can be programmed to execute specific trading strategies at hardware speeds, eliminating the software overhead entirely.

Data feed latency, the delay in receiving market data from exchanges, can be mitigated by subscribing to high-priority data feeds and using direct market access (DMA). DMA allows traders to interact directly with order books at various exchanges, reducing the latency associated with intermediaries. Additionally, employing compression algorithms and optimizing data parsing processes can further enhance the speed at which market data is processed and acted upon.

Another key area of optimization is the efficient management of computational resources. This includes techniques such as load balancing, where tasks are distributed evenly across available processors to prevent any single processor from becoming a bottleneck. Memory management also plays a crucial role; employing efficient data structures and avoiding memory leaks can ensure that the algorithm remains responsive even under high workloads.

Caching frequently accessed data can reduce the time spent on data retrieval operations. For instance, storing recent market data in high-speed caches can minimize the need to repeatedly access slower storage layers. Efficient database indexing and query optimization techniques can also reduce data retrieval times, enhancing overall algorithm performance.

The use of asynchronous processing methods can further optimize performance by allowing the algorithm to perform multiple tasks concurrently without waiting for each task to complete before starting the next one. For example, while one part of the algorithm processes incoming market data, another part can simultaneously be sending and monitoring orders, thus improving the throughput and responsiveness of the trading system.

Finally, continuous performance monitoring and iterative optimization are essential. This involves regularly collecting and analyzing performance metrics to identify any new bottlenecks or inefficiencies. Metrics such as order execution time, end-to-end latency, and system throughput should be continuously monitored. Leveraging machine learning techniques to dynamically adjust and optimize algorithm parameters in real-time can also be a powerful approach. These iterative optimizations ensure that the algorithm remains at peak performance despite changes in market conditions or trading environments.

By employing these optimization techniques, traders can ensure that their HFT algorithms are not only fast but also robust and efficient, capable of executing complex strategies within the stringent time constraints demanded by modern financial markets.

4.5 Error Handling and Fault Tolerance

In the highly competitive domain of High-Frequency Trading (HFT), the ability to handle errors swiftly and ensure fault tolerance is a critical component of algorithm design. While HFT systems strive for optimum performance, they are not immune to errors and unexpected failures, which can result from various sources such as software bugs, network issues, hardware malfunctions, or market anomalies.

Effective error handling and fault-tolerant design are imperative in maintaining the integrity, reliability, and consistent performance of trading algorithms. This section delves into sophisticated strategies for minimizing downtime and mitigating risks associated with algorithmic failures, ensuring the robustness of your HFT systems.

Anticipating Failure Scenarios

To build resilient algorithms, it is essential to anticipate and plan for potential failure scenarios. Begin by identifying common failure points within your trading system:

- **Software Bugs:** Coding errors or logical flaws that might result in incorrect decision-making.
- **Network Latency:** Delays in information transmission can affect order execution timing.
- **Hardware Faults:** Failures in servers, routers, or storage devices causing critical downtime.
- **Data Feed Errors:** Incorrect or delayed market data can lead to erroneous trades.

By recognizing these risks, you can institute preemptive checks and balances to mitigate their impact.

Incorporating Redundancy

Redundancy is a fundamental aspect of fault-tolerant systems. Implementing redundancy involves deploying multiple instances of critical components, thus ensuring that the failure of a single element does not incapacitate the entire system. Consider the following strategies:

- **Redundant Hardware:** Utilize backup servers and network devices that can take over automatically in the event of a primary component failure.
- **Multiple Data Feeds:** Subscribe to multiple market data providers to cross-verify information and ensure continuity.
- **Dual-Path Communication:** Establish alternative communication paths to handle network failures.

The application of redundancy enhances system availability and reliability, crucial for maintaining continuous trading activities.

Implementing Robust Monitoring and Alerts

Proactive monitoring and real-time alerts are vital for the early detection of anomalies and swift corrective action. Construct an extensive monitoring framework encompassing various aspects of the system:

- **System Health Monitoring:** Track CPU usage, memory allocation, and disk I/O operations to preempt hardware strain.
- **Network Performance Monitoring:** Regularly measure latency, packet loss, and throughput to detect network issues.
- **Trade and Order Monitoring:** Continuously monitor the status of orders, trade executions, and confirmation messages.

Deploy alert mechanisms to notify operators of irregularities, enabling rapid response before issues escalate into critical failures.

Utilizing Exception Handling Mechanisms

Incorporate comprehensive exception handling within your codebase to gracefully manage unexpected events. Exception handling involves catching errors during execution and systematically determining the appropriate recovery actions. The following principles are essential:

- **Define Clear Exception Types:** Establish specific exceptions for different error conditions, making it easier to identify and address issues.

- **Log Errors:** Implement detailed logging for error events to facilitate post-mortem analysis and future risk mitigation.
- **Fail Safe Mechanisms:** Ensure that the system transitions to a safe state upon encountering critical errors, such as halting trading operations to prevent unintended loss.

By intelligently handling exceptions, trading software can remain operational and resilient even under adverse conditions.

Designing for Scalability and Flexibility

Scalability and flexibility are hallmarks of fault-tolerant systems. Designing software that can scale horizontally, by adding more nodes, or vertically, by enhancing the capabilities of existing nodes, ensures that the system can handle increased loads and adapt to changing conditions. Emphasize these design principles:

- **Modular Architecture:** Design systems with interchangeable modules that can be independently updated or replaced.
- **Service-Oriented Architecture (SOA):** Utilize services that communicate over a network to facilitate scalability and fault isolation.
- **Asynchronous Processing:** Employ asynchronous operations to decouple processes, allowing continued functionality even if certain components are delayed or fail.

A scalable and flexible design helps in maintaining seamless operation and efficient management in dynamic and high-stakes trading environments.

Implementing Recovery Protocols and Procedures

Effective recovery protocols are paramount in restoring normal operations swiftly after a failure. Establish and routinely test recovery procedures:

- **Automated Failover:** Develop scripts and automated processes that initiate backup systems upon detecting failure.
- **Regular Backups:** Maintain frequent backups of critical data, configurations, and code repositories.

- **Disaster Recovery Plan:** Formulate and periodically test a comprehensive disaster recovery plan that encompasses all potential failure scenarios.

Structured recovery protocols ensure minimal disruption and expedite the return to full operational capacity, fortifying the trading system's resilience.

High-Frequency Trading, with its inherent complexities and rapid execution requirements, demands a robust framework for error handling and fault tolerance. Integrating these strategies not only safeguards against potential disruptions but also enhances the overall robustness and reliability of HFT algorithms. This resilience is a cornerstone of maintaining competitive advantage in the fast-paced arena of algorithmic trading.

4.6 Backtesting Algorithms

Backtesting is a critical component in the development and validation of high-frequency trading (HFT) algorithms. It involves simulating an algorithm's performance using historical market data to ensure its effectiveness before deploying it in a live trading environment. This process not only provides insights into how the algorithm would have performed in the past but also helps in identifying potential issues and refining the strategy.

The primary goal of backtesting is to evaluate the realistic viability of a trading strategy under historical market conditions. This requires an accurate and comprehensive representation of past market behaviors, which includes both the price movements and the order book dynamics. To achieve meaningful results, the backtesting process must be meticulously designed and implemented.

Let's delve into the key aspects of backtesting algorithms in high-frequency trading.

A fundamental aspect of backtesting is data integrity. Ensuring that the historical data used is accurate, complete, and free from errors is paramount. Historical tick data, which includes bid and ask prices, volumes, and timestamps, offers a granular view of the market, enabling a realistic simulation of trading conditions. Alongside market data, incorporating order book dynamics provides additional context, allowing the backtested algorithm to consider both the depth of the market and potential price impacts of trades.

Once the data is prepared, the next step is to set up the backtesting environment. This involves creating a simulation framework that replicates the trading conditions as closely as possible. The framework should account for latency, slippage, commissions, and other transaction costs to provide a realistic assessment of the algorithm's performance.

Consider the following pseudo-code for a basic backtesting loop:

```
for each timestamp in historical_data:
    process_market_data(timestamp)
    signal = algorithm.generate_signal()
    if signal == "buy":
        execute_buy_order()
    elif signal == "sell":
        execute_sell_order()
    update_portfolio()
```

This simple loop demonstrates the sequential nature of processing market data and executing trades based on the signals generated by the algorithm. Each step must be precisely time-synchronized to maintain the integrity of the simulation.

An important aspect of backtesting is the treatment of trading signals and the execution logic. The latency between the signal generation and the actual trade execution should be accurately modeled. In HFT, even microseconds of delay can significantly impact profitability. Therefore, simulating the network delays, order matching speeds, and other latency factors is crucial.

Moreover, the execution model must consider slippage, which occurs when the actual trade execution price differs from the intended price due to market movements. Ignoring slippage can lead to an overestimation of an algorithm's profitability. Including realistic assumptions about slippage and incorporating them into the backtesting framework ensures a more accurate performance assessment.

$$\text{Slippage} = \text{Actual Execution Price} - \text{Expected Price}$$

The formula above represents the slippage calculation, which should be factored into every trade during the backtesting process.

Another key consideration is the handling of transaction costs. These costs include commissions, market impact costs, and fees associated with trading. Accurately estimating these costs based on historical data is imperative, as they can erode the profitability of high-frequency trading strategies. The total transaction cost can be modeled as follows:

$$\text{Total Transaction Cost} = \text{Commission} + \text{Market Impact Cost} + \text{Exchange Fees}$$

Regularly calibrating these cost models with real-world data helps enhance the reliability of the backtest results.

Step by step, we need to incorporate risk assessment into the backtesting process. This involves evaluating the algorithm's performance across various risk measures, such as drawdown, Sharpe ratio, and maximum loss. Using these metrics, we assess the risk-adjusted returns and ensure the algorithm aligns with the overall risk management goals.

Given the complexity and numerous factors involved in backtesting HFT algorithms, it's crucial to use advanced statistical tools and techniques. Monte Carlo simulations, for example, can be employed to test the robustness of the algorithm under different market conditions and by generating thousands of scenarios. This helps in understanding the distribution of possible outcomes and the potential risk of extreme events.

$$\text{MC}_n = \frac{1}{N}\sum_{i=1}^{N} f(X_i)$$

Where MC_n represents the Monte Carlo estimate, N is the number of simulations, and $f(X_i)$ is the function applied to each generated scenario X_i.

Lastly, an essential part of backtesting is the validation and critical evaluation of the results. Look for overfitting, where the algorithm performs exceptionally well on historical data but fails to generalize to unseen data. Cross-validation techniques, out-of-sample testing, and walk-forward analysis are effective methods to mitigate overfitting. These techniques ensure that the backtest provides a realistic measure of the algorithm's performance and reliability.

By effectively integrating these elements, backtesting becomes a powerful tool to refine high-frequency trading algorithms, paving the way for robust strategies that perform well in live trading environments. Through rigorous backtesting, we build confidence in the algorithm's ability to handle real-world market dynamics while maximizing returns and managing risk.

4.7 Parameter Tuning and Sensitivity Analysis

The effective design of high-frequency trading (HFT) algorithms hinges on meticulous parameter tuning and rigorous sensitivity analysis. These two processes serve as cornerstones in ensuring that the algorithm performs optimally under a variety of market conditions. Proper parameter tuning involves adjusting the key parameters that guide the algorithm, while sensitivity analysis assesses how variations in these parameters can influence performance. This section delves into both processes in detail, providing a blend of theoretical foundations and practical guidance.

At the heart of parameter tuning lies a set of variables that could range from thresholds for trade execution, limits for position sizing, to time windows for calculating moving averages. The aim is to adjust these parameters so that the algorithm can maximize its performance metrics, such as Sharpe ratio, return on investment, and hit rate. However, this adjustment process is not straightforward. It demands a deep understanding of the algorithm's structure and the dynamics of the underlying market.

Consider an algorithm designed to execute trades based on moving average crossovers. In this context, the key parameters might include the lengths of the short-term and long-term moving averages (m_s and m_l respectively). To systematically explore the best settings for these parameters, one might use grid search—a brute force method where all possible combinations of m_s and m_l within a specified range are evaluated. While computationally intensive, grid search provides a comprehensive examination of the parameter space.

Alternatively, more sophisticated optimization techniques such as genetic algorithms or particle swarm optimization can be employed to expedite the search process. These methods rely on evolutionary principles or swarm intelligence to iteratively explore the parameter space, converging towards optimal settings more efficiently than grid search.

Mathematically, let $\Theta = \{\theta_1, \theta_2, ..., \theta_n\}$ represent the set of parameters to be tuned. The objective is to identify the optimal parameter set Θ^* that maximizes a performance function $P(\Theta)$. Formally, this can be expressed as:

$$\Theta^* = \arg\max_{\Theta} P(\Theta)$$

where $P(\Theta)$ typically encapsulates profitability, risk-adjusted returns, or other relevant performance metrics.

Once an initial set of optimal parameters is determined, sensitivity analysis comes into play. Sensitivity analysis involves perturbing each parameter slightly and observing the impact on the algorithm's performance. This step is crucial for understanding the robustness of the algorithm. If performance varies drastically with slight parameter adjustments, the algorithm may be overfitting to historical data, implying that it might not generalize well to unseen market conditions.

For sensitivity analysis, one approach is to compute partial derivatives of the performance function with respect to each parameter. Suppose P is the performance metric and θ_i is a specific parameter; the sensitivity of P with respect to θ_i is given by $\frac{\partial P}{\partial \theta_i}$. Large values of this derivative indicate high sensitivity, suggesting that the parameter has a significant influence on performance and might need precise tuning.

To facilitate sensitivity analysis, Monte Carlo simulations can be employed. By randomly varying parameters within a reasonable range and repeatedly evaluating the algorithm, one can build a distribution of performance outcomes. This distribution provides insights into the probable performance under slight variations in the parameter settings.

Visualization tools such as heatmaps and contour plots are invaluable in sensitivity analysis. For two parameters, say m_s and m_l, plotting the performance metric over a grid of these parameters can reveal regions of stability and instability. Such visualization helps in identifying not just the optimal parameters but also the safe zones where performance is relatively insensitive to parameter changes.

Beyond these methods, Bayesian optimization techniques offer another sophisticated means for parameter tuning. Bayesian optimization builds a probabilistic model of the performance function and uses it to guide the search for optimal parameters. This method is particularly useful when each evaluation of the performance metric is computationally expensive.

In practice, parameter tuning and sensitivity analysis are iterative processes. Initial tuning and analysis provide a baseline, which is then refined through successive iterations as more data and insights are gathered. This iterative approach ensures that the algorithm remains robust and adaptable to changing market conditions.

To conclude, parameter tuning and sensitivity analysis are pivotal in shaping an effective HFT algorithm. By systematically optimizing key parameters and rigorously testing their robustness, one can develop algorithms that not only perform well but also withstand the unpredictability of financial markets. As we move to the next section, we will shift focus to the metrics used for evaluating the overall performance of these finely tuned algorithms, further cementing our understanding of algorithmic trading efficacy.

4.8 Performance Metrics and Evaluation

Understanding and evaluating the performance of a high-frequency trading (HFT) algorithm is critical to its success and longevity in the market. This section delves into the various metrics and evaluation techniques employed to measure the efficiency, reliability, and profitability of HFT algorithms.

An essential first step is grasping the different types of metrics used. These can broadly be classified into profit-centric metrics, risk-centric metrics, and efficiency-centric metrics. Each serves a pivotal role in providing a comprehensive view of an algorithm's performance.

Profit-centric metrics are the most straightforward to understand and include measures such as total return, average return, and cumulative profit and loss (P&L). Calculating the total return is typically done by taking the final value of the portfolio and subtracting the initial investment, then dividing this by the initial investment:

$$\text{Total Return} = \frac{\text{Final Portfolio Value} - \text{Initial Investment}}{\text{Initial Investment}}$$

To present a clearer picture of performance over time, a common approach is to compute the average return per trade or per day.

Risk-centric metrics focus on the risk-adjusted returns and the potential downsides of your trading strategy. The most widely known risk-adjusted metric is the Sharpe Ratio, which measures the average return earned in excess of the risk-free rate per unit of volatility or total risk, represented by standard deviation. The Sharpe Ratio is calculated as follows:

$$\text{Sharpe Ratio} = \frac{\mathbb{E}[R - R_f]}{\sigma_R}$$

where $\mathbb{E}[R - R_f]$ is the expected return of the portfolio minus the risk-free rate, and σ_R is the standard deviation of the portfolio return.

Another critical risk metric is the Maximum Drawdown, which measures the largest peak-to-trough decline in the value of a portfolio (before a new peak is attained). It is an essential metric to evaluate as it emphasizes the worst-case scenario in terms of capital loss. Mathematically, the Maximum Drawdown is expressed as:

$$\text{Maximum Drawdown} = \max\left(\frac{\text{Peak Value} - \text{Trough Value}}{\text{Peak Value}}\right)$$

Efficiency-centric metrics are paramount in HFT due to the reliance on speed and execution quality. The average execution time, latency, and fill ratio are commonly evaluated. The average execution time measures the time taken from the decision-making process to the trade execution. Minimizing this time is crucial as milliseconds can be the difference between profit and loss in HFT.

Latency is the time delay between the initiation of a trade and its execution. A lower latency generally indicates superior technical infrastructure and can lead to better trading outcomes. Latency is influenced by various factors including network topology, data processing speed, and hardware performance.

The fill ratio is another significant performance metric, representing the proportion of orders that successfully get executed at the desired price. A higher fill ratio implies better order execution quality and market timing efficiency.

In addition to these metrics, it is essential to conduct a comprehensive evaluation using more advanced statistical measures like the Information Ratio, Sortino Ratio, and R-Squared values. The Information Ratio is similar to the Sharpe Ratio but it accounts for the benchmark's excess return instead of the risk-free rate, providing insight into the algorithm's ability to outperform the market.

The Sortino Ratio refines the Sharpe Ratio by focusing solely on downside volatility, thus penalizing only the negative returns:

$$\text{Sortino Ratio} = \frac{\mathbb{E}[R - R_f]}{\sigma_D}$$

where σ_D is the standard deviation of negative asset returns.

R-Squared measures the proportion of the algorithm's performance that can be explained by the performance of a benchmark index. High R-Squared values suggest that the algorithm's returns move closely with the benchmark, whereas low values indicate more independent performance.

Furthermore, Monte Carlo simulations serve as a robust tool to evaluate algorithm performance under various market conditions. These simulations generate a wide range of possible outcomes based on historical data, providing a probabilistic assessment of risk and potential returns.

Finally, real-time performance tracking and regular audits ensure the HFT algorithm continues to perform optimally. Techniques such as rolling window analysis and walk-forward optimization can be implemented to dynamically adjust parameters and models based on the latest market data, enhancing the algorithm's resilience and adaptability.

By thoroughly understanding and implementing these performance metrics and evaluation techniques, traders can develop more robust HFT algorithms that not only achieve superior profitability but also maintain manageable risk and operational efficiency.

No discussion on performance metrics and evaluation is complete without addressing the importance of continuous monitoring and adaptive improvements. The dynamic nature of financial markets requires that HFT algorithms are not only highly optimized at launch but also regularly reassessed to ensure sustained performance under ever-changing market conditions.

Chapter 5

Latency and Infrastructure

This chapter delves into the importance of latency and the infrastructure required to support High-Frequency Trading (HFT). It provides an understanding of different components contributing to latency, such as network, processing, and data latency. The chapter explores how to optimize network infrastructure, the benefits of colocation and proximity hosting, and the significance of precise time synchronization. It also highlights tools and techniques for monitoring and reducing latency, while addressing the challenges and limitations in achieving minimal delays in trade execution. These insights emphasize the critical role of infrastructure in the performance of HFT activities.

5.1 Understanding Latency in Financial Markets

Latency in financial markets refers to the delay between the initiation of a market action and the subsequent realization of that action. This delay can be crucial in high-frequency trading (HFT), where every microsecond can impact profitability. As financial markets become more electronically driven, understanding latency and its implications has become indispensable for traders looking to optimize their strategies and infrastructures.

At its core, latency impacts the speed at which various trading activities occur—from order placement and execution to the dissemination of market data. In an HFT environment, where thousands of trades might be executed in a second, even minor delays can aggregate into significant performance differentials.

One of the primary contributors to latency is network latency, which encompasses the time taken for data packets to travel from the trader's infrastructure to the exchange and back. This round-trip time is influenced by factors such as the physical distance between the servers and the quality of the network connections. For example, a trader situated in New York may experience lower latency when trading on the NASDAQ compared to an exchange located halfway across the globe in Tokyo.

Another important aspect is processing latency. This occurs within the trader's and exchange's systems, encompassing the time it takes to process incoming orders, match them with existing ones, and then send acknowledgments back to the trader. Faster processing speeds can be achieved through optimized hardware, high-performance trading algorithms, and efficient software code. For instance, using Field-Programmable Gate Arrays (FPGAs) can significantly reduce processing times by allowing for parallel processing, thus further minimizing delays.

Data latency is also a critical factor. This type of latency pertains to the time lag involved in capturing and interpreting market data, which can include prices, order book updates, and news feeds. High-frequency traders must access and react to this data as swiftly as possible. Employing advanced data feeds such as the Financial Information eXchange (FIX) protocol can offer faster and more reliable data delivery compared to traditional data sources. Moreover, implementing in-memory databases can reduce the time needed to fetch and analyze critical information, providing traders with a decisive edge.

The interplay between these different types of latency creates a complex environment where constant monitoring, analysis, and optimization are necessary to maintain competitive performance. For instance, a reduction in network latency might not yield optimal results if processing latency remains high or if data latency leads to outdated information. Thus, a holistic approach is required, where each latency component is jointly considered for overall system efficiency.

Understanding latency is also about recognizing its impacts on the broader market landscape. Lower latency leads to tighter bid-ask spreads, reduced market impact, and improved liquidity. High-frequency traders often provide liquidity through their rapid, small-scale trades, benefiting from the microscopic price movements. However, for non-HFT participants, this environment can pose challenges as their slower actions may be disproportionately disadvantaged.

The regulatory landscape is also evolving with regard to latency. Financial authorities are increasingly scrutinizing HFT activities to ensure market stability and fairness. For example, measures such as minimum resting times for orders and circuit breakers are being analyzed to mitigate potential risks associated with ultra-low latency trading. Traders must therefore stay abreast of regulatory changes to adapt their strategies and infrastructures accordingly.

Understanding and managing latency in financial markets is fundamental for traders, especially those engaged in HFT. By comprehensively addressing network, processing, and data latencies, traders can not only optimize their trading strategies but also enhance their ability to compete in an increasingly fast-paced market environment.

5.2 Components of Latency: Network, Processing, and Data Latency

Latency is a pivotal aspect of High-Frequency Trading (HFT) that can significantly influence the profitability and effectiveness of trading strategies. To fully comprehend the intricacies of latency, it is crucial to break it down into its core components: network latency, processing latency, and data latency. Each of these elements contributes in unique ways to the overall latency observed in HFT systems.

Network latency refers to the time it takes for data to travel from one point to another within a network. In the context of HFT, this encompasses the entire journey from the trading algorithm to the exchange server and back. Network latency is influenced by numerous factors, including the physical distance between nodes, the quality and speed of the transmission medium, and the efficiency of routing protocols. One common technique to reduce network latency is the utilization of colocation services, where trading servers are placed in close proximity to exchange servers, thus minimizing the physical distance data must travel.

Processing latency occurs during the computational process needed to execute trading strategies. This includes the time required for data input to be received, processed by algorithms, and output to be generated as trading instructions. Processing latency is heavily dependent on the computational resources at hand, such as the CPU and memory performance, as well as the efficiency of the trading algorithms. Advanced technologies like Field-Programmable Gate Arrays (FPGAs) and Graphics Processing Units (GPUs) are often employed to accelerate processing capabilities, thereby reducing the latency associated with this component.

Data latency involves delays in data retrieval, which can affect the timely execution of trades. This type of latency can stem from delays in accessing historical data, real-time market data feeds, or any other necessary data inputs that a trading algorithm requires to make informed decisions. To mitigate data latency, optimized data storage solutions, such as in-memory databases, can be used to facilitate faster access times. Additionally, data preprocessing techniques can be deployed to minimize the time spent on data transformation and normalization.

Understanding these different components of latency is fundamental for traders, as each offers distinct avenues for optimization. Network latency can be minimized by strategic infrastructure placement and advanced networking technologies. Processing latency can be reduced through hardware acceleration and efficient algorithm design. Data latency can be addressed by leveraging high-speed storage and preprocessing techniques. By addressing each component methodically, traders can achieve significant reductions in overall latency, thus enhancing the performance and profitability of their HFT systems.

5.3 Optimizing Network Infrastructure

In the realm of High-Frequency Trading (HFT), network infrastructure serves as one of the critical pillars underpinning the quest for minimizing latency. Achieving optimal network performance is imperative for ensuring that data transmission between trading systems and exchanges occurs as swiftly as possible. This section will explore various approaches and technologies aimed at optimizing network infrastructure for HFT, considering factors such as hardware selection, network architecture, and transmission protocols.

Network optimization begins with the careful selection of hardware components. High-performance network interface cards (NICs) are pivotal, given that they facilitate the rapid processing of network packets. Low-latency NICs, equipped with offload capabilities, can reduce CPU load and expedite data transfer, thereby enhancing overall performance. Additionally, switches and routers must be meticulously chosen to ensure minimal delay. Managed switches with low-latency specifications and high-throughput capabilities are preferred to avert congestion and quicken packet forwarding.

A crucial consideration in optimizing network infrastructure is the physical layout and architecture of the network. The topology should minimize the number of intermediary devices data packets traverse from the trading system to the exchange. Mesh topologies, although robust, may introduce unnecessary delays due to multiple hops. Conversely, a star topology can ensure that data routes are more direct, although it necessitates a reliable central hub. Hybrid approaches can also be employed whereby critical paths are kept minimal, and redundancy is built through strategic network design.

Fiber optics play an essential role in the optimal design of network connections due to their high-speed transmission capabilities and reduced latency compared to traditional copper wires. Trading firms often opt for direct fiber links to exchanges, ensuring that the communication path is as short and fast as possible. The use of Dense Wavelength Division Multiplexing (DWDM) technologies can further enhance bandwidth utilization within fiber optic cables, allowing multiple data streams to be transmitted simultaneously without added latency.

Protocols and software optimizations equally warrant attention. Traditional Transmission Control Protocol (TCP) can introduce delays due to its inherent congestion control and acknowledgment mechanisms. In contrast, User Datagram Protocol (UDP) eliminates such delays by offering less overhead and faster data transmission, although at the cost of reliability. In HFT systems, where latency outweighs data integrity considerations, UDP is commonly favored. For scenarios requiring reliable data transfer, hybrid protocols such as TCP offload engines can be utilized to balance speed and reliability.

Network latency can be further minimized through the implementation of kernel bypass techniques. Standard network processing typically involves the operating system's kernel, which introduces latency. Technologies like Data Plane Development Kit (DPDK) and Solarflare's OpenOnload can circumvent the kernel, allowing direct data transfers between the application and the NIC, significantly reducing latency.

Monitoring and management software is indispensable for ensuring that the network remains optimized. Real-time performance monitoring tools help identify latency spikes and congestion points. Software-defined networking (SDN) solutions can dynamically manage network paths and optimize data flows based on current network conditions, ensuring that latency remains minimized even during peak loads.

The strategic placement of trading servers near exchange facilities—often referred to as colocation—complements these network infrastructure optimizations. By housing servers in proximity to the exchange's server, firms can drastically curtail the physical distance data must travel, slashing round-trip times substantially.

Finally, ongoing maintenance and regular updates of network components are non-negotiable. Firmware updates, hardware replacements, and periodic assessments of network performance are vital to maintain an optimal, low-latency infrastructure. As network technology evolves, staying at the cutting edge with the latest advancements ensures that trading systems remain competitive in the relentless race to zero latency.

The endeavor for optimizing network infrastructure in HFT is a complex, multifaceted challenge that demands both technical acumen and strategic foresight. By integrating advanced hardware, streamlined architecture, efficient protocols, and proactive monitoring, trading firms can edge closer to achieving the near-zero latency essential for excelling in the high-stakes domain of high-frequency trading.

5.4 Collocation and Proximity Hosting

Collocation and proximity hosting are pivotal concepts in the realm of high-frequency trading (HFT), where milliseconds can determine the success of a trading strategy. These practices involve positioning servers in close physical proximity to the exchange's data centers, thereby reducing the round-trip time for data transmission. By minimizing the distance that trade orders and market data must travel, firms can achieve significant reductions in latency, ensuring faster trade execution and more accurate response times.

To understand the significance of collocation and proximity hosting, it is essential to first grasp the nature of latency and its impact on HFT strategies. Latency, as previously discussed, can be broken down into network latency, processing latency, and data latency. All these components can be minimized through effective infrastructure choices, with collocation and proximity hosting standing out as highly effective methods for reducing overall latency.

The primary benefit of collocation lies in its ability to virtually eliminate the geographic constraints of network latency. By housing trading servers within the same data centers as the exchanges or very nearby, traders can access the exchange's order book data and submit orders with minimal delay. This close positioning ensures that the physical distance, and consequently the time taken for data to travel between the trader's servers and the exchange's servers, is kept to an absolute minimum.

Implementing collocation typically involves renting server space within the data center facilities of the exchange. These facilities are equipped with high-speed networking hardware to handle vast amounts of data traffic efficiently. The infrastructure provided at these collocation centers is often optimized to support the demanding requirements of HFT operations, including advanced cooling systems, uninterrupted power supplies, and robust security protocols. This allows trading firms to maintain the reliability and speed necessary for executing high-frequency trades.

Proximity hosting, on the other hand, refers to the placement of trading servers in data centers that are geographically close to the exchange's data center but not necessarily within the same facility. While slightly increasing the physical distance compared to direct collocation, proximity hosting still offers substantial latency benefits compared to more distant locations. Data centers designated for proximity hosting are strategically located to ensure minimal latency and are often interconnected with the exchange through high-speed, low-latency network connections.

There are several key considerations when opting for collocation or proximity hosting. First, the proximity to the exchange not only impacts latency but also affects the cost. Collocation, being the closest form of hosting, typically commands higher fees due to the premium location and associated infrastructure benefits. However, for many HFT firms, the reduction in latency and the resulting edge in trade execution justify the additional expense.

Another critical factor is the choice of hardware and network equipment. Firms must invest in high-performance servers and low-latency network interfaces to maximize the advantages gained from reduced physical distance. Additionally, the infrastructure should be capable of handling large volumes of market data and executing rapid order transmissions. Enhanced hardware configurations, such as field-programmable gate arrays (FPGAs) or application-specific integrated circuits (ASICs), can be leveraged to further accelerate processing times and reduce latencies associated with computational tasks.

Moreover, regulatory considerations play a role in deciding between collocation and proximity hosting. Regulatory bodies in various jurisdictions may have specific guidelines or restrictions concerning the deployment of trading infrastructure. Firms must ensure compliance with these regulations to avoid legal repercussions and maintain operational integrity.

The implementation of collocation and proximity hosting also demands robust real-time monitoring systems. Continuous monitoring of network performance, server health, and data flow is essential to identify and mitigate latency bottlenecks quickly. Furthermore, maintaining redundant systems and failover mechanisms can ensure uninterrupted trading operations, even in the event of hardware or network failures.

Collocation and proximity hosting have become an arms race within the HFT industry, as firms strive to edge out competitors by achieving minimal latency. This drive for ultra-low latency often leads to significant investments in infrastructure, advanced technologies, and strategic location planning. Despite the associated costs, the potential rewards in terms of trading profits and competitive advantages make these strategies indispensable for serious HFT participants.

Effective utilization of collocation and proximity hosting represents a cornerstone in minimizing latency and enhancing the performance of high-frequency trading systems. Ensuring the optimal placement of trading servers relative to exchange data centers can deliver substantial improvements in trade execution speed, ultimately contributing to the success and profitability of HFT strategies.

5.5 Time Synchronization and Clock Precision

The precise synchronization of clocks within a trading system is a cornerstone of High-Frequency Trading (HFT) infrastructure. In the ultracompetitive world of HFT, even nanosecond discrepancies can lead to substantial financial advantages or losses. This section explores why time synchronization is essential, the methods and technologies used to achieve high precision, and the challenges inherent in maintaining this accuracy.

Understanding the critical nature of time synchronization begins with recognizing its impact on trade execution and order matching. In HFT, decisions are made in fractions of a second, and trades are executed at speeds approaching the limits of physical communication. Every system component, from market data feeds to execution algorithms, relies on timestamps to make coherent and synchronized decisions. Disparities in these timestamps can lead to out-of-order messages, incorrect sequencing of trades, and increased latency, undermining the very essence of high-frequency trading strategies.

Achieving precise time synchronization involves several technologies and standards:

- **Network Time Protocol (NTP):** NTP is widely used for general-purpose time synchronization across computer networks. While adequate for many applications, NTP's millisecond-level accuracy often falls short for the stringent demands of HFT.
- **Precision Time Protocol (PTP):** Also known as IEEE 1588, PTP offers much higher precision, capable of synchronizing clocks to within nanoseconds over a local area network. This level of accuracy is essential for the latency-sensitive operations of HFT.
- **Global Positioning System (GPS):** GPS time synchronization is another critical component, providing an external time reference. Many trading infrastructures rely on GPS as a primary time source, benefiting from its global reach and high precision.
- **Atomic Clocks:** For the ultimate in precision, some HFT firms utilize atomic clocks, which offer unparalleled accuracy and stability. These clocks, though costly, ensure that internal timekeeping devices remain synchronized with a highly stable time source.

Effective implementation of these synchronization technologies requires a robust and resilient infrastructure. Network design must minimize latency and jitter while ensuring that time signals are distributed accurately across the entire trading ecosystem. This often involves dedicated timing networks and specialized hardware, such as PTP Grandmasters and Boundary Clocks, which help maintain synchronization across various network segments.

$$t_{synchronized} = t_{server} + \left(\frac{d_{total}}{2}\right)$$

where $t_{synchronized}$ is the synchronized time at the server, t_{server} is the local time at the server, and d_{total} is the total round-trip delay measured between the time source and the server.

Despite best efforts, maintaining clock precision is fraught with challenges:

- **Network Delays:** Variations in network latency, even at the microsecond level, can skew synchronization. It's crucial to implement measures that account for and minimize these delays.

- **Hardware Limitations:** Variations in hardware capabilities and performance can introduce discrepancies. Therefore, selecting high-quality, certified equipment is essential.

- **Environmental Factors:** Temperature fluctuations and electromagnetic interference can affect clock stability and accuracy. Proper environmental controls and shielding can mitigate these issues.

- **Regulatory Compliance:** Financial regulations often mandate precise timestamping for trade audits and traceability, adding another layer of complexity and necessity to maintain stringent synchronization.

Trading firms often adopt a multi-layered strategy to mitigate these challenges, combining multiple time sources and constantly validating time synchronization against known benchmarks. Redundant systems, continuous monitoring, and real-time adjustments ensure that their timekeeping remains as precise as possible.

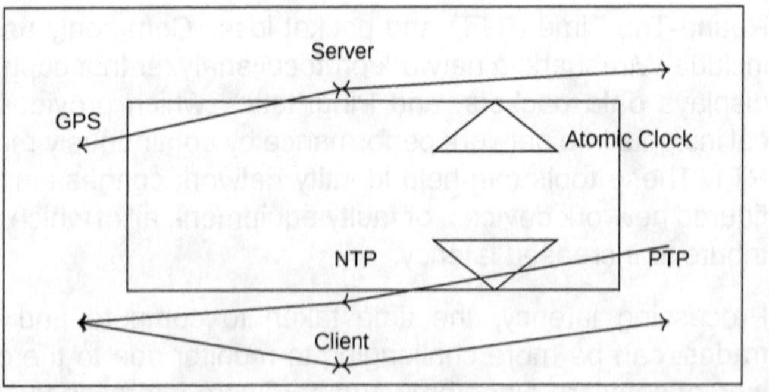

The pursuit of perfect time synchronization is an ongoing race, a continuous process of refinement and adaptation as new technologies emerge and trading environments evolve. Though intricate and technically challenging, mastering this aspect of trading infrastructure significantly enhances the performance and reliability of high-frequency trading systems, providing firms with the precise timing they need to stay competitive in the race to zero latency. Such meticulous attention to detail ensures that every nanosecond is optimally utilized, translating into tangible gains in trading effectiveness and profitability.

5.6 Latency Monitoring Tools and Techniques

Latency monitoring is a critical aspect of High-Frequency Trading (HFT) as it allows traders to identify and address performance bottlenecks in real time. Given the speed at which markets operate, even microsecond delays can significantly impact trading efficiency and profitability. Investing in sophisticated latency monitoring tools and techniques is essential for maintaining a competitive edge and ensuring optimal system performance.

To begin with, a solid understanding of the types of latency that can affect trading activities is paramount. These include network latency, processing latency, and data latency, each of which can be monitored using specialized tools. The primary objective of latency monitoring is to provide actionable insights that enable the fine-tuning of hardware and software components to minimize delays.

- Network latency, the time taken for data to travel from one point to another in a network, can be monitored using tools that measure

Round-Trip Time (RTT) and packet loss. Commonly used tools include Wireshark, a network protocol analyzer that captures and displays data packets, and PingPlotter, which provides graphical insights into network performance by continuously measuring RTT. These tools can help identify network congestion, misconfigured network devices, or faulty equipment, all of which can contribute to increased latency.

- Processing latency, the time taken to compute and process trades, can be more challenging to monitor due to the complexities of software algorithms and hardware interactions. Profiling tools like Intel VTune and AMD CodeXL offer detailed insights into CPU and GPU performance, pinpointing bottlenecks in code execution. Additionally, custom-built instrumentation within trading applications can log processing times at various stages, providing granular data that helps optimize algorithm performance.
- Data latency, the delay in receiving and processing market data, is another critical factor. Tools like Corvil and ITRS Geneos are designed to monitor and analyze real-time data feeds, offering insights into delays caused by the data acquisition, normalization, and distribution processes. These tools can help identify slow data sources, inefficient data processing pipelines, and other factors contributing to data latency.

Combining these tools with comprehensive monitoring frameworks can further enhance latency management. For example, Elastic Stack (formerly known as ELK Stack, comprising Elasticsearch, Logstash, and Kibana) can aggregate logs and metrics from various sources, providing a centralized platform for real-time monitoring, visualization, and alerting. Such frameworks enable traders to correlate events across the entire trading infrastructure, offering a holistic view of performance and latency issues.

Effective latency monitoring also involves setting up thresholds and alerts to detect anomalies promptly. By defining acceptable latency levels for different components and setting up automated alerts, traders can quickly respond to deviations from the norm. This proactive approach helps in maintaining optimal performance and avoiding potential financial losses due to unexpected latency spikes.

Furthermore, machine learning and artificial intelligence (AI) are increasingly being integrated into latency monitoring systems. These technologies can analyze historical data and identify patterns that might predict future latency issues, allowing traders to preemptively address potential problems. AI-driven tools can also automatically adjust system parameters to optimize performance, reducing the need for constant manual intervention.

Real-world examples of latency monitoring are evident in the setups used by leading financial institutions. For instance, JP Morgan Chase utilizes in-house developed latency monitoring tools alongside commercial solutions to maintain and optimize their trading infrastructure. These tools provide continuous insights into network performance, processing times, and data feed integrity, enabling quick adjustments to maintain low-latency trading environments.

In conclusion, effective latency monitoring tools and techniques are indispensable for High-Frequency Trading. By leveraging a combination of network analyzers, profiling tools, real-time monitoring frameworks, and AI-driven solutions, traders can gain comprehensive visibility into their trading infrastructure. This proactive and integrated approach not only minimizes delays but also enhances overall trading performance, ensuring a competitive edge in the fast-paced world of HFT.

5.7 Latency Reduction Strategies

As the quest for faster trade execution intensifies, deploying effective latency reduction strategies becomes an imperative priority for High-Frequency Trading (HFT) firms. In this section, we will explore various techniques that can be adopted to minimize latency, providing traders with a competitive edge in the financial markets.

Firstly, leveraging appropriate hardware choices is fundamental. Utilizing field-programmable gate arrays (FPGAs) can dramatically reduce latency compared to traditional software-based processing. FPGAs allow for parallel processing of tasks, significantly lowering the time required for data handling and execution. Custom-built hardware, such as application-specific integrated circuits (ASICs), further optimizes the performance by being tailored to specific trading operations, albeit at a higher cost and complexity.

Another significant approach is optimizing software architecture. High-frequency traders rely on extremely efficient algorithms that are designed to operate with minimal delay. These algorithms must be meticulously optimized for speed, which includes eliminating any redundant code and streamlining the data processing paths. Multi-threading and parallelism enable simultaneous execution of multiple components of the trading system, further cutting down on processing time.

Memory management is another critical area that can impact latency. Accessing data from memory (especially from high-speed caches) is considerably faster than reading from hard drives or even solid-state drives. Therefore, it is crucial to make use of in-memory databases and utilize techniques such as memory mapping to keep the frequently accessed data in the fastest accessible memory.

Next, network optimization plays a pivotal role. Utilizing low-latency network hardware such as InfiniBand and removing unnecessary layers or devices between trading systems and the exchange can minimize delays. Direct Market Access (DMA) servers that bypass the intermediary stages further enhance the speed. Employing advanced network protocols and fast transmission methods like User Datagram Protocol (UDP) also contribute to the reduction of network-induced latency.

Moreover, employing colocation and proximity hosting substantially cuts down on the geographical distance that data packets must travel, thereby reducing latency. Placing trading infrastructure in the same data centers or in close proximity to exchange servers ensures the fastest possible data transmission. This proximity might make the difference between landing a profitable trade or missing the opportunity entirely.

Time synchronization using high-precision clocks is critical in HFT. Ensuring that all components within the trading system are synchronized to a high degree of accuracy, typically using protocols such as Precision Time Protocol (PTP), ensures seamless coordination. This synchronization helps accurately timestamp trades and orders, reducing discrepancies and ensuring the system operates at peak efficiency.

Finally, conducting continuous latency monitoring and employing feedback loops to refine strategies is essential. Utilizing sophisticated monitoring tools can help identify bottlenecks in real time, and these insights enable traders to continually adjust and improve their approaches. Implementing real-time analytics and machine learning techniques can predict and preemptively address latency spikes, ensuring the trading system remains at its optimal operational efficiency.

Reducing latency is a multi-faceted challenge that demands a holistic understanding of both hardware and software components in high-frequency trading systems. By integrating advanced hardware solutions, optimizing software, managing memory efficiently, enhancing network infrastructure, colocating servers, ensuring precise time synchronization, and continuously monitoring the system, traders can significantly enhance their system's performance, thus gaining an advantageous position in the fast-paced trading environment.

5.8 The Race to Zero Latency: Challenges and Limitations

High-frequency trading (HFT) firms are relentlessly pursuing minimal latency in their trade execution processes. The term "zero latency" epitomizes the goal of instantaneous information flow and execution, underscoring the competitive edge that even nanoseconds can provide in this arena. Despite significant advancements, numerous challenges and limitations persist in this high-stakes race.

Achieving minimal latency necessitates addressing inherent delays within network, processing, and data components. The physical constraints imposed by the speed of light, the propagation delays in fiber optics, and other electronic transmission limits introduce unavoidable latencies. For instance, while light travels at approximately 299,792 kilometers per second in a vacuum, this speed is reduced to about 200,000 kilometers per second in fiber optics due to the refractive index. Consequently, geographical distance between trading venues and data centers fundamentally limits the achievable latency, as described by the equation:

$$\text{Latency}_{\text{propagation}} = \frac{\text{Distance}}{\text{Transmission Speed}}$$

In addition to physical constraints, network congestion and routing inefficiencies can further exacerbate delays. High-frequency trading relies on the uninterrupted and rapid transmission of massive volumes of data. Network bandwidth limitations and packet loss become significant concerns, especially during traffic spikes induced by market events or sudden surges in trading activity.

Processing latency, the time taken by algorithms to analyze data and make trading decisions, poses another significant challenge. Implementing highly efficient algorithms is crucial, but complexity often increases with the sophistication of trading strategies. Each micro-optimization needs balancing between computational time and accuracy, with more intricate models potentially introducing additional processing delays.

Data latency, particularly in the form of data retrieval and storage delays, also plays a critical role. Database query speeds, data fetching from remote sources, and the time taken to synchronize data across different systems all contribute to aggregate latency. These components are interdependent, necessitating harmonious optimization, where improvements in one area might lead to bottlenecks in another.

Collocation and proximity hosting are employed to shave off microseconds by positioning servers in close physical proximity to exchanges. Despite the benefits, this approach introduces its own limitations. The initial setup cost of collocation can be exorbitant due to the need for specialized hardware and premium real estate within data centers. Furthermore, maintenance and operational costs remain significant, pressuring firms to ensure the profitability of reduced latency against these fixed expenditures.

Accurate time synchronization across trading systems forms the backbone of latency-sensitive operations. However, attaining nanosecond-level precision is fraught with technical challenges. Atomic clocks and Global Positioning System (GPS) technology are leveraged to synchronize time, yet even these advanced systems carry limitations. Signal degradation, atmospheric conditions, and electronic interference can introduce timing inaccuracies, impacting the coherence of time stamps across distributed systems.

Monitoring latency necessitates sophisticated tools and methods capable of dissecting and analyzing milliseconds of time. However, the granularity and fidelity of these monitoring tools must be impeccable. Inadequate monitoring can lead to misdiagnosis of latency issues, causing firms to invest resources into non-productive areas. Effective latency monitoring thus requires an amalgamation of high-resolution timestamping, real-time analytics, and comprehensive logging of data flows across trading platforms.

Despite all these efforts, achieving absolute zero latency remains an elusive goal. Even with cutting-edge technology and strategies, the collective impact of physical, technical, and economic barriers limits the extent to which HFT firms can minimize latency. The marginal returns on investments in latency reduction diminish as firms approach the theoretical zero, requiring exponential increases in capital for increasingly smaller gains:

$$\text{Diminishing Returns on Latency Reduction} \propto \frac{1}{\text{Investment Magnitude}}$$

Furthermore, market dynamics continuously evolve, rendering any latency optimizations temporary at best. Competitors relentlessly innovate, regulatory changes alter the trading landscape, and technological advancements levied by the broader industry continually redefine the operating baselines.

Ultimately, the race to zero latency encapsulates a paradox: the more firms close in on zero, the harder and costlier each step becomes. By understanding the multifaceted challenges and inherent limitations, HFT firms can make informed decisions, balancing the pursuit of minimal latency against strategic, operational, and financial prudence. As the industry moves forward, the quest involves not just striving for lower latency, but also valuing sustainable and scalable efficiency gains. The journey itself propels technological progress, shaping the future of high-frequency trading.

Chapter 6

Risk Management in HFT

This chapter examines the various dimensions of risk management critical to High-Frequency Trading (HFT). It introduces the types of risks inherent to HFT, including market, credit, operational, and technological risks. The chapter delves into quantitative risk models and strategies for managing volatility and market risk, as well as addressing credit and counterparty risks. It explores operational and regulatory risks, along with effective mitigation strategies and tools used for risk management. These insights are essential for ensuring the stability and compliance of HFT operations in an environment marked by high speed and complexity.

6.1 Introduction to Risk Management

Risk management stands as the cornerstone of any successful high-frequency trading (HFT) strategy. In the fast-paced world of HFT, where trades are executed within microseconds, the ability to identify, assess, and mitigate risks is paramount. The dynamic nature of the market, coupled with the sophisticated algorithms driving the trades, introduces a multitude of risks that can swiftly impact performance and profitability if not meticulously managed.

In its most fundamental sense, risk management in HFT involves a systematic approach to understanding potential threats to operations and implementing measures to counteract them. This encompasses a broad spectrum of risks, including market volatility, technological failure, operational shortcomings, and regulatory changes, each of which can have far-reaching consequences.

Understanding Risk as an Integral Component: Traditionally, risk is perceived as a negative factor—a potential loss or adverse outcome. However, within the context of HFT, risk also represents inherent uncertainty that, when appropriately managed, can be transformed into an opportunity. Effective risk management is not merely a defensive mechanism but an integral component of a strategic plan aimed at maximizing returns.

Key elements of risk management include:

- **Risk Identification:** The first step involves identifying the multitude of risks that HFT firms are exposed to. This requires a comprehensive understanding of the trading environment, the algorithms used, and the various external factors that can influence trading activities.
- **Risk Assessment:** Once identified, these risks must be assessed to understand their potential impact. This involves quantifying the risks and examining their probability of occurrence, allowing traders to prioritize which risks require more immediate and stringent controls.
- **Risk Mitigation:** Risk mitigation involves developing strategies and tools to reduce the likelihood of risks materializing and minimizing their impact if they do. This can range from diversifying the portfolio to implementing robust technological safeguards.
- **Risk Monitoring:** Continuous monitoring is essential to ensure that risk management strategies remain effective under changing market conditions. Automated systems often play a crucial role in real-time risk monitoring within HFT environments.
- **Risk Reporting:** Clear and consistent reporting mechanisms are necessary to keep all stakeholders informed about the current risk landscape and any actions taken to address the risks. This enhances transparency and aids in informed decision-making.

The Role of Quantitative Models: In HFT, the reliance on quantitative models for risk management cannot be overstated. These models, which include statistical and mathematical frameworks, allow for precise calculation and prediction of potential risks. They enable traders to pre-emptively identify trends and anomalies, providing a tactical advantage in mitigating risks before they materialize.

Risk Management Frameworks: Establishing a robust risk management framework is critical. Such frameworks typically incorporate policies, protocols, and procedures tailored specifically to the unique landscape of HFT. They provide a structured approach to mitigating risks, orienting all aspects of the trading operations towards a common goal of stability and compliance. An effective framework will align with overall business objectives and regulatory requirements, ensuring that risk management practices are integrated seamlessly into daily trading activities.

Technological Considerations: Given the reliance on technology in HFT, managing technological risks is a significant component of the overall risk management strategy. This includes safeguarding against system failures, cyber-attacks, and ensuring the robustness of the trading algorithms. Fault tolerance, redundancy, and rigorous stress-testing of systems are some of the measures employed to mitigate technological risks. High-frequency trading firms invest heavily in their technological infrastructure to ensure minimal latency and maximum reliability.

Regulatory Compliance: Finally, the importance of adhering to regulatory requirements cannot be overlooked. Regulatory frameworks governing HFT are designed to maintain market integrity and protect against systemic risks. Therefore, compliance is not just a regulatory obligation but also a critical aspect of risk management. Firms must stay abreast of regulatory changes and ensure that their trading activities are compliant to avoid penalties and reputational damage.

Risk management in high-frequency trading is a dynamic and continuous process. It requires an intricate balance of proactive risk identification, robust risk control measures, and responsive risk mitigation strategies. By embedding effective risk management practices into their operational blueprint, HFT firms can navigate the complexities of the market with greater confidence and success.

6.2 Types of Risks in High-Frequency Trading

High-Frequency Trading (HFT) operates in a complex and dynamic environment where risk management is paramount. Understanding the different types of risks inherent in HFT is crucial for developing robust strategies that ensure stability and compliance. This section explores the various dimensions of risk that can impact HFT operations, including market risk, credit risk, operational risk, and technological risk.

Market Risk is one of the most prominent risks in HFT. It refers to the possibility of incurring losses due to adverse price movements in the market. Given the rapid pace at which HFT operations execute trades, even minor price fluctuations can result in significant financial losses. Strategies such as statistical arbitrage and market making inherently carry market risk since they rely on the assumption that prices will revert to their mean or follow predictable patterns. Effective management of market risk often involves the use of advanced analytical tools and algorithms designed to predict and hedge against unfavorable market conditions.

Credit Risk involves the potential for loss due to a counterparty's failure to fulfill their financial obligations. In HFT, this risk is particularly pronounced due to the high volume and frequency of trades executed. Credit risk can arise from various sources, including clearinghouses, brokers, and other financial institutions. Managing credit risk requires rigorous due diligence, real-time credit assessments, and the use of collateral to mitigate potential default scenarios. For instance, implementing strict margin requirements and actively monitoring counterparty creditworthiness can help reduce exposure to credit risk.

Operational Risk encompasses the risks associated with internal processes, systems, and human errors. In the context of HFT, operational risk can manifest through misconfigured algorithms, software bugs, or human oversight. Given the automated nature of HFT, ensuring the reliability and accuracy of trading algorithms is paramount. Firms typically employ rigorous testing and validation procedures, incorporating redundancy and fail-safe mechanisms to mitigate operational risk. Regular audits and continuous monitoring of systems and processes further contribute to minimizing operational disruptions.

Technological Risk is a critical consideration in HFT, where cutting-edge technology is both a driver of competitive advantage and a source of potential vulnerabilities. This risk includes hardware malfunctions, software failures, and cyber-attacks. The intense reliance on technology for executing trades, coupled with the need for ultra-low latency, makes HFT systems susceptible to technological disruptions. To mitigate technological risk, firms invest heavily in robust infrastructure, including high-speed data transmission lines and fault-tolerant servers. Additionally, implementing comprehensive cybersecurity protocols is essential to safeguard against data breaches and cyber threats.

The interconnected nature of these risks means that they often compound each other, amplifying the overall risk exposure in HFT scenarios. For instance, a technological failure could trigger market and operational risks by causing erroneous trades or disrupting trading activities. Consequently, a holistic approach to risk management, incorporating real-time monitoring and integrated risk assessment tools, is essential for managing the multifaceted risks in HFT.

By understanding and differentiating between these types of risks, HFT firms can develop targeted strategies that protect their operations from potential losses and maintain the delicate balance required for successful high-frequency trading. Advanced risk management tools and methodologies play a vital role in not only identifying and mitigating these risks but also in enabling firms to achieve optimal performance within a controlled risk framework.

6.3 Quantitative Risk Models

Quantitative risk models play a pivotal role in the rapidly evolving domain of High-Frequency Trading (HFT), where the ability to make split-second decisions can lead to substantial gains or significant losses. These models utilize mathematical and statistical techniques to quantify and manage risk, helping traders to make informed decisions under uncertainty.

One of the fundamental quantitative models used in HFT is the Value at Risk (VaR) model. VaR estimates the maximum potential loss a portfolio could face over a given time period, under normal market conditions, at a specific confidence level. For instance, a one-day VaR at the 95% confidence level of $1 million suggests there is a 5% chance that the portfolio could lose more than $1 million in a single day. Mathematically, VaR can be expressed as:

$$\text{VaR}_{\alpha}(X) = \inf\{x \in \mathbb{R} : P(X \leq x) > \alpha\}$$

where X represents the portfolio loss and α is the confidence level.

However, while VaR provides a snapshot of potential loss, it has its limitations, particularly in HFT environments characterized by extreme tail events and non-normal distributions. To overcome these limitations, Conditional Value at Risk (CVaR) is often employed. CVaR, also known as Expected Shortfall, measures the expected loss given that the VaR threshold has been exceeded. It is defined as:

$$\text{CVaR}_\alpha(X) = E[X|X \geq \text{VaR}_\alpha(X)]$$

where $E[X|X \geq \text{VaR}_\alpha(X)]$ signifies the expected value of the loss beyond the VaR threshold.

Another critical approach in quantitative risk modeling is the use of Stress Testing, which involves simulating the portfolio's performance under extreme market conditions. These tests enable HFT firms to evaluate the robustness and resilience of their trading strategies against severe market disruptions. Common stress scenarios include significant increases in volatility, abrupt market crashes, and liquidity squeezes. For example, an HFT strategy based on mean reversion may be stress tested to assess its performance during a sudden market trend reversal.

The advent of advanced machine learning techniques has further enhanced the capabilities of quantitative risk models in HFT. Algorithms such as Random Forests, Gradient Boosting Machines, and Deep Neural Networks are used to model complex non-linear relationships within the data. These techniques can uncover hidden patterns and correlations in market behavior that traditional models might miss. For instance, a neural network might be trained to predict crisis periods by learning from historical market data and identifying subtle pre-crisis indicators.

Moreover, the integration of Monte Carlo simulations provides an additional layer of robustness to risk assessment. Monte Carlo methods involve generating a large number of random scenarios for asset price movements and then calculating the distribution of potential portfolio outcomes. This approach helps in understanding the risk under various hypothetical situations and enhances the statistical reliability of the results. The process can be described as:

$$X_1, X_2, \ldots, X_n \sim F(\theta)$$

where θ is the parameter vector and F is the probability distribution function

This technique is especially valuable for evaluating the risk of complex derivative portfolios where analytical solutions are infeasible.

Factor models are another cornerstone of quantitative risk assessment in HFT. These models help in decomposing the risks into various underlying factors such as market indices, interest rates, or economic indicators. The Fama-French Three-Factor Model, for instance, expands on the traditional Capital Asset Pricing Model by incorporating factors for size and value:

$$R_p - R_f = \alpha + \beta_m(R_m - R_f) + \beta_s \times \text{SMB} + \beta_v \times \text{HML} + \epsilon$$

Here, R_p is the return on the portfolio, R_f is the risk-free rate, R_m is the return on the market portfolio, SMB (Small Minus Big) captures the size effect, and HML (High Minus Low) captures the value effect.

Incorporating these sophisticated quantitative models is essential for any effective risk management strategy in HFT. By continuously refining these models and integrating new techniques, traders can better navigate the intricate landscape of modern financial markets, transforming risks into opportunities.

6.4 Volatility and Market Risk Management

In the high-frequency trading (HFT) landscape, where trades are executed within fractions of a second, managing volatility and market risk is paramount. Volatility represents the degree of variation in the price of a financial instrument over time, often quantified by standard deviation. Market risk, on the other hand, encompasses the broader exposure to market fluctuations, which can negatively impact trading positions and portfolios. The swift and dynamic nature of HFT necessitates sophisticated strategies to manage these risks effectively.

Understanding the nuances of volatility is crucial for any HFT strategy. Volatility can be categorized into historical volatility, which is derived from past market prices, and implied volatility, which is gleaned from market expectations embedded in options pricing. Both types are invaluable in developing predictive models and setting risk parameters.

The first step in managing market risk is accurately measuring volatility. A commonly used metric is the GARCH (Generalized Autoregressive Conditional Heteroskedasticity) model, which excels in gauging time-varying volatility by incorporating past returns and volatility. The model is expressed as:

$$\sigma_t^2 = \alpha_0 + \alpha_1 \epsilon_{t-1}^2 + \beta_1 \sigma_{t-1}^2, \tag{6.1}$$

where ϵ_{t-1} represents the past errors and σ_{t-1}^2 the past variance. Through fitting this model, traders can obtain a dynamic forecast of future volatility, aiding in preemptive risk adjustments.

Another vital aspect is the Value at Risk (VaR) metric, which estimates the potential loss in the portfolio value with a given probability over a specific time horizon. The parametric VaR calculation relies on the assumption of normality and is given by:

$$\text{VaR}_\alpha = Z_\alpha \cdot \sigma \cdot \sqrt{\Delta t}, \tag{6.2}$$

where Z_α is the z-score under the standard normal distribution corresponding to the confidence level α, σ is the volatility, and Δt is the time horizon. In HFT, shorter timeframes and higher percentiles (such as 99% confidence level) are often utilized to capture the rapid market dynamics more accurately.

Managing exposure to market risk involves not only monitoring but also actively mitigating it. One prevalent approach in HFT is statistical arbitrage, which exploits short-term price inefficiencies between correlated securities. By constructing market-neutral strategies that involve simultaneous long and short positions, traders can hedge against market-wide movements and focus solely on the individual asset's relative performance.

Dynamic hedging is another tactic employed to adjust positions in real-time as market conditions change. This involves recalibrating the portfolio's delta—a measure of sensitivity to price movements—using options or other derivatives. The delta-hedging process incorporates both the initial setup and continuous adjustments based on the delta changes:

$$\Delta_{new} = \Delta_{old} + \Delta_{Options}, \tag{6.3}$$

where $\Delta_{Options}$ is the change in delta achieved through trading options contracts. The goal is to maintain a delta-neutral stance, minimizing the portfolio's exposure to price fluctuations.

Leverage control is critical in mitigating market risk. High leverage amplifies both potential gains and losses, necessitating stringent leverage ratio monitoring to avoid overexposure. Effective leverage limits are calculated considering the VaR and available capital, ensuring that positions remain within a manageable risk threshold.

Incorporating diversification is also a prudent strategy in HFT. Diversifying across various asset classes, sectors, and geographic regions can reduce unsystematic risk—the risk tied to a specific asset or sector—by ensuring that adverse movements in one area do not disproportionately affect the entire portfolio.

Lastly, real-time risk monitoring systems are indispensable for effective volatility and market risk management. Advanced algorithms and machine learning models can detect anomalies and alert traders to abrupt volatility spikes or market swings, enabling swift actions to mitigate potential losses. These systems continuously assess risk metrics, offering insights into evolving conditions and the overall risk profile of the trading strategies.

As we delve deeper into the realm of HFT, the concepts discussed form the bedrock upon which robust risk management strategies are built. Ensuring a comprehensive understanding of volatility dynamics and implementing diverse mitigation techniques can significantly enhance the stability and profitability of high-frequency trading operations. The intricate dance between speed and precision in HFT demands an unwavering focus on risk management, underscoring its paramount importance in navigating the high-stakes trading arena.

6.5 Credit and Counterparty Risk

Credit and counterparty risks are significant concerns in High-Frequency Trading (HFT), where the velocity of trades and the intricate network of counterparties amplify these risks. Understanding and managing these risks is crucial for any HFT firm aiming to maintain financial stability and operational integrity.

Credit risk refers to the possibility that a counterparty will fail to meet its obligations in accordance with agreed terms. In the context of HFT, this typically translates to the risk of a counterparty defaulting on a financial obligation, such as failing to settle a trade. Counterparty risk encompasses the broader scope of risks arising from the default or insolvency of any trading partner or intermediary involved in the transaction process.

Given the high-speed environment of HFT, the risk exposure periods are shortened, but the sheer volume and frequency of transactions raise the stakes. Effective risk management in this context necessitates a multi-layered approach that includes real-time risk assessment, rigorous counterpart screening, and robust credit risk modeling.

At the heart of managing credit and counterparty risks lies the credit risk assessment. This involves evaluating the creditworthiness of trading partners and determining appropriate credit limits. For HFT firms, this process is automated and continuous, leveraging real-time data feeds and sophisticated algorithms to dynamically adjust credit exposure limits based on market conditions and counterparty behavior.

To manage counterparty risk, HFT firms employ a set of stringent criteria for selecting counterparties. This includes assessing the financial health, market reputation, regulatory compliance, and operational robustness of potential trading partners. Moreover, many HFT firms rely on clearinghouses to mitigate counterparty risk. Clearinghouses act as intermediaries in trade settlements, ensuring that trades are executed smoothly even if one party defaults.

Metrics such as Credit Value Adjustment (CVA) are widely used to quantify the counterparty risk in HFT portfolios. CVA reflects the market value of counterparty credit risk inherent in derivative transactions. It adjusts the risk-free valuation of the portfolio by incorporating the likelihood of counterparty default, thereby providing a more accurate measure of potential exposure.

$$CVA = (1 - \text{Recovery Rate}) \times \sum_{i=1}^{n} EAD_i \times PD_i \times DF_i \tag{6.4}$$

In this equation:

- EAD_i represents the Exposure at Default for each trade i,
- PD_i is the Probability of Default,
- DF_i denotes the Discount Factor,
- while the Recovery Rate is the percentage of the exposure that can be recovered in the event of a default.

Additionally, HFT firms employ portfolio diversification to spread exposure across multiple counterparties and reduce the impact of any single counterparty failure. Automated stress testing and scenario analysis are also pivotal, enabling firms to assess the resilience of their portfolios under various adverse market conditions and counterparty default scenarios.

It is also critical to implement stringent internal controls and robust operational procedures to manage these risks effectively. Real-time monitoring systems should be in place to detect early warning signs of counterparty distress, while internal audit mechanisms ensure compliance with regulatory requirements and internal risk policies.

Engagement with external credit rating agencies can provide an added layer of assurance, although HFT firms must also be wary of the lag in ratings adjustments during rapidly changing market conditions. Thus, an integrated approach that combines external ratings with real-time internal assessments is often the most effective strategy.

By continuously refining these risk management practices and incorporating advanced machine learning models to predict counterparty behavior, HFT firms can enhance their resilience against credit and counterparty risks. Maintaining a proactive stance in risk management facilitates not only the mitigation of potential losses but also promotes a stable and compliant trading environment.

6.6 Operational and Technological Risks

Operational and technological risks are critical considerations in the high-stakes realm of High-Frequency Trading (HFT). These risks pertain to the internal processes, people, and systems that can impact trading operations. Given the rapid pace and complexity inherent to HFT, even minor flaws can lead to substantial financial repercussions. This section delves into the various dimensions of these risks and elucidates strategies to effectively manage and mitigate them.

Operational risks in HFT encompass a broad range of potential issues. One significant source of risk is human error. Despite the sophisticated algorithms and automated systems employed in HFT, the human element cannot be entirely eliminated. Traders and programmers might accidentally introduce bugs when coding algorithms, or operational staff may fail to respond adequately to system alerts. To minimize such risks, it is essential to implement comprehensive training programs, establish strict protocols for code reviews, and create a culture of accountability and continuous improvement within the trading organization.

Another aspect of operational risk is related to the organizational structure and internal processes. Inefficient workflow, lack of communication, and inadequate documentation can hinder effective risk management. Implementing robust operational procedures, such as standardized protocols for algorithm deployment, regular audits, and efficient incident response mechanisms, can significantly reduce the likelihood of operational failures.

Technological risks, meanwhile, are innately linked to the hardware and software infrastructure supporting HFT activities. Given the reliance on ultra-low latency performance, any technological failure can be catastrophic. These risks include hardware malfunctions, software bugs, and network disruptions. For example, server crashes or unexpected downtime can result in missed trading opportunities or an inability to execute critical trades.

To mitigate technological risks, it is crucial to have redundant systems and failover mechanisms in place. Redundancy ensures that if one component fails, another can seamlessly take over without significant disruption to trading activities. Implementing high-availability clusters and disaster recovery plans can provide additional layers of protection. Regular testing of these systems, including simulated stress tests and failover drills, is necessary to ensure their resilience and reliability under adverse conditions.

Another key technological risk is cybersecurity. HFT firms are prime targets for cyberattacks due to the sensitive nature of the data and the substantial financial stakes involved. A successful cyberattack can lead to data breaches, manipulation of trading algorithms, or unauthorized access to trading accounts. To combat these threats, HFT firms must adopt cutting-edge cybersecurity measures such as advanced encryption, multi-factor authentication, and real-time monitoring of network traffic for suspicious activities. Additionally, conducting periodic penetration testing and vulnerability assessments can help identify and address potential security gaps before they can be exploited.

Latency, while often discussed in the context of speed, also represents a technological risk factor in HFT. Variations in latency can lead to discrepancies in trading opportunities and execution quality. To manage latency risks, HFT firms should continuously monitor and optimize their network configurations, seek out the fastest connectivity options, and leverage co-location services to position their trading infrastructure as close as possible to the exchange servers.

Systematic risk can be another underestimated aspect of technological considerations. The interactions between multiple systems, both internal and external, can sometimes lead to unforeseen consequences. Implementing comprehensive system integration testing and maintaining clear, well-documented interfaces between systems are crucial steps to prevent such issues.

Algorithmic risks form a subset of technological risks, specifically related to the design and performance of trading algorithms. Flawed algorithms can result in significant losses, either through poor trading decisions or through triggering unintended market reactions. To mitigate algorithmic risks, a rigorous development and testing lifecycle must be adopted. This includes backtesting algorithms across historical data, conducting forward testing in simulated environments, and employing machine learning techniques to adapt and improve algorithm performance over time.

Effective risk management also involves real-time monitoring and analytics. Deploying a sophisticated monitoring system that provides real-time alerts on system performance, trade execution, and market conditions can enable rapid detection and rectification of issues before they escalate. Integrating artificial intelligence and machine learning technologies into these systems can enhance their predictive capabilities, allowing for proactive risk management.

Operational and technological risks, although daunting, can be managed through a combination of robust systems, comprehensive procedures, and a proactive approach to risk mitigation. By fostering a culture of vigilance, leveraging advanced technologies, and ensuring continuous improvement, HFT firms can navigate these risks and maintain their competitive edge in the fast-paced world of high-frequency trading.

6.7 Regulatory Risk and Compliance

Regulatory risk in High-Frequency Trading (HFT) pertains to the adverse impact of new or changing regulations on trading operations, strategies, and profitability. Unlike traditional market risks that are relatively predictable through historical data and models, regulatory risks can be abrupt, sometimes politically motivated, and often involve changes in the legal landscape that directly or indirectly affect HFT activities.

To understand regulatory risk, one must first appreciate the rationale behind financial regulations. Regulators aim to ensure market integrity, protect investors, and maintain systemic stability. HFT, being inherently complex and fast, poses unique challenges to these objectives, leading to targeted regulatory scrutiny and, consequently, frequent updates in regulatory frameworks.

A comprehensive approach to managing regulatory risk involves not only understanding the laws and guidelines but also anticipating regulatory changes and adapting trading strategies proactively.

One key regulatory requirement in many jurisdictions is the implementation of comprehensive risk control mechanisms. These mechanisms include pre-trade risk controls such as leveraged limits, order size, and order frequency filters, ensuring that each trade adheres to the regulatory framework and does not contribute to excessive market volatility.

$$\text{Pre\_trade\_limit} = \frac{\text{Account\_leverage\_limit}}{\text{Average order size}}$$

Adopting robust post-trade risk management practices is equally important. Post-trade compliance verifies that trades executed throughout the trading day adhere to risk policies and regulatory requirements. Automated systems for trade surveillance and reporting are essential tools for maintaining compliance. For example, trade surveillance algorithms can be designed to detect and prevent market manipulation behaviors like spoofing and layering.

Consider a scenario where the regulatory body mandates real-time reporting of large volume trades. The HFT firm needs an infrastructure capable of capturing trade executions instantaneously and transmitting the data to the relevant authority without delays.

$$\begin{aligned}\text{Reporting\_time} &= \frac{\text{Trade\_execution\_time} + \text{Data\_transmission\_time}}{2} \\ &\leq \text{Regulatory\_limit}\end{aligned}$$

Compliance extends beyond adhering to existing regulations; it also involves rigorous internal governance. This includes establishing compliance departments with roles dedicated to monitoring compliance, conducting regular audits, and maintaining a direct line of communication with regulators. Compliance officers must stay informed about regulatory developments, ensuring any amendments or new policies are integrated into the firm's practices.

Furthermore, incorporating advanced technologies like Artificial Intelligence (AI) and Machine Learning (ML) in compliance strategies can be immensely beneficial. These technologies enable the analysis of vast amounts of trading data, identifying patterns that may suggest non-compliance risks. For example, AI could rank trades by risk level, allowing compliance departments to prioritize their reviews efficiently.

Another critical aspect of regulatory compliance is international collaboration. HFT firms often operate across multiple jurisdictions, each with distinct regulatory requirements. Therefore, multinational HFT operations must establish a compliance framework that harmonizes with various international legal standards. This sometimes involves creating country-specific compliance protocols that align with local regulations without compromising the firm's global operational integrity.

$$\sum_{i=1}^{n} \text{Compliance\_Cost}_i = \text{Total\_Compliance\_Budget}$$

In an industry as dynamic as HFT, regulatory risk management and compliance are not static processes. They require continuous adaptation and investment. Successful firms harness the power of predictive analytics to foresee regulatory changes and prepare accordingly. These firms engage with regulators and industry bodies to remain ahead of the curve, ensuring that their trading systems can swiftly adapt to new regulatory environments.

To instill confidence in regulators and stakeholders, HFT firms also emphasize transparency. Clear documentation of trading strategies, risk controls, and compliance procedures goes a long way in demonstrating a commitment to ethical trading practices and regulatory adherence.

Ultimately, navigating regulatory risk and sustaining compliance in high-frequency trading necessitate a proactive, informed, and strategically integrated approach. By embracing regulatory changes and maintaining robust compliance frameworks, HFT firms can mitigate risks and capitalize on opportunities within the legal confines, thus ensuring their long-term viability and success.

6.8 Risk Mitigation Strategies and Tools

In High-Frequency Trading (HFT), the lightning-fast execution and razor-thin margins demand a robust approach to risk management.

Risk Mitigation Strategies and Tools are paramount for safeguarding operations, managing volatility, and ensuring compliance. This section delves into the specific strategies and tools employed to mitigate the multifaceted risks associated with HFT, providing practical and actionable insights for traders and investors.

Risk mitigation in HFT involves a blend of sophisticated mathematical models and technological solutions. These are tailored to address the unique risks posed by HFT, such as market, credit, operational, and technological risks. Effective risk management not only protects financial capital but also enhances the integrity and efficiency of trading operations.

1. Advanced Algorithmic Strategies

Algorithms lie at the heart of HFT and play a critical role in risk mitigation. Advanced algorithmic strategies are designed to minimize exposure to market volatility and facilitate optimal trade execution. These strategies include arbitrage, statistical arbitrage, and market making. By employing these algorithms, traders can exploit inefficiencies in the market while managing risk through precise and controlled execution.

Consider the implementation of *statistical arbitrage*, which leverages historical price relationships between correlated assets. By executing trades based on statistical models, traders can capitalize on temporary price divergences, thereby reducing directional market risk. The formula used in statistical arbitrage can be expressed as:

$$P_{\text{spread}} = P_{\text{asset1}} - \beta \cdot P_{\text{asset2}}$$

where P_{spread} represents the price spread between two correlated assets, and β is the regression coefficient obtained from historical data analysis.

2. Diversification and Portfolio Hedging

Diversification is a fundamental principle in risk management that involves spreading investments across various assets to mitigate individual asset risks. In the context of HFT, diversification can be applied by trading a wide range of instruments, including equities, futures, currencies, and commodities. This reduces the impact of market-specific events on the overall portfolio.

Portfolio hedging is another powerful tool for risk mitigation. By using derivative instruments such as options, futures, and swaps, traders can protect their portfolios from adverse price movements. For instance, a trader holding a large position in a volatile stock can use put options to hedge against potential losses. The cost of the option acts as an insurance premium, providing downside protection while allowing for upside potential.

3. Dynamic Risk Adjustment

The highly volatile and unpredictable nature of markets necessitates dynamic risk adjustment strategies. These strategies involve continuously monitoring and adjusting risk parameters based on real-time market conditions. One such method is *Value at Risk* (VaR), which quantifies the potential loss in a portfolio over a specified time frame, given normal market conditions.

A dynamic approach to VaR can be illustrated by recalculating the risk metric at regular intervals and adjusting the portfolio positions accordingly. The formula for VaR is typically:

$$\text{VaR}_\alpha = \mu + \sigma \cdot Z_\alpha$$

where μ is the mean return, σ is the standard deviation of returns, and Z_α is the z-score corresponding to the confidence level α.

4. Technological Solutions

Technology plays a critical role in mitigating operational and technological risks in HFT. High-performance computing (HPC) and advanced analytics enable traders to process vast amounts of data swiftly and efficiently. Implementing redundant systems and disaster recovery protocols ensures business continuity in the event of system failures or cyberattacks.

Additionally, the use of machine learning and artificial intelligence (AI) can enhance risk management by identifying patterns and anomalies that may not be apparent through traditional methods. For example, AI algorithms can detect unusual trading activities that could signal market manipulation or fraud, allowing for prompt corrective actions.

5. Real-Time Monitoring and Surveillance

A proactive approach to risk management involves real-time monitoring and market surveillance systems. These tools provide continuous oversight of trading activities, enabling immediate identification and response to irregularities. Real-time monitoring systems can track various metrics, including order execution rates, latency, and trade volumes.

Through automated alert systems, traders can receive instant notifications of potential issues, such as network outages or significant market moves. This allows for timely interventions to mitigate risks before they escalate. Furthermore, regulatory compliance is enhanced by maintaining detailed records of trading activity, ensuring transparency and accountability.

6. Stress Testing and Scenario Analysis

Stress testing and scenario analysis are critical components of risk mitigation, providing insights into how portfolios might perform under adverse market conditions. By simulating extreme scenarios, such as market crashes or liquidity crises, traders can evaluate the resilience of their strategies and identify potential vulnerabilities.

The process of stress testing involves defining hypothetical scenarios and applying them to the portfolio to assess the impact on asset values and risk metrics. For instance, a scenario might involve a sudden spike in interest rates or a sharp decline in equity prices. The results of these tests guide the development of contingency plans and risk mitigation measures.

As the complexity and speed of HFT continue to evolve, the importance of robust risk mitigation strategies and tools cannot be overstated. By leveraging advanced algorithms, diversification, dynamic risk adjustment, technological solutions, real-time monitoring, and stress testing, traders can navigate the intricacies of HFT with confidence and precision. These risk management practices not only protect financial capital but also ensure the stability and efficiency of trading operations in an ever-changing market landscape.

Chapter 7

Regulatory Environment and Compliance

This chapter provides a thorough overview of the regulatory environment and compliance requirements relevant to High-Frequency Trading (HFT). It identifies key regulatory bodies and their roles, delves into major regulations impacting HFT, such as Dodd-Frank and MiFID II, and outlines the necessary regulatory reporting requirements. The chapter discusses best practices for compliance processes, market surveillance, and monitoring, as well as the role of technology in ensuring regulatory adherence. Additionally, it looks forward to future trends in HFT regulation, emphasizing the importance of staying informed and compliant in an ever-evolving regulatory landscape.

7.1 Overview of Regulatory Environment

High-Frequency Trading (HFT) operates within a heavily regulated environment, reflecting the need to balance market efficiency with financial stability and investor protection. Understanding the regulatory landscape surrounding HFT is essential for market participants seeking to navigate this space effectively. This section provides a detailed overview of the key elements that define the regulatory environment for HFT, setting the stage for deeper exploration of specific regulations and compliance practices in subsequent sections.

At its core, the regulatory environment for HFT is shaped by the interplay between national and international regulatory bodies. These organizations establish rules and guidelines designed to mitigate risks associated with high-speed, automated trading while promoting fair and orderly markets. To appreciate the full scope of HFT regulation, one must first grasp the foundational principles and objectives that regulators aim to achieve.

The primary objectives of HFT regulation include enhancing market transparency, reducing systemic risk, protecting investors, and ensuring market integrity. Market transparency is improved through rigorous reporting requirements, mandating that trades and orders be documented in a manner accessible for oversight. Systemic risk reduction involves measures to prevent market disruptions caused by algorithmic trading errors, emphasizing the importance of robust risk management frameworks. Investor protection focuses on preventing manipulative practices such as spoofing and ensuring equitable access to markets. Market integrity is maintained through surveillance and monitoring mechanisms designed to detect and deter abusive trading behaviors.

Globally, the regulatory environment for HFT is influenced by both national policies and international agreements. In the United States, the Securities and Exchange Commission (SEC) and the Commodity Futures Trading Commission (CFTC) are pivotal in shaping the regulatory landscape. The SEC oversees securities markets, enforcing rules that enhance transparency and investor protection, while the CFTC regulates commodity futures and options markets, emphasizing the prevention of market manipulation.

In Europe, the Markets in Financial Instruments Directive II (MiFID II) plays a crucial role. MiFID II introduces comprehensive reforms to foster greater transparency and accountability in financial markets. It mandates extensive reporting and record-keeping requirements and sets stringent conduct standards for investment firms, particularly those engaging in high-frequency trading. MiFID II also aims to improve investor protection and enhance market resilience by addressing conflicts of interest and ensuring fair competition.

Internationally, the Financial Stability Board (FSB) and the International Organization of Securities Commissions (IOSCO) contribute to the regulatory discourse by establishing global standards and promoting cooperation among national regulators. These organizations focus on addressing cross-border challenges posed by HFT and ensuring coherent regulatory approaches across different jurisdictions.

Emerging markets and regions with developing financial infrastructures also play a critical role in the global regulatory environment for HFT. As these markets experience rapid growth in automated trading activities, they face unique challenges and opportunities. Regulators in these regions often draw on international best practices while adapting rules to local market conditions and developmental trajectories.

The evolving nature of technology and market structure necessitates a dynamic regulatory approach. Regulatory bodies must continually adapt to technological advancements in HFT, such as the increasing use of machine learning and artificial intelligence algorithms. This requires ongoing dialogue between regulators and market participants to ensure that rules remain relevant and effective in addressing new risks.

Ensuring compliance within this multifaceted regulatory framework demands that HFT firms develop comprehensive compliance programs. These programs must integrate ongoing education, internal audits, and technology solutions to monitor trading activities. Firms are also encouraged to engage in proactive communication with regulators, fostering a collaborative approach to regulatory adherence.

Understanding the regulatory environment for HFT is not merely about knowing the rules; it involves recognizing the underlying principles and objectives that drive regulatory actions. By appreciating the broader context, market participants can better anticipate regulatory shifts and align their strategies to maintain compliance. This awareness is crucial for sustaining a competitive edge while contributing to the overall integrity and stability of financial markets.

7.2 Key Regulatory Bodies and Their Roles

Navigating the regulatory environment of High-Frequency Trading (HFT) necessitates a comprehensive understanding of the key regulatory bodies and their respective roles. These entities are critical in shaping the rules, monitoring adherence, and enforcing compliance, thereby ensuring the integrity and stability of financial markets.

The first regulatory body to consider is the **Securities and Exchange Commission (SEC)** in the United States. The SEC has a pivotal role in protecting investors, maintaining fair, orderly, and efficient markets, and facilitating capital formation. Within the realm of HFT, the SEC's jurisdiction covers several aspects, from the registration of trading firms and their compliance with statutory requirements to the enforcement of rules designed to prevent market abuse, such as insider trading and market manipulation.

Another significant entity is the **Commodity Futures Trading Commission (CFTC)**, which oversees the derivatives markets, including futures, swaps, and options. The CFTC's regulatory framework is vital for HFT firms that engage in derivatives trading. The Dodd-Frank Wall Street Reform and Consumer Protection Act expanded the CFTC's authority to include the previously less-regulated swap markets, thus bringing a new dimension of oversight critical for HFT operations that deal in complex financial instruments.

Overseas, the **European Securities and Markets Authority (ESMA)** plays a similarly central role. ESMA is an independent EU authority that contributes to safeguarding the stability of the EU's financial system by ensuring the integrity, transparency, efficiency, and orderly functioning of securities markets. Through regulatory frameworks such as the Markets in Financial Instruments Directive (MiFID II) and the Markets in Financial Instruments Regulation (MiFIR), ESMA imposes stringent requirements on HFT firms, including algorithm testing and risk management controls.

In Asia, notable regulatory bodies include the **Financial Services Agency (FSA)** in Japan and the **Monetary Authority of Singapore (MAS)**. The FSA demands robust internal controls and detailed reporting from HFT firms to prevent systemic risk and ensure market fairness. Similarly, MAS regulates to maintain market orderliness and transparency, often instituting guidelines that closely mirror those of international counterparts like the SEC and ESMA.

Central to these regulatory bodies' roles is their function in surveillance and enforcement. For example, the SEC employs sophisticated market surveillance systems, such as the Market Information Data Analytics System (MIDAS), to monitor trading activities and detect anomalies indicative of manipulative practices. Likewise, the CFTC's use of trade surveillance technology helps it in identifying and prosecuting illegal trading practices.

Each regulatory body also places a significant emphasis on the development and enforcement of best practices in risk management and compliance for HFT firms. This includes requirements for pre- and post-trade risk controls, periodic compliance audits, and comprehensive reporting standards. For instance, MiFID II mandates the use of circuit breakers and volatility interruption mechanisms to mitigate the risks associated with high-frequency trading.

Moreover, collaboration and information sharing among these regulatory bodies are crucial in addressing the global nature of modern financial markets. For instance, the International Organization of Securities Commissions (IOSCO) provides a forum for securities regulators worldwide to cooperate and exchange information, thus ensuring a coordinated approach to market supervision and risk management.

Understanding the roles of these key regulatory bodies and their interactions is essential for any HFT firm striving for compliance in this highly regulated environment. It is not just about adhering to the rules but also proactively engaging with regulators, participating in industry consultations, and staying ahead of regulatory developments. This strategic engagement helps firms not only to avoid penalties but also to shape the future regulatory landscape in ways that balance innovation with market integrity.

Ultimately, the evolving regulatory environment requires that HFT firms remain agile and informed. Establishing a robust compliance framework that aligns with the directives of these key regulatory bodies can thus provide a significant competitive advantage, fostering trust among market participants and enhancing the overall robustness of the financial system.

7.3 Major Regulations Impacting HFT: Dodd-Frank, MiFID II, and More

High-Frequency Trading (HFT) operates within a complex regulatory framework designed to maintain market integrity, protect investors, and mitigate systemic risk. Among the multitude of regulations, the Dodd-Frank Wall Street Reform and Consumer Protection Act (Dodd-Frank) and the Markets in Financial Instruments Directive II (MiFID II) are paramount. This section delves into these cornerstone regulations, as well as other significant regulatory initiatives, to elucidate their scope, impact, and implications for HFT practitioners.

Dodd-Frank Act, enacted in the United States in 2010 following the financial crisis of 2007-2008, brought comprehensive reforms aimed at increasing transparency and reducing risks in the financial system. This legislation has several provisions specifically relevant to HFT. Title VII, which deals with over-the-counter (OTC) derivatives, mandates the clearing of standardized derivatives through central counterparties (CCPs) and reporting to trade repositories. This enhances transparency and reduces counterparty risk. Moreover, the Volcker Rule restricts banking entities from engaging in proprietary trading and limits their investments in hedge funds and private equity—a move intended to separate speculative trading from traditional banking activities.

MiFID II, implemented in the European Union in January 2018, represents another fundamental regulatory overhaul. It introduces extensive requirements for HFT firms, including mandatory registration with national competent authorities and stringent organizational obligations. One of the critical stipulations of MiFID II is the requirement for firms engaging in algorithmic trading to have effective systems and risk controls in place to ensure their trading systems are resilient and have sufficient capacity. Furthermore, MiFID II mandates detailed transaction reporting to enhance market transparency and surveillance. It also addresses issues related to market integrity by imposing limits on trading in dark pools and enforcing rules against market manipulation.

Another pivotal regulation is the European Market Infrastructure Regulation (EMIR), which complements MiFID II by focusing on OTC derivatives, central clearing, and trade repository reporting. EMIR aims to reduce systemic risk and increase transparency in OTC derivatives markets, similar to Dodd-Frank's Title VII.

The Commodity Futures Trading Commission (CFTC) in the United States also plays a crucial role through regulations such as Regulation Automated Trading (Reg AT) and the Market Reform Act. Reg AT, although not yet finalized, proposes risk controls, transparency measures, and testing standards for automated trading systems. The Market Reform Act, meanwhile, grants the CFTC authority to enforce rules against practices like spoofing and layering, which can distort market prices and liquidity.

Additionally, the Financial Stability Oversight Council (FSOC) established under Dodd-Frank, monitors systemic risks and can impose stringent regulatory standards on financial entities deemed systemically important, potentially affecting large HFT firms.

In Asia, jurisdictions like Japan and Singapore have introduced their own frameworks. Japan's Financial Services Agency (FSA) has enhanced regulations around algorithmic trading, requiring firms to register and adhere to specific standards of conduct. The Singapore Exchange (SGX) has implemented the Trading Rules to regulate automated and high-frequency trading, focusing on the integrity and resilience of its markets.

The regulatory landscape is continually evolving, and firms must stay abreast of ongoing developments and proposed regulations, such as the U.S. Securities and Exchange Commission's (SEC) initiatives on market structure modernization, which may introduce additional compliance requirements.

Ultimately, Dodd-Frank, MiFID II, and other regulations collectively aim to enhance market stability, transparency, and fairness. Practitioners in the HFT space must ensure robust compliance mechanisms, adapt to regulatory changes, and engage in proactive risk management practices to navigate this intricate regulatory environment effectively. Adhering to these regulations not only fulfills legal obligations but also promotes a stable and trustworthy market ecosystem.

"'

This section is designed to seamlessly fit within the chapter on "Regulatory Environment and Compliance" by ensuring it builds on the foundational knowledge established in earlier parts of the book, providing both educational value and practical insights. The direct and supportive tone, combined with detailed explanations, ensures clarity and accessibility for readers of all levels of expertise.

7.4 Regulatory Reporting Requirements

Regulatory reporting requirements for High-Frequency Trading (HFT) encompass a broad array of obligations that aim to maintain market integrity and protect investors. Accurate and timely reporting is essential for compliance with various regulatory frameworks. These requirements can vary significantly depending on the jurisdiction, with notable differences between regions such as the United States and the European Union. This section provides a detailed examination of the key regulatory reporting obligations that HFT firms must adhere to.

First, it is crucial to understand the primary objectives of regulatory reporting in the context of HFT. Regulatory authorities mandate reporting to achieve several critical goals:

- **Market Transparency:** Ensuring that all market participants have access to pertinent information about trading activities, which helps prevent market manipulation and fosters a fair trading environment.

- **Market Integrity:** Identifying and mitigating practices that could undermine the orderly functioning of financial markets.
- **Investor Protection:** Safeguarding investors by providing them with reliable information and protecting them from fraudulent activities.
- **Systemic Risk Monitoring:** Enabling regulators to detect and manage risks that could threaten the stability of the financial system.

To achieve these objectives, various reporting requirements are enforced. Let's delve into the specifics of these requirements.

1. Transaction Reporting:

Transaction reporting forms the cornerstone of regulatory reporting for HFT firms. Key regulations such as the European Union's Markets in Financial Instruments Regulation (MiFIR) and the United States' Consolidated Audit Trail (CAT) mandate detailed transaction reports. These reports must include comprehensive information about each trade, such as:

- **Instrument Details:** Identification of the financial instruments traded, including International Securities Identification Number (ISIN) codes.
- **Trade Details:** Precise time stamps, trade volume, price, and the execution venue for each trade.
- **Counterparty Information:** Identification of the clients or other market participants involved in the trades.
- **Trader Identifiers:** Unique identifiers for the traders executing the transactions.

Regulators utilize transaction reports to reconstruct trading activities and monitor for any attempts at market abuse or irregularities. Compliance with MiFIR, for instance, requires transaction reports to be submitted to the relevant regulatory authorities no later than the end of the following business day.

2. Order Record-Keeping:

Apart from transaction reporting, HFTs must maintain detailed records of all orders and quotes submitted to trading venues. This requirement is crucial for providing a complete audit trail of trading activities. Records must typically include:

- **Order Details:** The time the order was placed, modified, or canceled, the quantity and price of the order, and the type of order (e.g., limit or market order).
- **Quote Details:** Similar information for all quotes submitted, including the trader ID associated with each action.
- **Routing Information:** Data indicating the origin and destination of each order and quote.

These records must be stored in a format that allows for timely retrieval and analysis. For instance, under the SEC's Rule 613, all National Market System (NMS) securities must be reported to the CAT, facilitating comprehensive oversight.

3. Electronic Blue Sheets (EBS):

In the United States, Electronic Blue Sheets (EBS) are another critical reporting mechanism, requested by the Securities and Exchange Commission (SEC) and the Financial Industry Regulatory Authority (FINRA). EBS requests require firms to submit detailed trade data, especially in the context of investigations or examinations. The required information typically includes trade dates, quantities, prices, and counterparties involved. EBS serves as an investigative tool that enables regulators to analyze historical trading patterns and identify any suspicious activity.

4. Large Trader Reporting:

The SEC's Large Trader Reporting Rule mandates HFT firms that qualify as large traders to register and report their trading activity. A large trader is defined based on specified thresholds of trading volume or market impact. Registered large traders must file Form 13H, providing information about their trading activities and any relevant changes. By tracking large traders, the SEC can better understand market dynamics and identify risks related to large-scale trading activities.

5. Algorithmic Trading Reporting:

Given the unique characteristics of HFT, specific regulations target algorithmic trading disclosures. For example, MiFID II requires detailed reporting on the algorithms used in trading, including:

- **Algorithm Identification:** Detailed descriptions and identifiers for each algorithm employed in trading.
- **Algorithmic Behavior:** Information about the strategy, risk controls, and conditions under which the algorithm operates.
- **Performance Metrics:** Data concerning the performance and impact of algorithms, such as trade execution quality and market impact.

This level of transparency helps regulators monitor and assess the influence of algorithmic and high-frequency trading activities on market stability and integrity.

Compliance with these diverse regulatory reporting requirements necessitates significant technological and operational infrastructure. HFT firms must implement robust systems capable of capturing, storing, and transmitting large volumes of data accurately and promptly. Automation and real-time monitoring tools are often essential to meet the stringent timelines and data integrity standards set by regulators.

In navigating these obligations, the collaboration between compliance teams and technology experts is critical. Firms must stay abreast of evolving regulations and adapt their reporting frameworks accordingly. Through diligent adherence to these reporting requirements, HFT firms contribute to the overarching goals of market transparency, integrity, and investor protection, thereby fostering a more stable and trustworthy financial environment.

7.5 Compliance Processes and Best Practices

Success in high-frequency trading (HFT) necessitates a robust compliance framework to navigate the intricate landscape of regulatory requirements effectively. This section explores the essential components of HFT compliance processes, highlighting best practices that ensure market participants operate within legal boundaries while maintaining high efficiency.

An effective compliance process begins with a thorough understanding of the legal and regulatory framework. Engaging with knowledgeable legal advisors and compliance experts can provide the necessary insights to interpret complex regulations accurately. This foundational knowledge forms the basis upon which the compliance strategy is constructed.

The next critical element is the establishment of a comprehensive compliance program. This program should include clearly defined policies and procedures tailored to align with the specific requirements of the regulatory environment. These policies must cover all aspects of HFT operations, from pre-trade analytics to post-trade reporting.

Clear communication is vital in any compliance strategy. Ensuring that all team members, from executives to traders and IT staff, are aware of the compliance obligations is essential. Regular training sessions should be conducted to keep the team updated on new regulations and compliance tools. Additionally, creating a culture of compliance where every team member understands their role can significantly mitigate the risk of inadvertent non-compliance.

To implement these policies effectively, institutions should leverage technology to automate compliance tasks, thereby reducing the potential for human error. Integrating compliance management systems can streamline the monitoring of trading activities against pre-defined regulatory criteria. For instance, rule-based systems can automatically flag trades that breach regulatory limits, enabling swift corrective action.

Documentation is another cornerstone of a sound compliance process. Maintaining detailed records of trading activities, decision-making processes, and compliance checks is crucial. These records provide an audit trail that can be invaluable during regulatory inspections and audits. The use of standardized templates for documentation can enhance consistency and ease of access.

Internal audits play a significant role in ensuring ongoing compliance. Regular audits help in identifying gaps in the compliance framework and offer an opportunity to rectify issues before they escalate. Engaging with external auditors can provide an objective assessment of the compliance program's effectiveness, adding a layer of accountability and reassurance.

Regulatory reporting is an area where meticulous attention to detail is indispensable. Firms should implement automated solutions to manage regulatory reporting requirements efficiently. These solutions must be capable of generating accurate reports that comply with the format and timing stipulated by regulators. Consistent testing and validation of these systems are necessary to ensure their reliability.

Best practices in compliance also emphasize the importance of continuous improvement. The regulatory landscape is ever-evolving, and hence, compliance processes must be adaptable. Regular reviews of the compliance program, taking into account the latest regulatory changes, can help in updating policies and procedures as required. Feedback from regulatory bodies, as well as from the firm's own employees, should be used constructively to enhance the compliance framework.

Engagement with regulatory bodies can be strategically beneficial. Building a cooperative relationship with regulators helps in staying ahead of regulatory changes. Being proactive in seeking guidance on complex compliance issues can prevent potential non-compliance scenarios.

Risk management is integral to any compliance strategy. Identifying and assessing potential compliance risks enables firms to develop mitigation strategies. For example, conducting scenario analyses to understand the impact of various regulatory changes can help in formulating contingency plans. Embedding compliance risk management into the broader risk management framework ensures a holistic approach to risk mitigation.

Moreover, third-party compliance solutions can be an effective way to enhance an in-house compliance framework. These solutions offer tailored services that keep the firm updated with the latest regulatory changes and provide specialized tools for compliance monitoring and reporting.

Finally, transparency and accountability should be principles guiding the compliance strategy. Transparent communication with stakeholders, including clients, investors, and regulatory bodies, fosters trust and enhances the firm's reputation. Establishing accountability structures ensures that compliance responsibilities are clearly defined and managed effectively.

Adhering to these best practices can not only safeguard a firm's operations from regulatory penalties but also enhance its operational efficiency and reputation in the market. The pursuit of compliance should be viewed as an ongoing commitment to excellence and integrity in the fast-paced world of high-frequency trading.

This approach, grounded in a deep understanding of the regulatory landscape and underpinned by sophisticated technology and robust internal controls, forms the bedrock of a resilient and effective compliance framework.

7.6 Market Surveillance and Monitoring

In the rapidly evolving landscape of High-Frequency Trading (HFT), market surveillance and monitoring have emerged as crucial components in maintaining market integrity and ensuring compliance with regulatory standards. Effective surveillance systems enable regulatory bodies and trading firms to detect and prevent market abuses, such as spoofing, layering, and other manipulative behaviors that can distort the fair and orderly functioning of financial markets.

Market surveillance refers to the systematic observation and analysis of trading activities, with the primary objective of identifying suspicious patterns and behaviors that might indicate market manipulation or abuse. Monitoring, on the other hand, involves the continuous, real-time tracking of trading activities to ensure adherence to regulatory norms and firm-specific compliance policies.

The first step in developing a comprehensive market surveillance and monitoring system is to understand the different types of market manipulations commonly associated with HFT:

- **Spoofing:** This involves placing large orders with the intention to cancel before execution, creating a false impression of demand or supply and manipulating the market price.
- **Layering:** A technique where multiple, incremental orders are placed across various price levels with the intent to manipulate the market price by creating artificial depth in the order book.
- **Quote Stuffing:** The practice of rapidly placing and canceling a large number of orders to overwhelm the market with excessive data, potentially delaying other traders' execution.
- **Front-Running:** Using advance knowledge of large pending transactions to place orders ahead of the anticipated price movements.

To effectively monitor and surveil these behaviors, robust technological solutions are essential. These systems must be capable of processing vast amounts of data in real-time, employing sophisticated algorithms and machine learning techniques to identify abnormal trading patterns. Below we explore key components and best practices for implementing an efficient market surveillance and monitoring system.

Data Collection and Management:

An effective surveillance system begins with comprehensive data collection, encompassing all relevant trading activities across multiple exchanges and asset classes. High-frequency trading generates immense volumes of data, making it imperative to have advanced data management solutions. The following capabilities are crucial:

- *Real-Time Data Processing:* Ensuring that the system can handle the high throughput of HFT data with minimal latency.
- *Scalability:* The ability to scale up processing power to accommodate growing data volumes without compromising performance.
- *Accuracy and Integrity:* Implementing robust data validation checks to ensure the accuracy and completeness of collected data.

Advanced Analytical Tools:

Once data is collected, advanced analytical tools are used to detect and analyze suspicious activities. These tools leverage various methodologies, including pattern recognition, statistical analysis, and machine learning models. Key features include:

- *Algorithmic Pattern Detection:* Algorithms designed to sift through large datasets to identify anomalies indicative of manipulative behaviors.
- *Historical Analysis:* Comparing current trading data with historical patterns to identify deviations that may signal potential abuse.
- *Predictive Analytics:* Employing machine learning models to predict and identify emerging threats based on historical data and evolving market conditions.

Real-Time Alerts and Reporting:

The ability to generate real-time alerts is critical in a market surveillance system. These alerts should be customizable to meet specific regulatory and firm requirements. Some best practices include:

- *Threshold-Based Alerts:* Setting predefined thresholds for various trading activities that, when exceeded, trigger an alert.

- *Contextual Analysis:* Integrating contextual data, such as market news and economic indicators, to enhance the relevance and accuracy of alerts.
- *Comprehensive Reporting:* Providing detailed reports that document detected manipulative behaviors, facilitating regulatory reporting and internal audits.

Audit Trails and Regulatory Reporting:

Maintaining detailed audit trails is essential for demonstrating compliance during regulatory audits. An effective market surveillance system should:

- *Record Keeping:* Maintain detailed logs of all monitoring activities, including the rationale for alerts and any subsequent investigations.
- *Regulatory Compliance:* Ensure that the system's reporting capabilities align with the requirements of regulatory bodies such as the SEC, CFTC, and ESMA.
- *Transparency:* Provide transparent and accessible audit trails that can be readily accessed for regulatory inspections or compliance reviews.

Integration and Adaptability:

The rapidly changing nature of HFT and financial markets necessitates that surveillance systems are adaptable and integrative. They should:

- *Modularity:* Be built with a modular design to allow for easy updates and integration of new analytical tools without requiring complete system overhauls.
- *Interoperability:* Ensure compatibility with other internal systems and external regulatory platforms to streamline data exchange and reporting processes.
- *Continuous Improvement:* Incorporate feedback mechanisms and regular updates to refine algorithms and analytical models, adapting to new regulatory requirements and evolving market behaviors.

The effectiveness of market surveillance and monitoring systems ultimately hinges on the synergy between advanced technologies and well-defined processes. By leveraging state-of-the-art tools and adhering to industry best practices, firms can not only ensure compliance but also contribute to the integrity and stability of financial markets, fostering a trustworthy trading environment.

7.7 The Role of Technology in Regulatory Compliance

As high-frequency trading (HFT) continues to evolve, the role of technology in regulatory compliance becomes increasingly critical. The complexity and speed of HFT operations necessitate the use of advanced technological solutions to ensure adherence to a rapidly changing regulatory landscape. This section explores the pivotal role that technology plays in enhancing regulatory compliance within HFT, highlighting key technological tools and methodologies.

At the forefront of technological compliance solutions are automated compliance systems designed to monitor trading activity in real-time. These systems leverage machine learning algorithms and sophisticated data analytics to detect anomalies and potential breaches of regulatory guidelines swiftly. By continuously examining vast datasets for patterns indicative of misconduct or non-compliance, these systems mitigate the risk of regulatory infractions.

$$\text{Compliance\_Score} = \sum_{i=1}^{n} w_i \cdot f_i(x_i)$$

In this equation, Compliance_Score is a quantitative measure of adherence to regulatory standards, where $f_i(x_i)$ represents the compliance function applied to the i-th piece of data, weighted by w_i. Such scoring mechanisms enable firms to maintain a proactive stance towards regulatory compliance, flagging issues before they escalate into significant problems.

Another crucial technological advancement is the implementation of blockchain technology. Blockchain provides an immutable and transparent ledger of all transactions, which is invaluable for regulatory reporting and audit trails. The decentralized nature of blockchain ensures data integrity, making it exceedingly difficult to alter transaction records without detection. This level of transparency and security aligns perfectly with the stringent requirements set forth by regulations like MiFID II and Dodd-Frank.

Code compliance is equally important, requiring firms to embed regulatory checks directly into their trading algorithms. This practice ensures that trades are automatically evaluated against compliance rules before execution. Exchanges of such evaluations can be illustrated with pseudocode:

```
if check_compliance(trade_details):
    execute_trade()
else:
    flag_trade_non_compliant()
```

In the above pseudocode, check_compliance() is a function that assesses a trade against regulatory criteria. If the trade is compliant, it is executed; otherwise, it is flagged for further review.

Artificial Intelligence (AI) and natural language processing (NLP) facilitate the analysis of regulatory text, enabling systems to interpret and adapt to new rules without substantial manual intervention. These technologies can automatically update compliance frameworks based on changes in legislation, ensuring that HFT firms remain aligned with current regulations.

Moreover, surveillance technologies incorporating AI provide enhanced market monitoring capabilities. These systems not only track trading activities but also predict potential market abuses such as spoofing and insider trading by analyzing historical and real-time data. By incorporating AI models trained on extensive datasets, these technologies better identify patterns that precede regulatory breaches.

The role of cloud computing in regulatory compliance cannot be understated. Cloud platforms offer scalable and flexible infrastructure to handle the enormous data processing requirements of HFT regulatory compliance. They provide robust security protocols, data encryption, and regular compliance audits, ensuring that sensitive financial data is protected and accessible only to authorized entities. Cloud services like Amazon Web Services (AWS) and Microsoft Azure come with built-in compliance frameworks that help firms align with global regulatory standards efficiently.

Effective data management is also integral to the compliance technology ecosystem. Technologies such as big data analytics facilitate the consolidation and analysis of diverse data sources, providing a holistic view of trading activities and compliance status. These insights are critical for regulatory reporting and also for internal audits and assessments.

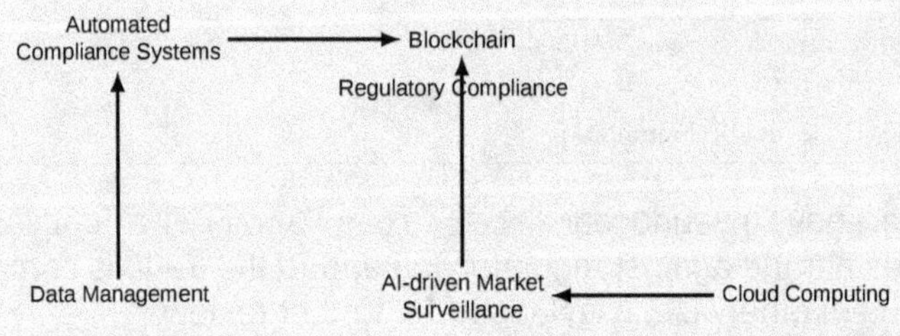

The above figure illustrates an integrated compliance framework that leverages multiple technological solutions to ensure regulatory adherence. This comprehensive approach combines automated compliance systems, blockchain technology, AI-driven market surveillance, and robust data management strategies to create a resilient compliance infrastructure.

Technological advancements have undoubtedly transformed the landscape of regulatory compliance in HFT. By leveraging cutting-edge solutions, firms can not only meet regulatory requirements with greater accuracy and efficiency but also gain a strategic edge through better risk management and operational transparency. Staying abreast of these technological innovations is essential for any HFT firm aiming to navigate the intricate world of regulatory compliance successfully.

7.8 Future Trends in HFT Regulation

As financial markets continue to evolve, so too does the regulatory landscape that governs High-Frequency Trading (HFT). Understanding future trends in HFT regulation is crucial for market participants who aim to stay compliant and competitive. Emerging trends suggest that regulations will continue to adapt to technological advancements and market behaviors, focusing on transparency, fairness, and market stability. This section explores several key trends anticipated in the regulatory environment for HFT.

One significant trend is the increasing emphasis on transparency. Regulatory bodies around the world are recognizing the need for greater visibility into the operations of HFT firms. Enhanced transparency measures are likely to include more detailed reporting requirements and real-time data disclosures. For instance, firms might be mandated to provide granular order and trade data to regulators, enabling closer scrutiny of activities that could disrupt market integrity.

Collaborative regulatory efforts on a global scale are also expected to intensify. Given the global nature of financial markets, a coordinated approach to HFT regulation is essential to prevent regulatory arbitrage, where firms exploit differences in regulations across jurisdictions. Initiatives such as the Financial Stability Board (FSB) and the International Organization of Securities Commissions (IOSCO) will likely play pivotal roles in harmonizing regulatory standards, ensuring a balanced and unified framework that can be enforced worldwide.

Further, technological innovation within regulatory frameworks is poised to transform compliance monitoring and enforcement. Regulators are increasingly adopting sophisticated technology solutions, such as machine learning algorithms and artificial intelligence, to better detect and analyze suspicious trading patterns. These technologies not only enhance the capability of regulators to catch market manipulation but also streamline the compliance requirements for HFT firms by automating aspects of reporting and surveillance.

Another anticipated trend is the tightening of rules governing the speed and frequency of trading activities. While speed has been a core advantage of HFT, concerns about its impact on market stability have prompted regulators to consider measures that limit extreme high-frequency trades. Such measures might include the introduction of minimum resting times for orders or constraints on the number of orders that can be submitted within a given time frame, aimed at mitigating the risk of market abuse and flash crashes.

The emphasis on ethical and responsible trading practices is also gaining traction within the regulatory discourse. Regulators are expected to push for stronger codes of conduct and ethical standards to be adopted by HFT firms. This trend reflects a broader move towards ensuring that market participants act in ways that promote trust and confidence in the financial markets. Comprehensive guidelines on best practices in algorithmic trading, focusing on fairness and accountability, are likely to be developed and enforced.

Cybersecurity is another critical area where future HFT regulations are expected to evolve. With the increasing reliance on advanced technology and connectivity, HFT firms face significant cybersecurity risks. Regulatory frameworks will likely require more stringent risk management protocols, including regular security audits and robust incident response strategies. Ensuring that HFT infrastructures are resilient against cyberattacks will be paramount in safeguarding market integrity and participant data.

Lastly, environmental, social, and governance (ESG) factors are becoming an integral part of the regulatory narrative. As investors and regulators alike place greater emphasis on sustainable and responsible investing, HFT firms may be required to align their strategies with ESG principles. This shift will necessitate transparent reporting on ESG metrics and adherence to guidelines that promote sustainable trading practices.

Staying ahead in the dynamic regulatory environment of HFT entails continuous engagement with regulatory bodies, adaptation to new rules, and proactive investment in compliance technologies. Market participants must strive to maintain robust internal control systems and cultivate a culture of compliance to navigate the evolving landscape successfully. By doing so, they can ensure not only regulatory adherence but also contribute positively to the overall stability and integrity of financial markets.

Chapter 8

Data Analysis and Machine Learning in HFT

This chapter explores the integral role of data analysis and machine learning in High-Frequency Trading (HFT). It covers the types of data used in HFT and the processes of data cleaning and preprocessing. The chapter introduces statistical methods for data analysis and provides an overview of machine learning, including both supervised and unsupervised learning techniques. It delves into the implementation of machine learning models in HFT, alongside methods for model validation and performance metrics. The chapter also addresses the challenges and limitations associated with applying machine learning in the high-speed trading environment, highlighting its transformative potential.

8.1 Introduction to Data Analysis in HFT

High-frequency trading (HFT) is a domain that operates at the intersection of finance, technology, and mathematics, with data analysis serving as its backbone. In this section, we will delve into the fundamental role that data analysis plays in HFT, highlighting its importance and the basic techniques employed to transform raw data into actionable trading strategies.

In the realm of HFT, data is paramount. The capacity to interpret and react to data in microseconds can be the difference between profit and loss. Data analysis in HFT encompasses a variety of processes, including the collection, cleaning, preprocessing, and analysis of vast quantities of market data. This data includes not only price and volume information but also Level II data, news feeds, and numerous other types of market signals.

The first step in data analysis is the acquisition of data. Given the speed at which markets operate, HFT firms rely on low-latency data feeds to minimize delays. These feeds provide real-time data streams from exchanges and other sources. However, raw data in its initial form is often noisy and unstructured. To make it useful, it requires meticulous cleaning and preprocessing, a topic that will be covered in subsequent sections.

Once the data is cleaned, various statistical and computational techniques are applied to extract meaningful insights. Basic statistical methods such as descriptive statistics, correlation analysis, and time series analysis serve as the foundation. Advanced techniques, such as mathematical modeling, machine learning algorithms, and artificial intelligence, build upon these basics to develop more sophisticated trading strategies.

In HFT, one critical aspect of data analysis is the detection of patterns that indicate trading opportunities. Pattern recognition techniques, such as moving averages, Bollinger Bands, and other technical indicators, are widely used. These techniques are employed to identify trends, reversals, and momentum in the data, allowing traders to make predictions about future price movements.

Given the high-stakes nature of HFT, it is crucial not only to detect patterns but also to assess the reliability and significance of these patterns. Statistical measures such as the *p-value*, confidence intervals, and hypothesis testing are used to evaluate the strength and validity of found patterns. This ensures that the strategies based on these patterns have a higher probability of success in live trading.

Another essential component of data analysis in HFT is the continuous monitoring and updating of trading models. The financial markets are dynamic, with conditions constantly changing due to various factors such as economic events, market sentiment, and regulatory changes. As such, trading models must be adaptable, continuously learning from new data to refine their predictions and strategies. This iterative process involves backtesting algorithms on historical data, performing stress tests under various market conditions, and adjusting the models based on their performance metrics.

Furthermore, the integration of machine learning in HFT has brought a new dimension to data analysis. Machine learning algorithms, particularly deep learning networks, have demonstrated remarkable success in identifying complex patterns and making predictions. These algorithms can process vast amounts of data more efficiently than traditional methods, offering new insights that were previously unattainable. Machine learning techniques will be explored in greater depth in later sections, specifically focusing on their implementation and the challenges they present.

To sum up, data analysis is the lifeblood of high-frequency trading. It transforms raw data into meaningful insights, driving the development of trading strategies that leverage speed and precision. By employing a combination of statistical methods, pattern recognition techniques, and machine learning, HFT practitioners can stay ahead in the fast-paced financial markets. This section lays the groundwork for understanding how data is processed and utilized in HFT, setting the stage for more detailed discussions on specific techniques and technologies in the chapters to follow. '''

This text has been formatted according to the specified LaTeX guidelines, ensuring that it is ready for integration into the broader document.

8.2 Types of Data Used in HFT

High-Frequency Trading (HFT) relies heavily on a diverse array of data types to execute trades at lightning speeds and to generate profitable trading strategies. This section will delve into the primary categories of data utilized in HFT, elucidating their significance and application in developing HFT models. Understanding these data types is crucial for anyone engaging in or analyzing HFT strategies.

Market Data: This is the most fundamental type of data in HFT and consists of real-time information generated by financial markets. Market data can be divided into two main categories: price data and order book data.

Price data includes the last traded price, bid and ask prices, and trade volumes. It provides insights into recent market transactions and current market sentiments. For illustrative purposes, consider the follow-

Time	Bid Price	Ask Price
T_1	100.50	100.55
T_2	100.48	100.53
T_3	100.45	100.50

Ticker Symbol	ISIN	Corporate Action
ABC	US1234567890	Dividend
XYZ	US0987654321	Stock Split

ing matrix representation of price data for a specific stock:

Order book data, on the other hand, provides a deeper look into market dynamics by displaying the queued buy and sell orders at various price levels. This data is essential for understanding the liquidity of an asset and identifying potential price movements. The complexity of order book data typically necessitates visualization tools, such as heat maps, for effective analysis.

Reference Data: Reference data is the static or slowly changing data essential for contextualizing market data. This includes data such as security identifiers (e.g., ISIN, CUSIP), corporate actions (e.g., dividends, stock splits), and exchange membership lists. Proper comprehension of reference data is vital for ensuring accuracy in trade execution and model backtesting.

Consider the following example of reference data for securities:

News and Sentiment Data: In the fast-paced world of HFT, news can significantly impact market prices. News and sentiment data analyze text from various sources such as financial news websites, social media platforms, and regulatory filings. Algorithms then parse this data to gauge market sentiment, which can drive trading strategies. Sentiment analysis gauges the tone of news, categorizing it as positive, negative, or neutral, and correlates this information with potential price movements.

A machine learning model utilizing sentiment data may represent it as follows:

$$\text{Sentiment Score} = \sum_{i=1}^{n} \text{weight}_i \times \text{sentiment}_i$$

where weight_i represents the importance of the source, and sentiment_i is the scored sentiment of the i-th news piece.

Derived Data: Derived or synthetic data is information that has been processed or inferred from raw data, often through mathematical models or statistical techniques. Examples include technical indicators (e.g., moving averages, Bollinger bands), signal generation (like buy/sell signals), and risk metrics (e.g., Value-at-Risk, Sharpe ratio). This data aids in constructing high-frequency trading models and backtesting strategies.

An example of a derived data formula is the Moving Average Convergence Divergence (MACD) indicator, calculated as follows:

$$\text{MACD} = \text{EMA}_{12}(\text{Close}) - \text{EMA}_{26}(\text{Close})$$

where EMA_{12} and EMA_{26} are the 12-day and 26-day exponential moving averages of the closing price, respectively.

Alternative Data: Alternative data encompasses non-traditional data sources that can offer alpha-generating insights. This includes satellite imagery, credit card transaction data, web scraping, and sensor data. For instance, satellite images of retail store parking lots can predict a company's performance before earnings announcements. The integration of alternative data into HFT models can provide a competitive edge through unique market insights.

In conclusion, the array of data types used in HFT is vast and multifaceted, each serving a distinct purpose in forming a comprehensive trading strategy. A robust understanding of these data types enhances the precision and effectiveness of HFT models, essential for achieving superior trading performance in a highly competitive arena.

8.3 Data Cleaning and Preprocessing

In the realm of High-Frequency Trading (HFT), the speed and accuracy with which decisions are made rest heavily on the integrity and quality of the data fed into the system. Before any sophisticated machine learning models or statistical analysis can be applied, it is imperative to ensure that the data used is both clean and well-preprocessed. This section delves into the meticulous processes involved in data cleaning and preprocessing, demonstrating why these steps are crucial in the fast-paced and data-intensive world of HFT.

Consider an extensive dataset capturing millisecond-level trade executions or order book updates. Raw data of this nature often contains noise, missing values, and inconsistencies that can significantly skew analysis or model performance if left unaddressed. To illustrate, let D be a dataset with n observations, defined as $D = \{x_1, x_2, \ldots, x_n\}$, where each x_i holds multiple attributes such as timestamp, price, volume, and trading venue.

Identifying and handling missing values is crucial in datasets. The process begins with the identification of missing or NULL values. In LaTeX, this can be represented as follows:

$$x_{i,j} = \text{NULL} \quad \text{where} \quad x_{i,j} \in x_i \quad \text{and} \quad 1 \leq j \leq m$$

Here, $x_{i,j}$ represents the j-th attribute of the i-th observation, and NULL indicates a missing value. Strategies to address missing values include:

- **Omission:** Dropping rows or columns with missing values, suitable if the proportion of missing data is minimal.
- **Imputation:** Replacing missing values with estimates based on the mean, median, or mode of the observed data. Advanced methods involve using machine learning algorithms to predict the missing values.
- **Forward/Backward Fill:** For time-series data, propagating the last non-missing value forward or backward to fill gaps.

Assume we choose mean imputation for simplicity. Let $\bar{x}_j$ denote the mean of the j-th attribute:

$$\bar{x}_j = \frac{1}{n} \sum_{i=1}^{n} x_{i,j}$$

The missing value is then replaced:

$$x_{i,j} = \bar{x}_j \quad \text{if} \quad x_{i,j} = \text{NULL}$$

Outlier detection and treatment are also critical. Outliers can unduly influence machine learning models and statistical tests, leading to erroneous conclusions. Detecting outliers involves statistical techniques or machine learning-based methods. One common statistical technique is the z-score, defined as:

$$z_{i,j} = \frac{x_{i,j} - \mu_j}{\sigma_j}$$

where μ_j and σ_j are the mean and standard deviation of the j-th attribute, respectively. Observations with $|z_{i,j}| > 3$ are typically considered outliers.

Remedial actions for outliers include:

- **Removal:** Simply removing the outlier data points.
- **Transformation:** Applying transformations such as logarithmic or square root to reduce the impact of extreme values.
- **Replacement:** Replacing the outlier values with statistical measures like median or mean.

Normalization and scaling are essential for machine learning models to perform optimally. To prevent attributes with larger scales from dominating those with smaller scales, it is important to normalize or scale the data. Two popular techniques are min-max scaling and standardization.

Min-Max Scaling transforms data to a specified range, typically [0, 1]:

$$x'_{i,j} = \frac{x_{i,j} - \min(x_j)}{\max(x_j) - \min(x_j)}$$

Standardization transforms data to have zero mean and unit variance:

$$x'_{i,j} = \frac{x_{i,j} - \mu_j}{\sigma_j}$$

Here, $x'_{i,j}$ denotes the scaled value of the j-th attribute for the i-th observation.

Feature engineering involves creating new features from existing data to better capture the underlying patterns within the data, enhancing the model's predictive power. Example actions include generating time-based features (e.g., minute of the hour) from timestamps or calculating the moving averages of price data:

$$\text{MA}_t = \frac{1}{k} \sum_{i=t-k+1}^{t} x_i$$

where MA_t represents the moving average at time t over k periods. This can help smooth out short-term fluctuations and highlight longer-term trends.

Feature selection, on the other hand, involves identifying the most relevant attributes that contribute to the predictive performance, thereby reducing dimensionality and improving model efficiency. Techniques include:

- **Filter Methods:** Using statistical tests or correlation measures to score each feature.
- **Wrapper Methods:** Iteratively selecting features based on model performance.
- **Embedded Methods:** Feature selection conducted during the model training process (e.g., Lasso regression).

These preprocessing steps are fundamental to preparing high-quality datasets that ensure accurate, reliable, and efficient model performance in the context of HFT.

The intricacies of data cleaning and preprocessing cannot be overstated. Implementing these techniques rigorously guarantees that any noise, inconsistencies, or irrelevant information that could potentially corrupt the insights or predictions derived from the data are mitigated. In doing so, the foundation is laid for the subsequent application of statistical and machine learning models, which rely heavily on clean, well-structured data to generate meaningful results in HFT operations.

8.4 Statistical Methods for Data Analysis

In the realm of high-frequency trading (HFT), data-driven decision-making is paramount. Understanding the statistical methods for data analysis forms the bedrock of robust trading strategies. These methods help traders and algorithms discern patterns, identify anomalies, and make predictions based on historical data. This section delves into various statistical techniques that are essential for analyzing high-frequency trading data, providing insights into how these methods can be leveraged to optimize trading performance.

To begin with, let's explore descriptive statistics, which are fundamental in summarizing the key features of a data set. Metrics such as mean, median, mode, variance, and standard deviation offer a snapshot of the data's central tendency and dispersion. In HFT, understanding these measures is crucial because they can reveal the underlying market conditions and the behavior of financial instruments over time. For instance, calculating the rolling mean and standard deviation for a stock's price series can provide insights into its volatility trends, which are critical for devising volatility-driven trading strategies.

Moving from descriptive statistics to inferential statistics, we encounter hypothesis testing and confidence intervals. Hypothesis testing allows traders to make probabilistic statements about market behaviors or trading strategies. For example, a trader might test whether the mean return of a trading strategy differs significantly from zero. The choice of test—be it a t-test, chi-square test, or ANOVA—depends on the data's characteristics and the hypothesis in question. Confidence intervals, on the other hand, give a range of values within which we expect the true parameter to lie with a certain level of confidence, typically 95% or 99%. These intervals are particularly useful for assessing the reliability of model parameters estimated from historical data.

Regression analysis is another cornerstone of statistical methods in HFT. Linear regression, in its simplest form, models the relationship between a dependent variable and one or more independent variables. For HFT practitioners, this means understanding how factors such as trading volume, time of day, or news events impact asset prices. The linear model, expressed as

$$Y = \beta_0 + \beta_1 X + \epsilon$$

where Y is the dependent variable, X is the independent variable, β_0 and β_1 are coefficients, and ϵ is the error term, provides a straightforward way to quantify these relationships. Moreover, the coefficients β_0 and β_1 are estimated using methods like Ordinary Least Squares (OLS), and their significance is tested using t-tests.

Beyond linear regression, more advanced methods such as logistic regression are crucial, especially when dealing with binary outcomes like buy/sell signals or the occurrence of a market event. Logistic regression models the probability that a given event occurs, and it is particularly adept at handling non-linearly separable data. The model is expressed as:

$$P(Y = 1) = \frac{1}{1 + e^{-(\beta_0 + \beta_1 X)}}$$

where $P(Y = 1)$ is the probability of the event (such as a price spike), and the β coefficients are estimated using maximum likelihood estimation (MLE).

Time series analysis, a subset of statistical methods, warrants special mention due to its relevance in tracking data points at successive time intervals. In HFT, models like the Autoregressive Integrated Moving Average (ARIMA) are widely used to understand and predict price movements. The ARIMA model, denoted as ARIMA(p,d,q), combines differencing (integrated part) to make the series stationary, autoregression terms (p) where the model regresses on its past values, and moving average terms (q) which incorporate past forecast errors. Seasonal ARIMA (SARIMA) models further address seasonality patterns in data by incorporating seasonal terms.

Additionally, stochastic processes are integral to understanding and modeling market dynamics in HFT. Concepts such as Brownian motion and geometric Brownian motion provide a framework for modeling the random behavior of price movements, crucial for simulating and optimizing trading strategies.

Each of these statistical methods offers unique benefits and insights, allowing traders to analyze historical data and make informed decisions. The effective application of these techniques requires not just theoretical knowledge but practical expertise in handling and interpreting large datasets typical of the HFT environment.

By mastering these statistical tools, traders can enhance their predictive accuracy, minimize risk, and ultimately, improve their trading outcomes in the fast-paced world of high-frequency trading.

8.5 Introduction to Machine Learning

Machine Learning (ML) represents a transformative approach in high-frequency trading (HFT), where algorithms can learn from and make predictions based on data. Leveraging machine learning in HFT requires a shift from traditional programming paradigms to a model where the system discerns trading patterns by processing historical and real-time data. This section illuminates the core aspects of machine learning, its fundamental principles, and its integration into HFT.

Machine learning can generally be divided into three major categories: supervised learning, unsupervised learning, and reinforcement learning. Each category holds unique significance and applications in the context of HFT.

Supervised learning involves training a model on a labeled dataset, which means that each training example is paired with an output label. This process allows the model to learn the mapping from inputs to the target output. Supervised learning is extensively used in predicting asset prices, classifying trade signals, or estimating trading volumes. For example, consider a scenario where we train a model to predict the price of a stock based on its historical prices and other market indicators. Mathematically, this can be expressed as:

$$y = f(X) + \epsilon$$

where y represents the target variable (e.g., future stock price), X represents the input features (e.g., past prices, volumes, technical indicators), f denotes the function learned by the model, and ϵ is the error term.

Unsupervised learning, on the other hand, deals with unlabeled data. The goal is to infer the natural structure present in a set of data points. In HFT, unsupervised learning can be employed to identify patterns, clusters, or anomalies that are not apparent through supervised methods. Two common techniques in this category are clustering and dimensionality reduction. For instance, clustering algorithms like K-means can group similar trading events together, helping traders identify common market behaviors or anomalies. Dimensionality reduction techniques, such as Principal Component Analysis (PCA), are valuable for condensing a large number of predictors into a smaller set of orthogonal factors, thus simplifying the modeling process while retaining essential information.

Reinforcement learning (RL) is a distinctive category where an agent learns to make decisions by interacting with the environment to maximize some notion of cumulative reward. The agent receives feedback in the form of rewards or penalties and iteratively improves its strategy. In HFT, reinforcement learning can be utilized for developing automated trading strategies that adapt based on market conditions. It involves a balance between exploration (trying new strategies) and exploitation (using known strategies that yield high rewards). Mathematically, this can be represented using value functions and policies, often solved by techniques like Q-learning or Deep Q-Networks (DQN). The value function $V(s)$ measures the expected cumulative reward from a state s:

$$V(s) = \mathbb{E}\left[\sum_{t=0}^{\infty} \gamma^t R_t \mid S_t = s\right]$$

where γ is the discount factor, R_t is the reward at time t, and S_t represents the state at time t.

Integrating machine learning in HFT involves several stages: data collection and preprocessing, feature engineering, model selection, training, and evaluation. Given the vast amount of data generated in financial markets, robust data preprocessing is essential for building reliable machine learning models. This process often includes handling missing values, normalizing or standardizing features, and removing outliers to enhance model performance. Feature engineering—designing relevant inputs to the model—is a critical step where domain knowledge about financial markets can significantly influence the efficacy of the model. Effective features might include technical indicators, statistical measures, or macroeconomic variables.

Selecting the appropriate model depends on the specific problem at hand. Linear models, decision trees, support vector machines, and neural networks are all viable choices, each with their strengths and weaknesses. Model training involves optimizing the model parameters to minimize prediction error, typically achieved through algorithms like gradient descent.

Evaluating machine learning models in HFT necessitates a careful consideration of financial performance metrics, such as the Sharpe ratio, maximum drawdown, and profit and loss (P&L). Additionally, cross-validation techniques are imperative to ensure that the model generalizes well to unseen data, mitigating the risk of overfitting.

The potential of machine learning in HFT is profound, offering capabilities to uncover hidden patterns, optimize trading strategies, and improve decision-making processes. However, deploying these models in a live trading environment poses its own set of challenges, including the need for real-time processing, algorithmic latency, and the dynamic nature of financial markets. As we continue through this chapter, we will delve deeper into specific machine learning techniques and their applications in HFT, providing practical guidance for implementing these models effectively.

8.6 Supervised Learning Techniques

Supervised learning remains at the forefront of machine learning applications in High-Frequency Trading (HFT) due to its robust predictive capabilities. The essence of supervised learning lies in its methodology; it utilizes historical data, comprising input-output pairs, to train models that can predict future outcomes. In HFT, the ability to foresee price movements, execute trades within milliseconds, and adjust strategies in real-time can lead to significant profits. This section provides a comprehensive examination of supervised learning techniques, exploring their implementation and application in the high-stakes environment of HFT.

Supervised learning techniques are broadly categorized into regression and classification algorithms. The distinction between these two hinges on the nature of the predicted output; regression models predict continuous values, whereas classification models predict discrete categories. Both types of models are indispensable in HFT, often used in tandem to optimize trading strategies.

To begin, regression techniques are fundamental in predicting price movements and other continuous financial metrics. Linear regression, one of the simplest and most widely used regression techniques, models the relationship between a dependent variable and one or more independent variables by fitting a linear equation to the observed data. The linear regression model can be mathematically represented as:

$$y = \beta_0 + \beta_1 x_1 + \beta_2 x_2 + \ldots + \beta_n x_n + \epsilon$$

where y is the dependent variable (e.g., future stock price), β_0 is the intercept, $\beta_1, \beta_2, \ldots, \beta_n$ are the coefficients, $x_1, x_2, \ldots, x_n$ are the independent variables (e.g., trading volume, previous prices), and ϵ represents the model's error term. The goal of linear regression is to minimize this error term, typically using methods such as Ordinary Least Squares (OLS).

However, linear relationships often fall short in capturing the complexities of financial markets. Polynomial regression extends linear regression by considering polynomial relationships between the variables, thus allowing for more accurate representations of non-linear trends.

$$y = \beta_0 + \beta_1 x + \beta_2 x^2 + \ldots + \beta_n x^n + \epsilon$$

Another powerful regression model is the Support Vector Regression (SVR), which utilizes the principles of Support Vector Machines (SVM) for regression tasks. SVR aims to fit the best line within a threshold value, ensuring robustness against outliers and volatility—key features for HFT applications.

For supervised learning to be maximally effective in HFT, it must also incorporate classification techniques. Classification models, such as Logistic Regression, support vector machines, and Neural Networks, are crucial for tasks like predicting the direction of price movement (up or down), classifying stock statuses (bullish or bearish), and other binary or multi-class categorizations.

Logistic Regression, although named similarly, is a classification technique used for binary outcomes. The logistic regression model predicts the probability that a given input belongs to a certain class by using the logistic function:

$$P(Y=1) = \frac{1}{1+e^{-(\beta_0+\beta_1 x_1+\beta_2 x_2+\ldots+\beta_n x_n)}}$$

where $P(Y=1)$ is the probability of the binary outcome Y being 1 (indicating, for example, a bullish trend).

Support Vector Machines (SVMs) are highly effective for classification tasks in high-dimensional spaces. SVMs find the optimal hyperplane that separates the classes by maximizing the margin between data points from different classes. For non-linear classification problems, they can employ kernel functions to transform the input space, making it easier to find a linear separation in the transformed space.

Deep learning, a subset of machine learning, has proven to be revolutionary in its ability to handle large volumes of unstructured data. Neural Networks, and more specifically Deep Neural Networks (DNNs), can capture intricate patterns in market data through their stacked layers and complex architectures. A typical neural network consists of an input layer, multiple hidden layers, and an output layer, each containing neurons that are weighted connections representing the learned model. The network learns through backpropagation, adjusting weights to minimize prediction error.

$$y = \sigma\left(\sum_{j=1}^{n} w_{ij} x_j + b_i\right)$$

where σ is an activation function, w represents weights, x are inputs, and b is a bias term. Popular activation functions include the sigmoid, hyperbolic tangent, and rectified linear unit (ReLU).

The choice of supervised learning model in HFT is contingent upon the specific trading strategy and market conditions. Rigorous cross-validation and performance metrics, such as Mean Absolute Error (MAE) and F1-score, are critical to evaluating model effectiveness. Regularly refining and retraining models ensure they adapt to evolving market dynamics—an imperative practice for staying competitive in high-frequency trading.

The synthesis of supervised learning techniques into HFT strategies exemplifies the cutting-edge convergence of financial acumen with computational prowess. As traders harness these models, they gain predictive precision and tactical agility, transforming raw data into actionable insights. This alignment not only enhances profitability but also fortifies the resilience of trading systems in the ever-volatile financial markets.

8.7 Unsupervised Learning Techniques

In the realm of high-frequency trading (HFT), unsupervised learning techniques are invaluable for uncovering hidden patterns within large datasets. Unlike supervised learning, which relies on labeled datasets, unsupervised learning algorithms operate without predefined outputs. This empowers traders to identify structures and correlations in the market data that might not be immediately evident. The primary applications of unsupervised learning in HFT include clustering, dimensionality reduction, and anomaly detection.

Clustering is one of the cornerstone techniques in unsupervised learning. It involves grouping data points in such a way that those within the same group (or cluster) are more similar to each other than to those in other groups. This can be particularly useful in HFT for segmenting financial instruments into similarly behaving clusters, enabling the development of specialized trading strategies for each cluster. Among the most popular clustering algorithms are the k-means algorithm and hierarchical clustering.

The k-means algorithm partitions the data into k clusters, where k is a user-defined parameter. The steps include initializing k centroids randomly, assigning each data point to the nearest centroid, and recalculating the centroids based on the mean of the points assigned to each cluster. This process iterates until convergence. The mathematical formulation of the *k*-means objective function can be expressed as:

$$J = \sum_{i=1}^{k} \sum_{x \in C_i} \|x - \mu_i\|^2$$

where C_i denotes the set of points in cluster i and μ_i is the centroid of cluster i. The goal is to minimize the sum of squared distances between points and their respective centroids.

Hierarchical clustering, on the other hand, builds a tree of clusters. It can be performed in an agglomerative (bottom-up) or divisive (top-down) manner. In agglomerative clustering, each data point starts as its own cluster, and pairs of clusters are merged based on a predefined linkage criterion until a single cluster encompassing all data points is formed. This technique does not require the number of clusters to be specified in advance, unlike *k*-means, making it flexible but computationally more intensive.

Beyond clustering, dimensionality reduction techniques serve a critical function in HFT by simplifying datasets while retaining essential information. Principal Component Analysis (PCA) and t-distributed Stochastic Neighbor Embedding (t-SNE) are widely used dimensionality reduction methods. PCA transforms the original variables into a new set of uncorrelated variables (principal components) ordered by the amount of variance they capture from the data. Mathematically, PCA involves the eigen decomposition of the covariance matrix of the data:

$$\Sigma = \frac{1}{n-1} \sum_{i=1}^{n} (x_i - \mu)(x_i - \mu)^T$$

where Σ represents the covariance matrix, n is the number of data points, x_i is a data point, and μ is the mean of the data points. The principal components are the eigenvectors of this matrix, with the magnitude of the eigenvalues indicating the amount of variance explained by each component.

t-SNE, in contrast, is a non-linear technique aimed at preserving the local structure of data, often yielding more visually interpretable results when projecting high-dimensional data into two or three dimensions. This method is particularly beneficial for visualizing complex market behaviors, thereby aiding in the development of intuitive trading tactics.

Anomaly detection is another pivotal application of unsupervised learning in HFT. It involves identifying unusual patterns that may indicate potential opportunities or risks. Techniques such as isolation forests and autoencoders are routinely employed to detect anomalies. Isolation forests work by randomly selecting a feature and a split value, recursively partitioning the data until each observation is isolated. Anomalies tend to be isolated quickly due to their distinct patterns, reflected in shorter path lengths in the tree structure. Autoencoders, a type of neural network, learn a compressed representation of the data (encoding) and then reconstruct it (decoding). The reconstruction error, which is higher for anomalies, serves as an indicator of abnormal data points.

```
autoencoder = Sequential([
    Dense(128, input_dim=784, activation='relu'),
    Dense(64, activation='relu'),
    Dense(32, activation='relu'),
    Dense(64, activation='relu'),
    Dense(128, activation='relu'),
    Dense(784, activation='sigmoid')
])
autoencoder.compile(optimizer='adam', loss='mean_squared_error')
```

The aforementioned techniques underscore the transformative potential of unsupervised learning in high-frequency trading. By leveraging these methods, traders can navigate the complexities of financial markets, uncovering patterns and anomalies that inform robust and sophisticated trading strategies. As the market evolves, the continuous advancement in unsupervised learning algorithms will undoubtedly enhance the efficacy of HFT systems.

8.8 Implementing Machine Learning Models in HFT

Implementing machine learning models in High-Frequency Trading (HFT) environments requires a comprehensive understanding of both the theoretical underpinnings of machine learning and the practical aspects of deploying these models in a fast-paced trading context. This section will elaborate on the critical steps involved in model implementation, from selecting the appropriate algorithms to ensuring seamless integration with trading systems.

To begin with, the selection of machine learning algorithms plays a pivotal role in the overall success of the trading strategy. In HFT, where speed and accuracy are paramount, algorithms need to be both computationally efficient and capable of handling high-dimensional data. Some commonly used algorithms in HFT include logistic regression, support vector machines, decision trees, and, increasingly, deep learning models like neural networks. The choice of algorithm depends on the specific use case, such as price prediction, pattern recognition, or anomaly detection.

Once the appropriate algorithm is selected, the next step involves data preparation and feature engineering. High-quality, clean data is essential for the performance of any machine learning model. This requires robust data cleaning and preprocessing pipelines, which were discussed in earlier sections. Feature engineering, the process of creating relevant features that can help the model learn patterns, is particularly crucial in HFT. Features might include technical indicators, order book imbalances, trade volumes, or time-based signals. Techniques such as Principal Component Analysis (PCA) can be employed to reduce the dimensionality of the feature space, ensuring faster and more efficient model training.

Following data preparation, the model training process begins. This involves splitting the data into training, validation, and test sets to ensure that the model generalizes well and does not overfit. The training process is computationally intensive and requires careful tuning of hyperparameters, such as the learning rate, regularization strength, and the depth of decision trees. Cross-validation techniques are often used to fine-tune these parameters and select the optimal model configuration.

Once the model is trained, it needs to be integrated into the trading system. This step is crucial in HFT, where millisecond or even microsecond delays can significantly impact trading performance. Implementing the model involves several sub-steps, including:

- **Model Serialization**: Saving the trained model in a format that can be loaded and utilized efficiently during trading.
- **Model Deployment**: Integrating the model with the trading infrastructure, ensuring it can process real-time data streams and generate trading signals with minimal latency.
- **System Optimization**: Fine-tuning the entire trading system, including hardware optimizations and network configurations, to ensure that the model operates at peak performance.

In practice, the deployed model continuously receives data, makes predictions, and communicates trading signals to order management systems. This integration necessitates rigorous performance monitoring and logging mechanisms to identify and address any issues promptly. Latency measurements, throughput analysis, and error rates are some of the key metrics monitored on an ongoing basis.

Moreover, implementing machine learning models in HFT requires a robust risk management framework. Given the high stakes and potential for significant financial loss, it is crucial to incorporate risk metrics such as Value at Risk (VaR), Expected Shortfall, and other stress testing scenarios. These metrics help in dynamically adjusting trading strategies in response to changing market conditions.

Ultimately, the successful implementation of machine learning models in HFT is an iterative process. It involves continuous learning and adaptation, leveraging feedback loops to refine models and improve trading performance. Scalability is another essential consideration, enabling the system to handle increasing data volumes and complexities without degrading performance.

In summary, deploying machine learning models within HFT systems demands a meticulous balance between computational efficiency and predictive accuracy. Leveraging advanced algorithms, fine-tuned feature sets, and robust integration strategies ensures that these models not only meet the high-speed requirements of HFT but also achieve sustainable trading profitability.

8.9 Model Validation and Performance Metrics

The evaluation of machine learning models in high-frequency trading (HFT) is a critical phase that ensures both robustness and reliability of predictive algorithms. Model validation and performance metrics are indispensable components in this process, providing the frameworks and criteria essential for assessing the accuracy, efficiency, and applicability of the models to real-time trading environments.

Before deploying a machine learning model in HFT, it must undergo rigorous validation to minimize the risks associated with false predictions and suboptimal performance. Validation involves partitioning the dataset into two or more subsets: typically, a training set, a validation set, and a testing set. This approach helps in measuring how well the model performs on unseen data, thereby preventing overfitting—a common pitfall where the model excessively tailors itself to the training data, compromising its generalizability.

A widely adopted technique in model validation is k-fold cross-validation. In this method, the entire dataset is randomly divided into k equally sized folds or subsets. The model is trained using $k-1$ folds and tested on the remaining fold. This process is repeated k times, with each fold serving as a testing set exactly once. The k performance scores from the different iterations are then averaged to produce a single estimation.

$$\text{CV\_Score} = \frac{1}{k}\sum_{i=1}^{k} \text{Score}_i \tag{8.1}$$

where Score_i denotes the performance metric for the ith fold.

In addition to cross-validation, techniques such as holdout validation, time-series split, and bootstrap aggregating (bagging) may also be employed, especially when dealing with non-stationary time-series data common in financial markets. It is crucial to acknowledge the time-dependent nature of trading data, hence methods like time-series split respect the chronological order of the data by ensuring that past information is only used to predict future states.

Once models are validated, the next step involves assessing their performance via appropriate metrics. Various performance metrics cater to different aspects of a model's predictive power and suitability for HFT. Key metrics include:

- **Accuracy and Precision:** Accuracy measures the proportion of correct predictions out of the total predictions made. Precision, specifically relevant in classifier models, calculates the ratio of true positive predictions to the total predicted positives.

$$\text{Accuracy} = \frac{\text{True Positives} + \text{True Negatives}}{\text{Total Predictions}} \tag{8.2}$$

$$\text{Precision} = \frac{\text{True Positives}}{\text{True Positives} + \text{False Positives}} \tag{8.3}$$

- **Recall and F1-Score:** Recall, or sensitivity, measures the ratio of true positive predictions to the total actual positives. The

F1-score harmonizes precision and recall by computing their harmonic mean, offering a balanced evaluation criterion.

$$\text{Recall} = \frac{\text{True Positives}}{\text{True Positives} + \text{False Negatives}} \tag{8.4}$$

$$\text{F1\_Score} = 2 \cdot \frac{\text{Precision} \cdot \text{Recall}}{\text{Precision} + \text{Recall}} \tag{8.5}$$

- **Mean Squared Error (MSE) and Root Mean Squared Error (RMSE):** For regression models, MSE measures the average of the squares of the errors, while RMSE provides a more interpretable scale by taking the square root of MSE.

$$\text{MSE} = \frac{1}{n}\sum_{i=1}^{n}(y_i - \hat{y}_i)^2 \tag{8.6}$$

$$\text{RMSE} = \sqrt{\frac{1}{n}\sum_{i=1}^{n}(y_i - \hat{y}_i)^2} \tag{8.7}$$

  where y_i represents the actual values and $\hat{y}_i$ denotes the predicted values.

- **Area Under the Curve (AUC) and Receiver Operating Characteristic (ROC):** For classification problems, AUC and ROC curves depict the true positive rate against the false positive rate at varying threshold levels, highlighting the model's discrimination capability.

In the context of HFT, it is also vital to consider metrics reflecting trading performance, such as Sharpe ratio, Profit and Loss (PnL), and Maximum Drawdown. These metrics are essential for evaluating the financial viability and risk-adjusted returns of algorithmic strategies.

$$\text{Sharpe Ratio} = \frac{E[R_i - R_f]}{\sigma_i} \tag{8.8}$$

where R_i denotes the return of the portfolio, R_f is the risk-free rate, and σ_i represents the standard deviation of the return.

Effective model evaluation further necessitates backtesting against historical market data, ensuring the strategy remains robust over different market conditions. Incorporating walk-forward optimization, where models are periodically retrained and tested on new data, maintains their relevance and adaptability in the ever-evolving markets.

By implementing these robust validation methodologies and performance metrics, traders can confidently leverage machine learning models in high-frequency trading, converting data-driven insights into successful trading strategies.

8.10 Challenges and Limitations of Machine Learning in HFT

High-frequency trading (HFT) leverages cutting-edge technology and sophisticated algorithms to execute trades at breathtaking speeds. While machine learning (ML) offers substantial potential for enhancing HFT strategies, its application is fraught with unique challenges and limitations. Identifying and addressing these barriers is crucial for traders aiming to optimize their HFT systems. This section explores the key obstacles in integrating ML into HFT, offering insights that are both strategic and practical.

One significant challenge is the sheer speed required in HFT. Trades are executed in a matter of milliseconds, leaving little room for computational delays. While traditional ML models can provide profound insights over extended periods, their real-time application in HFT necessitates models that can deliver instantaneous predictions. Developing such high-speed algorithms requires not only advanced ML techniques but also highly optimized coding practices and powerful hardware, which can be prohibitively costly.

Another critical limitation is the quality and quantity of data. HFT strategies often hinge on vast datasets comprising market data, order books, and financial news. However, the effectiveness of ML models is highly contingent on the quality of these data inputs. Noisy, incomplete, or biased data can significantly impair the model's performance, leading to erroneous trading decisions. The necessity of data cleaning and preprocessing cannot be overstated, as even minute inaccuracies can have amplified consequences in the high-speed realm of HFT.

Model overfitting presents an additional hurdle. In the pursuit of creating models that capture every nuance of financial markets, there's a risk of developing overly complex algorithms that perform exceptionally well on historical data but fail to generalize in live trading scenarios.

Overfitting can lead to significant financial losses, as the model may react inaccurately to new market conditions. Regularization techniques, cross-validation, and careful feature selection are essential practices to mitigate the risk of overfitting, yet they add layers of complexity to the modeling process.

Another limitation surrounds the dynamic nature of financial markets. Market dynamics can shift due to economic events, regulatory changes, or sudden large trades, making it challenging for ML models to maintain their accuracy over time. These shifts require continuous retraining and adaptation of models, demanding constant vigilance and resources. Additionally, models must be designed to recognize and adapt to sudden, unanticipated changes, which is a non-trivial task.

The interpretability of ML models is also a pertinent issue. Many powerful ML techniques, such as deep learning algorithms, operate as black boxes, meaning their internal workings are not easily interpretable. This lack of transparency can be problematic in trading because traders and regulatory bodies often require a clear understanding of why certain decisions are made. Developing interpretable models or employing methods to explain predictions is crucial, but achieving this without sacrificing performance is challenging.

Moreover, the competitive nature of HFT means that strategies employed must be proprietary and cutting-edge to offer any substantial advantage. This necessitates continuous investment in research and development, as well as safeguarding intellectual property. The implementation of ML in HFT demands significant resources in terms of time, expertise, and capital, making it an endeavor not feasible for all trading firms.

Regulatory constraints are an external factor that can limit the application of ML in HFT. Financial markets are heavily regulated to ensure fairness, stability, and transparency. ML models must comply with these regulations, which may restrict certain trading activities or impose requirements that complicate the development and deployment of models. Ensuring regulatory compliance adds another layer of complexity and risk to the use of ML in HFT.

Finally, the integration of ML models into existing HFT infrastructure poses practical challenges. Legacy trading systems may not be compatible with modern ML algorithms, requiring extensive modifications or complete overhauls. This integration process is both time-consuming and costly, often involving rigorous testing to ensure that the new system operates seamlessly and without introducing new risks.

While the integration of machine learning in high-frequency trading presents formidable challenges, these should not dissuade determined traders from exploring this frontier. By acknowledging and addressing these limitations, traders can devise robust, adaptive strategies that harness the full potential of machine learning, carving out a competitive edge in the fast-paced world of HFT. It is through persistent innovation and meticulous refinement that the synergy between machine learning and HFT can be fully realized.

Chapter 9

Market Impact and Liquidity

This chapter addresses the concepts of market impact and liquidity within the context of High-Frequency Trading (HFT). It differentiates between temporary and permanent market impacts and methods for measuring them. The chapter delves into the role of liquidity in market impact, contrasting liquidity takers and providers. It explores strategies to minimize market impact and discusses various market impact models. Additionally, regulatory aspects of market impact and liquidity are examined, supplemented with real-world case studies to provide practical insights and applications.

9.1 Understanding Market Impact

To grasp the intricacies of High-Frequency Trading (HFT) and its influence on today's financial markets, one must first understand the concept of market impact. Market impact refers to the effect that trading a substantial volume of assets can have on the price of those assets. This effect is critical for traders, especially those engaged in high-frequency strategies, as it can significantly influence their profits and strategies.

Market impact is essentially the change in the market price of an asset caused by the execution of a trade. When a trader places a large order, it can affect the balance of supply and demand, thereby altering the asset's price. High-frequency traders often encounter market impact due to the sheer volume and frequency of their transactions, making it a pivotal consideration in their trading decisions.

The market impact can be intuitively understood through the law of supply and demand. When a large buy order is placed in the market, it can deplete the available supply at the current price level, causing subsequent transactions to occur at higher price points. Conversely, a large sell order can increase supply, pushing prices down as buyers take advantage of the increased availability.

Mathematically, market impact can be expressed using various models, but a foundational understanding can be derived from considering a simple linear model:

$$P(t) = P_0 + \alpha \cdot Q$$

In this model, $P(t)$ is the new price after a transaction, P_0 is the initial price before the order, Q is the size of the order, and α is a coefficient representing the market impact per unit of traded volume. While this model is overly simplistic for real-world applications, it serves as a useful baseline for understanding the relationship between trade size and price change.

The market impact can be classified into two main categories: temporary and permanent. Although this classification will be discussed in more detail in the subsequent sections, it is essential to introduce the basic distinction here.

Temporary market impact refers to the short-term price changes that occur as a result of the trade but revert to the initial price over time as the market absorbs the traded volume. This form of market impact is often driven by liquidity constraints and the immediate reaction of market participants to the new order.

On the other hand, permanent market impact results in a lasting change in the asset's price due to the trade. Such impact reflects a shift in the market's perception of the asset's value, driven by the information conveyed by the trade. For instance, a large purchase might signal to the market an increased interest or positive information about the asset, leading to a sustained price increase.

Efficient management of market impact is crucial for high-frequency traders. Deploying strategies that minimize adverse price movements while executing large volumes can protect profits and enhance trading performance. Techniques such as order fragmentation, where a large order is broken into smaller trades and executed over time, can mitigate market impact by avoiding noticeable disruptions in the market.

High-frequency traders also utilize advanced algorithms specifically designed to judge the optimal execution paths and timing to minimize market impact. For example, Volume-Weighted Average Price (VWAP) algorithms execute trades in proportion to the total volume traded in the market over a specific period, thereby blending the orders with the market flow to reduce noticeable price shifts.

Moreover, understanding the broader market structure, including liquidity conditions and the behavior of other market participants, is indispensable in managing market impact. Traders must be adept at interpreting market signals and adjusting their strategies dynamically to align with prevailing market conditions.

In encapsulating the concept of market impact, it is evident that it forms the bedrock of strategic decision-making in high-frequency trading. Recognizing the dual nature of market impact—temporary and permanent—and employing sophisticated strategies to manage it are essential skills for any trader looking to succeed in the high-paced world of HFT.

The upcoming sections will delve deeper into the classification of market impact, refine our understanding with precise measurement techniques, and elucidate the interplay between liquidity and market impact, ultimately equipping readers with a comprehensive toolkit for navigating the complexities of modern financial markets.

9.2 Classification of Market Impact: Temporary vs. Permanent

In high-frequency trading (HFT) and broader financial markets, understanding the classification of market impact is essential for developing effective trading strategies that minimize costs and enhance profitability. Market impact refers to the change in the price of a security caused by a trade. To fully grasp how market impact influences trading outcomes, it is crucial to distinguish between temporary and permanent impacts.

Temporary market impact, as the name suggests, is short-lived. It arises due to the immediate reaction of the market to the trade. When an order is executed, the increased demand (or supply) momentarily moves the price up (or down). This transient price movement is often a result of market participants adjusting their quotes and spreads in response to the trade. However, as time progresses and no further trades reinforce this movement, the impact diminishes, and the security's price tends to revert to its pre-trade level.

Temporary impacts are typically a consequence of liquidity dynamics. When a large trade is executed, it may temporarily deplete the available liquidity at the best bid or ask prices. Market makers and liquidity providers quickly step in to replenish the order book, restoring the balance over a short period. To quantify this effect, one could model the price change immediately following the trade and track its reversion over time.

Consider the formula to model temporary impact:

$$I_{\text{temp}} = f(Q) \cdot \sigma \cdot \sqrt{\frac{2\kappa}{\lambda}}.$$

Here, I_{temp} represents the temporary impact, $f(Q)$ is a function of the order quantity Q, σ is the volatility of the security, κ is a constant reflecting market resilience, and λ signifies the liquidity.

Conversely, permanent market impact refers to a lasting change in the security's price due to the trade. This impact arises when the trade conveys new information to the market, leading participants to reassess the security's value. For example, a significant buy order might signal to the market that an informed trader anticipates future positive developments, prompting others to adjust their valuations upward permanently.

Permanent market impacts are linked to the informational content of trades. If a trade reveals information about the trader's expectations or the security's underlying value, market participants will adjust their quotes to reflect this new information. This adjustment leads to a persistent shift in the price level, as the market incorporates the updated information into the security's valuation.

To model permanent impact, we consider

$$I_{\text{perm}} = \phi \cdot Q.$$

Here, I_{perm} represents the permanent impact, ϕ is a coefficient that translates order size Q into a durable price change. ϕ incorporates factors such as the extent of the information revealed by the trade and the market's reaction to this information.

Both types of market impact are crucial in constructing trading strategies. High-frequency traders, in particular, need to account for temporary impacts to manage short-term price movements and exploit brief inefficiencies. Simultaneously, understanding permanent impacts is essential for longer-term strategies, such as those based on fundamental analysis, where the longer-term price trend matters more.

To mitigate market impact, traders often break large orders into smaller, less conspicuous parcels. This technique, known as order slicing, aims to minimize both temporary and permanent impacts by spreading out the trades over time to avoid raising suspicion and to blend into the market's natural flow.

In practice, high-frequency trading systems continuously analyze market data to adjust their strategies and execution algorithms dynamically. By integrating real-time analytics and sophisticated models, these systems can estimate the potential temporary and permanent impacts of trades and adapt their actions accordingly. This adaptive approach helps HFT firms maintain a competitive edge while managing the dual challenges posed by temporary and permanent market impacts.

Understanding the distinction between temporary and permanent market impacts not only enhances the effectiveness of trading strategies but also aids in managing execution costs and risks. By leveraging this knowledge, traders can develop more nuanced approaches that optimize trade execution and capitalize on market dynamics efficiently.

9.3 Measuring Market Impact

In the sophisticated ecosystem of high-frequency trading (HFT), accurately measuring market impact is crucial for optimizing trading strategies and preserving profitability. Market impact refers to the change in the price of a security caused by trading activity, particularly significant in high-volume transactions. Understanding and quantifying this impact allows traders to anticipate and mitigate adverse effects on their trades, ultimately enhancing their performance. This section delves into the methods and metrics used to measure market impact, equipping readers with practical tools and insights for better trade execution.

Market impact can be broadly categorized into two types: temporary and permanent impact. Temporary market impact refers to the immediate price change caused by a trade, which partially or fully reverts over time. Permanent market impact, on the other hand, represents a lasting price change resulting from the trade, reflecting new information or reassessment of the security's value.

To measure market impact effectively, traders and analysts employ various quantitative approaches, leveraging both historical data and real-time metrics. A few commonly used methods include:

- **Price Slippage:** Price slippage occurs when there is a difference between the expected price of a trade and the actual execution price. This discrepancy is often a direct consequence of market impact. For instance, if a trader intends to buy a large quantity of shares at the current market price, the surge in demand might push the price higher before the order is fully executed. The formula for price slippage is given by:

$$\text{Slippage} = \frac{\sum_{i=1}^{N}(P_{\text{actual},i} - P_{\text{expected},i})}{N}$$

  where $P_{\text{actual},i}$ is the actual execution price of the i-th trade, $P_{\text{expected},i}$ is the expected price, and N is the number of trades observed. Analyzing slippage helps in understanding the immediate cost of trading large volumes and adjusting strategies accordingly.

- **Implementation Shortfall:** Also known as the transaction cost analysis (TCA), implementation shortfall measures the difference between the decision price (the price at the time the trading decision is made) and the final execution price. This metric captures the cost of market impact alongside other factors such as delays in execution and bid-ask spreads. The formula for implementation shortfall is:

$$\text{Implementation Shortfall} = (P_{\text{decision}} - P_{\text{execution}}) \times \text{Trade Size}$$

  where P_{decision} is the price at the decision time, and $P_{\text{execution}}$ is the final execution price. This metric is valuable for assessing the overall efficiency and effectiveness of the trading strategy.

- **Volume-Weighted Average Price (VWAP):** VWAP is a trading benchmark that calculates the average price of a security over a specified period, weighted by volume. Comparing the execution price to the VWAP provides a measure of how the trade performed relative to the market's average price, offering insights into market impact. The VWAP is calculated as follows:

$$\text{VWAP} = \frac{\sum_{i=1}^{N}(P_i \times Q_i)}{\sum_{i=1}^{N} Q_i}$$

where P_i is the price of the i-th trade, Q_i is the quantity of the i-th trade, and N is the total number of trades. Executing trades close to the VWAP can help minimize market impact, as it indicates alignment with the market's average trading activity.

- **Market Depth Analysis:** Market depth refers to the market's ability to absorb large orders without significant price changes. By analyzing the order book, traders can gauge the level of liquidity at different price levels and anticipate potential market impact. Metrics such as the Order Book Imbalance (OBI) provide insights into market depth:

$$\text{OBI} = \frac{\text{Bid Volume} - \text{Ask Volume}}{\text{Total Volume}}$$

  where Bid Volume represents the quantity of buy orders and Ask Volume represents the quantity of sell orders. A higher OBI indicates higher buying pressure, which could lead to greater market impact when executing large sell orders.

- **Impact Cost Estimation Models:** Various econometric models estimate the cost of market impact based on historical trading data, order size, and market conditions. One popular model is the Almgren-Chriss framework, which quantifies the trade-off between market impact costs and volatility risks:

$$\text{Total Expected Cost} = \alpha Q^2 + \beta \sigma Q$$

  where α and β are coefficients derived from historical data, Q is the order size, and σ is the price volatility. By optimizing these parameters, traders can plan their orders to minimize market impact while managing risk.

By proactively measuring market impact through these methods, traders can refine their strategies to maintain profitability and reduce transaction costs. Understanding the nuances of market impact allows traders to navigate the dynamic landscape of high-frequency trading more effectively, achieving better execution outcomes and sustainable success in the financial markets.

9.4 The Role of Liquidity in Market Impact

Liquidity plays a crucial role in determining the extent and nature of market impact, particularly within the realm of High-Frequency Trading (HFT). In general terms, liquidity refers to the ability to buy or sell a security in the market without causing a significant change in its price. The more liquid a market is, the easier it is to execute large orders without affecting the price. Conversely, in less liquid markets, even relatively small trades can lead to substantial price changes.

To understand the influence of liquidity on market impact, it is essential to differentiate between various forms of liquidity and their implications. Market liquidity can be broadly categorized into three main types: immediacy, depth, and resiliency.

- **Immediacy** pertains to the speed at which trades can be executed. In highly liquid markets, traders can swiftly enter or exit positions, meeting their demand for immediate action. When immediacy is high, the market impact tends to be lower since orders can be quickly absorbed by the available liquidity without substantial price movements.
- **Depth**, on the other hand, refers to the volume of orders available at different price levels around the current market price. A market with considerable depth can accommodate larger trades, as there are sufficient buy and sell orders close to the prevailing price. Depth helps to distribute the impact of substantial trades over a larger volume, thus mitigating sharp price fluctuations. It is often assessed through order book analysis, where the volume of pending buy and sell orders at different price points is examined.
- **Resiliency** is the market's ability to recover from price changes caused by trades. In a resilient market, prices quickly revert to their equilibrium levels after being impacted by large trades. This characteristic is crucial in reducing the lasting effects of any substantial orders, hence lowering the permanent market impact. Resiliency is typically quantified by evaluating the speed at which price disturbances diminish and return to their fundamental value.

The interplay of these types of liquidity directly affects trading strategies and their execution. For instance, in markets where liquidity is high, the impact of executing a large order can be minimal, thereby making it feasible to implement aggressive trading strategies. On the other hand, in less liquid markets, the same order might cause significant price disruptions, necessitating the use of more sophisticated execution techniques to spread out the trade and minimize impact.

Market makers and liquidity providers play a pivotal role in sustaining the level of liquidity within the market. These entities submit limit orders that provide liquidity by offering to buy or sell at specified prices, thus creating a buffer against price volatility caused by market orders from liquidity takers. Their presence stabilizes the market, reducing the temporary impact of trades. High-frequency trading firms often engage in market-making activities, leveraging advanced algorithms to continuously provide liquidity and capture the bid-ask spread.

One of the prime metrics used to measure liquidity and its effect on market impact is the bid-ask spread. A narrower bid-ask spread indicates higher liquidity, as the cost of trading is lower. Conversely, a wider spread suggests lower liquidity, reflecting higher trading costs and potential for larger market impact. By scrutinizing the bid-ask spread, traders can gauge the liquidity environment and adjust their strategies accordingly.

Volume also serves as a significant indicator of liquidity. Higher trading volumes typically signal healthier liquidity, where large orders can be executed more efficiently with reduced price impact. However, it is essential to differentiate between routine volume and volume spikes driven by news or events, as the latter can temporarily alter the liquidity landscape and amplify market impact.

To illustrate, consider the case of a high-frequency trader looking to execute a substantial buy order in a moderately liquid stock. If the trader attempts to execute the order all at once, the market depth may not be sufficient to absorb the trade without a significant price spike, leading to adverse price movements and signaling other market participants of the ongoing activity. Alternatively, employing a time-weighted average price (TWAP) or volume-weighted average price (VWAP) strategy can enable the trader to distribute the order over time, better utilizing available liquidity and reducing market impact.

Additionally, the type of liquidity provider influences market conditions. Traditional market makers might rely on fundamental price analysis and human judgment, while algorithmic market makers use advanced statistical models and real-time data to provide continuous liquidity. The latter can react swiftly to market conditions, enhancing market resiliency and reducing impact.

Understanding liquidity's role in market impact is indispensable for developing effective trading strategies, particularly in the high-frequency trading domain. By analyzing liquidity metrics and employing sophisticated execution algorithms, traders can minimize market impact, optimize execution, and achieve superior trading outcomes. The nuances of liquidity dynamics underscore its critical importance in shaping market behavior and guiding trading decisions.

9.5 Liquidity Takers vs. Liquidity Providers

In the dynamics of financial markets, a fundamental dichotomy exists between liquidity takers and liquidity providers. Understanding this distinction is essential for comprehending the mechanics of High-Frequency Trading (HFT) and its impact on market structure.

Liquidity providers, often likened to market makers, play a pivotal role in enhancing market efficiency. They continuously post buy (bid) and sell (ask) orders, thereby offering liquidity to other market participants. These entities profit primarily from the bid-ask spread, the difference between the buy and sell prices. By maintaining a presence in the market, liquidity providers facilitate trade execution and contribute to price discovery, ensuring that assets can be bought and sold with relative ease.

On the other hand, liquidity takers are participants who execute trades against the posted orders of liquidity providers. Their actions are driven by an immediate need to enter or exit positions, often prioritizing speed over price. This urgency generally results in paying the bid-ask spread, making liquidity takers more susceptible to trading costs associated with market impact.

The interaction between these two groups is critical for a functional and vibrant market. Liquidity providers supply the necessary depth that helps stabilize prices, while liquidity takers generate the volume needed to keep markets active. However, the balance between the two is delicate. An excess of liquidity takers can deplete market depth, leading to higher volatility and increased transaction costs. Conversely, a predominance of liquidity providers could result in narrower spreads and more stable prices, but with reduced trading activity.

To illustrate the mechanics further, consider an example involving a widely traded stock:

Price	Bid Size	Ask Size
$100.00	500	600
$99.90	400	700
$99.80	300	800

In this simplified order book, liquidity providers have posted bids to buy the stock at $100.00, $99.90, and $99.80, while offers to sell (asks) are placed at corresponding levels. A liquidity taker wanting to purchase a large quantity of shares quickly might impact the market by lifting the asks sequentially, thereby moving the price upwards. This action, known as *market impact*, demonstrates how liquidity takers influence prices due to their urgent need to trade.

High-frequency traders often engage as both liquidity takers and providers, dynamically adjusting their strategies in response to market conditions. Their ability to rapidly post and cancel orders allows them to manage risk effectively and capitalize on fleeting opportunities. For instance, through statistical arbitrage, an HFT firm might act as a liquidity provider by posting limit orders in correlated markets, profiting from minor price discrepancies.

Moreover, lifecycle strategies in HFT highlight the dual roles traders may embody. At times, they provide liquidity to harvest the bid-ask spread, while in other instances, they take liquidity to capitalize on arbitrage opportunities or to avoid adverse selection risk. The latter occurs when traders only execute against the most attractive quotes, leaving the less competitive ones, a situation often mitigated by sophisticated algorithms designed to optimize execution across fragmented markets.

The distinction between liquidity takers and providers extends beyond individual trading strategies, impacting broader market phenomena. For example, during periods of market stress, the behavior of liquidity takers can amplify price movements, exacerbating volatility. Conversely, robust liquidity provision can dampen such effects by ensuring that substantial buying or selling pressure is absorbed efficiently.

In conclusion, the dynamic interplay between liquidity takers and providers shapes market resilience, efficiency, and the overall trading ecosystem. Recognizing the importance of both roles and their interplay enables traders and investors to devise more informed strategies, capable of navigating the complexities of modern financial markets.

9.6 Strategies to Minimize Market Impact

In high-frequency trading (HFT), minimizing market impact is crucial to optimizing trading performance and preserving profitability. Market impact refers to the change in asset prices caused by trading activities, and it can significantly affect execution prices and trading costs. This section outlines various strategies that traders can employ to mitigate market impact, ensuring more efficient and cost-effective trading.

One effective strategy is algorithmic trading, which involves using computer algorithms to execute trades in a manner designed to reduce market visibility. These algorithms can slice large orders into smaller, less noticeable trades that are dispersed over time and across different trading venues. Common algorithms include the Volume Weighted Average Price (VWAP), which targets a price close to the average market price over a specific time period, and the Time Weighted Average Price (TWAP), which disperses orders evenly throughout a trading session. By concealing the size and intent of the trade, these algorithms help minimize the price movement induced by large orders.

Another strategy is to leverage dark pools, which are private exchanges where trade orders are not displayed publicly. Dark pools allow traders to execute large trades without revealing their intentions to the broader market, thus mitigating potential adverse price impacts. While dark pools offer reduced transparency, they enable large institutional investors to trade significant volumes with minimal market disturbance. However, it is imperative to balance the benefits of dark pools with the potential for reduced price improvement and liquidity.

Time optimization is another critical approach. Traders can strategically time their trades to coincide with periods of high market liquidity or lower volatility. By executing trades during peak trading hours or following key market events, traders can take advantage of increased trading activity and tighter bid-ask spreads, thus reducing the likelihood of significant market impact. Additionally, avoiding trades during low liquidity periods, such as immediately after market open or close, can prevent adverse price movements.

Order placement techniques also play a significant role in minimizing market impact. Utilizing limit orders, as opposed to market orders, allows traders to control the price at which an order is executed, thereby avoiding unfavorable price concessions. Placing invisible orders, such as iceberg orders, where only a small portion of the order is visible to the market at any given time, can further reduce market visibility and impact. These techniques enable the execution of large trades without alarming other market participants.

Risk management is integral to minimizing market impact. By diversifying trading strategies and spreading orders across different asset classes and markets, traders can dilute the impact of any single transaction. Employing statistical arbitrage strategies, which exploit price inefficiencies between correlated assets, can further mitigate market impact by ensuring trades are driven by relative value rather than absolute size.

Technology and infrastructure also play a vital role in mitigating market impact. High-speed, low-latency trading systems enable traders to react swiftly to market conditions, ensuring timely execution and reducing slippage. Co-location services, where trading systems are physically located close to exchange servers, minimize transmission delays and enhance execution speed. These technological advancements provide a significant edge in reducing market impact, particularly in the realm of HFT.

Knowledge and predictive analytics are equally important. By utilizing advanced data analytics and machine learning models, traders can predict market movements and identify optimal execution strategies. These models analyze historical trading data, order book dynamics, and market sentiment to forecast price changes and inform trading decisions, thus minimizing unintended market impact.

Incorporating market microstructure knowledge is also essential. Understanding how various market participants, including retail traders, institutional investors, and market makers, interact within the market helps traders anticipate liquidity and price movements. By aligning trading strategies with the behaviors of different market players, traders can navigate the market more effectively and reduce adverse impacts.

Lastly, regulatory compliance and ethical practices must not be overlooked. Adhering to trading regulations and best practices ensures market integrity and avoids potential legal repercussions. Transparent and fair trading practices foster a healthier market environment, ultimately benefiting all market participants.

By combining these strategies, traders can significantly minimize market impact, thereby enhancing execution quality and achieving better trading outcomes. These approaches, when tailored to specific trading goals and market conditions, provide a robust framework for mitigating the adverse effects of high-frequency trading.

9.7 Market Impact Models

Understanding and accurately modeling market impact is crucial for High-Frequency Trading (HFT) algorithms to optimize execution strategies and manage costs effectively. Market impact refers to the change in the price of an asset caused by a trader entering or exiting positions. Developing robust market impact models allows traders to predict the price movement associated with their trades and minimize adverse effects. This section delves into various theoretical and empirical models used to quantify and forecast market impact.

- **Linear Models**

  Linear market impact models are among the simplest and most intuitive frameworks. These models assume a proportional relationship between trade size and price movement. The fundamental equation for a linear impact model can be expressed as:

  $$\Delta P = \gamma Q$$

  where ΔP represents the price change, Q is the quantity of the asset traded, and γ is the impact coefficient. Despite their simplicity, linear models often fail to capture the non-linear nature of large trades and can lead to underestimating the true market impact.

- **Non-linear Models**

  Given the limitations of linear models, non-linear approaches offer a more nuanced perspective. One common non-linear model is the square-root model, which posits that the market impact grows with the square root of the order size:

  $$\Delta P = \eta \sqrt{Q}$$

  In this equation, η is a scaling factor that varies based on market conditions. The square-root model recognizes that larger trades tend to have disproportionately higher impacts, reflecting the fragility and capacity of financial markets.

- **Market Microstructure Models**

  Market microstructure models delve into the intricate dynamics of how trades are processed and matched in the marketplace.

These models consider factors such as order book depth, bid-ask spread, and limit order dynamics. An influential market microstructure model is the Almgren-Chriss framework, which balances the trade-off between market impact and trading speed to minimize execution costs. The impact cost C in the Almgren-Chriss model is expressed as:

$$C = \frac{\sigma S}{\lambda}\left(2\sqrt{\frac{\lambda Q}{\sigma S}}\right)^{\frac{2}{3}}$$

where σ represents the volatility, S is the stock price, Q is the order size, and λ is a liquidity parameter. This model is particularly useful for algorithmic traders looking to optimally split large orders over time to reduce market impact.

- **Empirical Models**

  Empirical models rely on historical trade data to estimate and validate market impact functions. Such models can be highly tailored to specific assets and trading environments. An empirical approach involves regression analysis to fit a curve to past trade impacts and extracting parameters that reflect current market conditions. For instance, a generalized form of an empirical model might be:

  $$\Delta P = \alpha + \beta Q^{\delta} + \epsilon$$

  where α, β, and δ are coefficients derived from empirical data, and ϵ is the error term representing random noise. The flexibility of empirical models makes them a preferred choice for high-frequency traders who can frequently recalibrate their models to align with evolving market dynamics.

- **Machine Learning Models**

  The advent of machine learning has introduced new capabilities for modeling market impact with higher accuracy and adaptability. Machine learning models, such as decision trees, neural networks, and random forests, can capture complex, non-linear interactions within the trading data that traditional models might miss. These models are trained on vast datasets and can predict market impact by identifying hidden patterns and relationships.

  For instance, a neural network model for market impact might involve multiple layers of interconnected nodes, each performing nonlinear transformations on the input features like trade size, market volatility, and liquidity measures. These advanced models are particularly useful in dynamic environments where market conditions are rapidly changing.

Incorporating sophisticated market impact models into trading algorithms allows HFT firms to mitigate costs and enhance their execution performance. By selecting and fine-tuning the right model for their specific needs, traders can better navigate the complexities of financial markets.

9.8 Regulatory Aspects of Market Impact and Liquidity

The regulatory landscape surrounding market impact and liquidity is a critical factor in shaping the behavior of market participants, particularly in the realm of High-Frequency Trading (HFT). This section examines the various regulatory frameworks that govern market impact and liquidity, assessing their implications for traders, brokers, exchanges, and other stakeholders. By understanding these regulations, market participants can better align their strategies with legal requirements and ethical standards, thereby ensuring compliance and optimizing performance.

Regulators worldwide have implemented a series of measures to monitor and control the activities associated with HFT and its potential market impacts. Among the foremost objectives are the maintenance of fair and orderly markets, protection against market abuse, and preservation of market integrity and investor confidence. Several key regulations and directives form the cornerstone of these efforts.

The *Markets in Financial Instruments Directive II* (*MiFID II*) is one of the most comprehensive regulatory frameworks in the European Union that directly impacts HFT activities. MiFID II introduces stringent requirements for HFT firms, mandating robust risk controls and transparency measures. Firms must now maintain accurate and complete records of all trading activity and are subject to periodic reporting to regulators. One notable requirement is the implementation of circuit breakers and minimum tick sizes to mitigate the risks associated with excessive market volatility and ensure smoother price formation.

In the United States, the *Dodd-Frank Wall Street Reform and Consumer Protection Act* has been instrumental in shaping the regulatory environment for market impact and liquidity. The act introduced several provisions aimed at enhancing transparency and reducing systemic risks. The *Volcker Rule*, a key component of Dodd-Frank, restricts proprietary trading by commercial banks, thereby limiting their ability to engage in speculative HFT practices. Additionally, the *Consolidated Audit Trail* (CAT) system was established to enable regulators to track and analyze trading data comprehensively, aiding in the identification and investigation of potentially manipulative activities.

Another significant regulatory concern is the prevention of *market abuse*, including activities like spoofing and layering, which can artificially influence market prices and liquidity. The *European Market Abuse Regulation* (*MAR*) explicitly prohibits such practices, imposing hefty fines and sanctions on offenders. Similarly, the U.S. Securities and Exchange Commission (SEC) and the Commodity Futures Trading Commission (CFTC) have enacted stringent anti-manipulation rules and actively pursue enforcement actions against those breaching these regulations.

Beyond national and regional regulations, international bodies such as the *International Organization of Securities Commissions* (IOSCO) play a pivotal role in harmonizing global regulatory standards. IOSCO's principles for financial market infrastructures and secondary markets seek to ensure that trading venues adopt practices promoting resilience, efficiency, and transparency across different jurisdictions.

Compliance with these regulatory frameworks necessitates advanced technological and procedural adjustments by HFT firms. This includes enhancing surveillance systems to detect irregular trading patterns, implementing robust pre-trade risk controls, and maintaining comprehensive audit trails. Partnering with regulatory technology (RegTech) providers has become increasingly common, offering HFT firms specialized solutions to meet their complex compliance requirements effectively.

Firms must also stay informed about the evolving regulatory landscape, as new rules and amendments frequently arise in response to emerging market dynamics and technological advancements. Active engagement with regulators and industry associations can provide valuable insights and enable proactive adaptation to upcoming regulatory changes.

Moreover, adherence to these regulatory requirements extends beyond mere compliance; it embodies a commitment to ethical trading practices and the broader goal of market stability. By fostering transparency and reducing market abuse, these regulatory frameworks contribute to a more equitable trading environment that benefits all market participants, from retail investors to institutional players.

As we consider the various regulatory aspects of market impact and liquidity, it becomes evident that a well-regulated market is fundamental to the long-term sustainability and growth of financial markets. Understanding and complying with these regulations not only mitigate risks but also enhance the credibility and effectiveness of trading strategies in an increasingly competitive and scrutinized marketplace.

Navigating the complexities of the regulatory landscape is undoubtedly challenging, but it is essential for the successful operation of HFT activities. By aligning their practices with regulatory expectations, firms can achieve a harmonious balance between innovative trading methods and the overarching need to maintain market integrity and investor trust, ensuring their sustained participation and success in the financial markets.

9.9 Case Studies: Market Impact in Real-world Scenarios

To truly understand the subtleties of market impact and liquidity, examining real-world scenarios offers invaluable insights. By analyzing these case studies, we can observe the practical application of theoretical concepts and derive actionable lessons for high-frequency trading (HFT) strategies.

One notable case study involves the May 6, 2010 Flash Crash, which marked one of the most dramatic examples of market impact. Within mere minutes, major U.S. stock indices plummeted, wiping out nearly $1 trillion in market value, only to recover similarly swiftly. An investigation revealed that a large sell order executed via an algorithm significantly impacted market liquidity. The algorithm, designed to sell $4.1 billion in E-mini S&P 500 contracts, operated without any regard for time, price, or market conditions. This lack of adaptive strategy overwhelmed the available liquidity and triggered a domino effect, causing a cascade of sell orders and an exceptional market plunge.

This example underscores the importance of intelligent order execution in high-frequency trading. Employing algorithms that adapt to real-time market data, rather than utilizing fixed rules, can mitigate abrupt market impacts. Strategies such as VWAP (Volume Weighted Average Price) or TWAP (Time Weighted Average Price) could help in dispersing large orders over time, minimizing adverse market reactions.

Another instructive instance is the significant market impact observed during Facebook's IPO on May 18, 2012. An overwhelming volume of orders led to technical glitches on the Nasdaq exchange, delaying the initial trading and causing widespread confusion among traders. The anticipation and subsequent high volume of orders consumed the available liquidity swiftly, exacerbating the market impact. This case highlights the sensitivity of market impact to order flow and system resilience. HFT strategies that consider potential system constraints and liquidity interfaces can avoid such disruptions.

Moreover, examining the impact of the Swiss Franc's unpegging from the Euro in January 2015 provides a perspective on the effect of sudden, unexpected announcements on market dynamics. The Swiss National Bank's decision led to a swift appreciation of the Swiss Franc by nearly 30% against the Euro, creating massive dislocations in various markets. High-frequency traders who could adapt quickly to the news benefitted significantly, while others experienced severe losses. This scenario exemplifies the importance of real-time news processing algorithms that can rapidly interpret and react to exogenous shocks.

A further example can be drawn from the ETFs' behavior during the August 24, 2015 market sell-off. ETFs experienced unprecedented volatility, with numerous funds trading at deep discounts to their net asset values (NAVs). High-frequency algorithms attempting to arbitrage these discrepancies were caught in a loop of continuous price adjustments, amplifying market dislocation. This event brings to light how under certain stressed conditions, the liquidity of ETFs, which is typically high, can evaporate swiftly, making market impact models more complex. Strategies involving dynamic hedging and circuit breakers might offer more resilience in such turbulent scenarios.

Additionally, consider the impact of the Brexit referendum on June 23, 2016, when the UK voted to leave the European Union. The unexpected outcome led to a rapid depreciation of the British Pound and substantial volatility across global markets. Traders who had pre-existing algorithms to handle such market-moving news were able to capitalize, while others faced significant adverse impacts. This emphasizes the need for maintaining situational awareness and having preemptive strategies in place for geopolitical events.

Finally, the March 2020 COVID-19 pandemic-induced crash offers a contemporary case study. The sheer speed and magnitude of the market's decline, accompanied by extreme illiquidity, provided a challenging environment for high-frequency trading strategies. Liquidity dried up in multiple asset classes simultaneously, rendering traditional market impact models less effective. Algorithmic traders who swiftly reduced their exposure and adapted to the elevated volatility levels were better positioned.

By examining these real-world scenarios, traders can grasp the multifaceted nature of market impact and the critical role of liquidity. Each case provides distinct lessons on order execution, the necessity of adaptable algorithms, and the potential benefits of incorporating advanced risk management practices. As the market evolves, continuously learning from such instances is crucial for refining HFT strategies and ensuring robust, resilient trading operations.

Chapter 10

Backtesting and Simulation

This chapter focuses on the critical practices of backtesting and simulation in High-Frequency Trading (HFT). It outlines the importance of backtesting for evaluating trading strategies and the data requirements necessary for accurate simulations. The chapter explains how to design a robust backtesting framework and simulate market conditions to test HFT strategies. It covers the analysis of backtest results, highlights potential pitfalls and limitations, and discusses methods to enhance simulation accuracy. Through these practices, traders can refine their strategies and improve their performance before deploying them in real market scenarios.

10.1 Introduction to Backtesting

Backtesting is a foundational cornerstone in the development and evaluation of trading strategies within High-Frequency Trading (HFT). At its core, backtesting involves the retrospective testing of trading strategies using historical market data to assess their potential performance in real-world scenarios. This section seeks to elucidate the fundamental principles of backtesting, establishing a robust understanding that will serve as the bedrock for the more advanced discussions that follow.

In essence, backtesting is predicated on the assumption that patterns and relationships observed in past market data may persist into the future. By applying trading strategies to historical data, traders can gauge how these strategies might have performed, thereby gaining insights into their viability, strengths, and potential weaknesses. This process is crucial for several reasons, as it allows traders to fine-tune their strategies before committing capital in live markets, reduces the risk associated with untested strategies, and aids in the identification of strategies with a higher probability of success.

To begin, one must understand the basic workflow of backtesting. It typically starts with the formulation of a trading hypothesis or strategy. This could be as simple as a moving average crossover strategy or as complex as an algorithmic pattern recognition system. Next, historical market data relevant to the strategy must be meticulously gathered. The quality and granularity of this data play a pivotal role in the accuracy of the backtesting results. For HFT algorithms that execute trades in fractions of a second, high-resolution tick data is often required.

Once the data is sourced, the strategy is applied to this dataset within a backtesting environment. This simulated environment mimics market conditions, incorporating various parameters such as order execution latency, transaction costs, and market impact. The results generated from the backtest provide numerous key performance metrics, such as the return on investment (ROI), Sharpe ratio, maximum drawdown, and win/loss ratio, offering a detailed picture of the strategy's historical performance.

However, backtesting is not without its challenges and caveats. One major consideration is the phenomenon of overfitting, where a strategy performs exceptionally well on historical data but fails to generalize to unseen data. Overfitting occurs when a strategy becomes excessively tailored to past noise rather than to genuine market signals, sacrificing future performance. To mitigate this, techniques such as cross-validation and out-of-sample testing are employed. Additionally, practitioners must be wary of look-ahead bias and survivorship bias, which can skew backtesting results and lead to overly optimistic performance estimates.

Moreover, the backtesting process must be iterative and reflective. A single backtest cannot definitively determine the efficacy of a strategy. Instead, continuous refinement and optimization are necessary. It is imperative to adapt and evolve strategies in response to backtest feedback, adjusting for market regime changes, evolving market dynamics, and the introduction of new technologies.

As we delve deeper into the nuances of backtesting, we will explore the importance of data quality, the intricacies of designing a robust backtesting framework, and the simulation of realistic market conditions. Mastery of these concepts will significantly enhance the precision of your strategy evaluations, ultimately leading to more informed and confident trading decisions.

Backtesting, therefore, is more than just a preliminary check; it is an essential practice that underpins the discipline and rigor of professional trading. By systematically applying trading strategies to historical data within a controlled and methodical framework, traders can uncover critical insights and develop robust, high-performing strategies tailored for the fast-paced realm of HFT.

10.2 Importance of Backtesting in HFT

In the rapidly evolving world of High-Frequency Trading (HFT), backtesting serves as a cornerstone for strategy development and refinement. Backtesting involves simulating a trading strategy using historical data to evaluate its performance. This section underscores the critical role that backtesting plays in HFT and explores the various facets that make it indispensable for both novice and seasoned traders aiming to optimize their trading strategies.

Understanding the performance of a trading strategy prior to live deployment is paramount. Backtesting enables traders to gain insights into how their strategies would have performed under past market conditions. By doing so, traders can identify potential strengths and weaknesses, allowing them to adjust their strategies accordingly before committing real capital. This process mitigates risk and enhances the likelihood of success in live trading environments.

One of the primary benefits of backtesting is its ability to provide a sense of confidence in a trading strategy. By rigorously testing a strategy against historical data, traders can ascertain its robustness and efficacy. This is especially crucial in HFT, where the markets are highly volatile and trades are executed in fractions of a second. A well-backtested strategy can provide reassurance that it can withstand different market regimes and yield positive returns even in adverse conditions.

Backtesting also facilitates the fine-tuning of trading parameters. In the world of HFT, strategies typically involve a multitude of parameters, such as entry and exit points, stop-loss levels, and order sizes. Through backtesting, traders can systematically adjust these parameters to achieve optimal performance. This iterative process of optimization helps in fine-tuning the strategy to align with specific objectives, such as maximizing profit or minimizing risk.

Moreover, backtesting allows for the comparison of different strategies. Traders can backtest multiple strategies to determine which one performs best under the same market conditions. This comparative analysis is invaluable for deciding which strategy to deploy. It also provides a benchmark for strategy development, motivating continual improvement and innovation in trading approaches.

In addition to optimization and comparison, backtesting serves as a powerful tool for identifying the potential for overfitting. Overfitting occurs when a trading strategy is too closely tailored to historical data, capturing noise rather than genuine market patterns. This can lead to poor performance in live trading. By thoroughly backtesting and validating strategies on multiple datasets, traders can detect overfitting and take steps to improve the generalizability of their strategies.

Furthermore, backtesting helps traders understand the risk and reward profile of a strategy. Detailed analysis of backtest results reveals metrics such as maximum drawdown, Sharpe ratio, and volatility, which are crucial for assessing the risk associated with the strategy. By understanding these risk metrics, traders can make informed decisions about whether a strategy aligns with their risk tolerance and investment goals.

High-Frequency Trading inherently involves substantial transaction costs due to the high volume of trades. Backtesting allows traders to incorporate these costs into their simulations, providing a more realistic picture of net profitability. By accounting for slippage, bid-ask spreads, and other transaction costs, traders can evaluate whether a strategy remains viable after considering these expenses.

The regulatory environment is another area where backtesting proves essential. In many jurisdictions, regulators require thorough documentation of trading strategies and their expected performance. Backtesting provides the empirical evidence needed to satisfy these regulatory requirements. It demonstrates that a strategy has been rigorously tested and is not designed to exploit market anomalies in a manner contrary to market integrity and fairness.

Ultimately, backtesting fosters a deeper understanding of market behavior. By analyzing how a strategy performs across different market conditions—bullish, bearish, and sideways—traders gain insights into underlying market dynamics. This knowledge is instrumental in developing adaptive strategies that can respond to changing market environments, which is a key attribute of successful HFT systems.

In essence, the importance of backtesting in HFT cannot be overstated. It is a fundamental practice that underpins the development, validation, and optimization of trading strategies. Through diligent backtesting, traders can enhance their strategy's robustness, gain confidence in its performance, and ensure it aligns with their financial objectives. The meticulous work done during the backtesting phase pays dividends when the strategy is finally deployed in the fast-paced world of high-frequency trading.

10.3 Data Requirements for Backtesting

Data is the lifeblood of backtesting in High-Frequency Trading (HFT). The accuracy and reliability of a backtest are contingent on the quality and completeness of the data used. Therefore, understanding the data requirements for backtesting is pivotal for developing robust trading strategies.

The primary data types necessary for backtesting HFT strategies include high-resolution tick data, order book data, and market event data. Each type of data plays a crucial role in reconstructing the market conditions precisely as they were when the trades took place.

- **Tick Data:** Tick data encompasses all the information about each transaction that occurs in the market. This includes the timestamp of the trade, the price at which the trade occurred, and the traded volume. For HFT, the granularity of this data is paramount; even the smallest deviation can alter the outcome of a backtest. High resolution, down to the nanosecond, ensures that every single trade and price movement is captured accurately.

- **Order Book Data:** The order book is a real-time list of buy and sell orders at various price levels. Capturing this data allows traders to understand the liquidity and market depth at any given moment. The order book data should include timestamps, bid and ask prices, and the corresponding volumes for each price level. In high-frequency scenarios, changes in the order book occur rapidly, and hence, capturing these changes with high precision is essential for realistic backtesting.

- **Market Event Data:** Market events, such as news releases, economic reports, and company-specific announcements, can significantly impact the price movements and liquidity of the market. Integrating this data into backtesting helps in mimicking the effect of these events on trading strategies. The data should include the type of event, the time it occurred, and any associated quantifiable metrics, such as volatility spikes or sudden changes in trading volume.

It is not sufficient to merely collect these data types; their quality must be meticulously verified. Common issues that need to be addressed include missing data points, incorrect timestamps, and discrepancies between reported and actual traded prices. Filtering out erroneous data and filling in gaps is a necessary preprocessing step. Approaches such as interpolation, smoothing, and thresholding may be employed to ensure the dataset's integrity.

Moreover, the historical data utilized for backtesting should cover diverse market conditions, including volatile periods, calm markets, and significant economic events. This variety ensures that the backtesting framework can assess the resilience and adaptability of the trading strategy under different market scenarios.

Another critical factor to consider is the synchronization of data streams. In HFT, even the slightest delay or mismatch in data timestamps can lead to erroneous backtesting results. Ensuring that all data sources, whether from different exchanges or different types of data, are harmonized to a common time standard is crucial. Techniques like cross-referencing timestamps with a reliable time server or employing time-sync technologies can mitigate such issues.

To handle the vast amounts of data required for backtesting HFT strategies, robust data storage and retrieval systems are essential. Efficient data management techniques, such as indexing and partitioning, can significantly speed up access times and enable faster backtesting processes. Leveraging distributed computing frameworks can further enhance the capability to process large datasets in parallel, substantially reducing computational overhead.

Finally, regulatory considerations must be accounted for when sourcing data for backtesting. Traders must ensure compliance with data usage policies stipulated by exchanges and data providers. Licensing agreements, data privacy laws, and intellectual property rights are critical aspects that must be evaluated to avoid legal repercussions.

Effective management and utilization of data for backtesting can greatly influence the success of HFT strategies. By using high-quality, precisely synchronized, and comprehensive data, traders can enhance the reliability of their backtesting results, providing a solid foundation for deploying strategies in live markets.

10.4 Designing a Backtesting Framework

Designing a backtesting framework is a fundamental aspect of evaluating the viability of High-Frequency Trading (HFT) strategies. The framework serves as the bedrock upon which trading ideas are rigorously tested against historical data, allowing traders to analyze performance, identify weaknesses, and optimize strategies before live deployment. To achieve a robust and reliable backtesting framework, several key components and considerations must be addressed:

1. Establishing Clear Objectives

The first step in designing a backtesting framework is to define clear objectives. These objectives should align with the specific goals of your trading strategy. For instance, are you aiming to maximize returns, minimize drawdown, or optimize for a specific risk-adjusted performance metric? Clarifying these objectives will guide the structure and emphasis of your backtesting process.

2. Selecting Appropriate Data Sources

Choosing the right data sources is crucial for accurate backtesting. High-quality data that closely represents actual market conditions is essential. For HFT, this typically involves high-frequency data such as tick-by-tick prices, order book data, and trade timestamps. Effective data sources should be:

- Clean and pre-processed to eliminate errors and anomalies.
- Sufficiently comprehensive to include diverse market conditions (e.g., varying volatility, different trading hours).
- Updated regularly to incorporate the latest market dynamics.

For accurate simulations, it's vital to use data from reputable sources known for reliability and precision.

3. Defining the Strategy Logic

A clear and well-documented definition of the trading strategy is paramount. This involves specifying the rules and conditions under which trades are executed. Incorporate elements such as:

- Entry and exit signals, defined based on technical indicators, price action, or other criteria.
- Position sizing rules to determine the volume of each trade.
- Risk management protocols, including stop-loss and take-profit levels.

By precisely defining these parameters, you create a reproducible and testable model that can be accurately backtested.

4. Implementing the Backtesting Engine

Developing the backtesting engine—software that simulates trades according to the strategy's rules—is a critical technical task. The backtesting engine should process historical data, execute trades, and record performance metrics. Key considerations include:

- *Computational Efficiency*: Ensure the engine can handle large datasets efficiently, as HFT strategies often require processing vast amounts of data.
- *Accuracy*: Precision in executing trades according to the defined logic without introducing biases or errors.
- *Modularity*: Design the engine in a modular way to allow for easy updates and integration of new strategies or modifications.

Here is a simple example of a backtesting engine core in Python using pseudo-code:

```
for each bar in historical_data:
    execute_trading_logic(bar)
    update_positions()
    record_performance_metrics()
```

5. Accounting for Transaction Costs

In the realm of HFT, transaction costs—spreads, commissions, and slippages—can significantly impact strategy profitability. Therefore, it is essential to incorporate realistic transaction costs into the backtesting framework. This involves:

- *Modeling Spreads*: Estimate bid-ask spreads based on historical market conditions.
- *Commissions*: Include broker fees and exchange fees as applicable.
- *Slippage*: Factor in the real-world delay and market impact cost of executing large orders.

By simulating these costs accurately, the backtest results will provide a more realistic assessment of strategy performance.

6. Validating Performance Metrics

To evaluate the effectiveness of the strategy, it is essential to define and validate a set of performance metrics. Beyond just net profits, consider metrics such as:

- *Sharpe Ratio*: Measures risk-adjusted return.
- *Max Drawdown*: Indicates the largest peak-to-trough decline.
- *Win Rate*: Percentage of profitable trades.
- *Profit Factor*: Ratio of gross profits to gross losses.

These metrics provide a deeper insight into the strategy's risk and reward characteristics.

7. Implementing Robustness Checks

A sound backtesting framework must include robustness checks to ensure the strategy is not overfitted to historical data. This involves techniques such as:

- *Walk-Forward Analysis*: Sequentially testing and optimizing the strategy over multiple time periods.
- *Out-of-Sample Testing*: Assessing strategy performance on data not used during development.

- *Monte Carlo Simulation*: Evaluating strategy performance across a wide range of random market conditions.

These checks ensure that the strategy remains viable and adaptable to future market changes.

By rigorously addressing these elements, you can construct a robust and reliable backtesting framework. This framework is a critical tool in the trader's arsenal, offering a detailed and accurate assessment of how a trading strategy would have performed under historical market conditions. With this foundation, traders can continuously refine and improve their strategies, reducing risks and enhancing their potential for success in live trading environments.

10.5 Simulating Market Conditions

Simulating market conditions is a critical step in backtesting high-frequency trading (HFT) strategies, as it allows traders to evaluate their approaches in a controlled yet dynamically realistic environment. Replicating real market situations as closely as possible ensures that the strategies tested are robust and capable of handling the complexities and volatility of live trading. This section dives into various aspects of market simulation, including selecting appropriate simulation models, incorporating liquidity and order book dynamics, and handling transaction costs and market impact.

Market simulation begins with choosing a model that can accurately represent the trading environment. Various models exist, each with its advantages and trade-offs. Among the most popular are the agent-based models, Monte Carlo simulations, and historical replay.

Agent-based models are particularly valuable as they simulate the interactions of various market participants (agents) who act based on predefined rules or behaviors. This method captures the microstructure elements of the market, such as order flow, price formation, and the impact of different trading strategies. By modeling individual agents, from retail traders to institutional investors, it is possible to observe emergent phenomena typical of real markets, such as liquidity imbalances and volatility clustering.

Monte Carlo simulations, on the other hand, use repeated random sampling to model the probability distribution of prices and other market variables. This approach is useful for stress-testing strategies under different market conditions, including extreme scenarios. By adjusting the input parameters, traders can generate a wide range of market scenarios and examine how their strategies perform across these varied conditions.

Historical replay is another powerful technique where historical market data is used to reconstruct past market conditions. By replaying actual market events, traders gain insights into how their strategies would have performed in real-world scenarios. This method leverages high-fidelity data to provide a close approximation to actual trading, making it easier to spot deficiencies and areas for improvement in the strategy.

A critical element of market simulation involves accurately modeling the order book dynamics. The order book represents the supply and demand at various price levels and is a fundamental component of market structure. Simulating the order book requires detailed data on order flow, including the submission, modification, and cancellation of orders. This data allows the construction of a realistic order book, including the spread, depth, and liquidity at different prices.

Liquidity simulation is also paramount, as liquidity impacts the execution of trades and the overall strategy performance. A simulated environment must account for varying liquidity levels throughout the trading day, different trading venues, and market conditions. Realistic liquidity modeling helps in assessing the potential slippage and the ability of the strategy to find counterparties for trades without significant market impact.

Transaction costs and market impact can significantly influence the profitability of HFT strategies. Including these elements in simulations ensures that backtests reflect the real costs of trading. Transaction costs encompass commissions, fees, and other costs associated with executing trades, while market impact refers to the effect that executing a trade has on the price of the asset. Accurately modeling these factors involves analyzing historical transaction cost data and incorporating models that estimate the price impact of various order sizes and execution speeds.

Incorporating these elements into market simulations allows traders to stress test their strategies under realistic conditions. By doing so, they can identify strengths, weaknesses, and areas for improvement. This comprehensive approach ensures that strategies are not only theoretically sound but also practical and resilient in real market environments.

Simulation accuracy can be further enhanced by adopting advanced techniques such as machine learning and artificial intelligence, which can model complex market behaviors and predict future price movements. Techniques like reinforcement learning enable the development of adaptive strategies that continuously improve as they interact with the simulated market.

Ultimately, robust market simulation frameworks are indispensable in the development and refinement of high-frequency trading strategies. By closely mimicking the real market and incorporating critical factors such as liquidity, order book dynamics, transaction costs, and market impact, traders can gain a realistic assessment of their strategies' viability and readiness for live deployment.

Through diligent and thorough market simulation, traders are well-equipped to navigate the intricate and fast-paced world of high-frequency trading, fostering confidence and precision in their trading decisions.

10.6 Testing HFT Strategies

In high-frequency trading, the efficacy of any trading strategy is contingent upon rigorous testing. This process helps in identifying the strengths and weaknesses of a strategy before it is deployed in live market conditions. Testing HFT strategies requires a combination of precise data, advanced algorithms, and robust backtesting frameworks to simulate market conditions and gauge the projected performance.

The initial step in testing any HFT strategy is to clearly define the rules and logic that the strategy will follow. This includes specifying entry and exit points, order types, risk management protocols, and other factors that influence decision-making. Once the strategy is clearly defined, it needs to be encoded into an algorithm that can execute trades based on these rules without human intervention.

Given the speed and volume characteristic of HFT, it is imperative that the algorithm operates with minimal latency. High-frequency traders often employ co-located servers and optimized code to ensure that the trading logic is executed as swiftly as possible. In HFT, even microsecond delays can lead to significant differences in trade execution and profitability.

After coding the algorithm, the next phase involves subjecting the strategy to backtesting against historical market data. High-quality, granular data is essential here to accurately replicate market conditions. The dataset should include high-resolution information with tick-level data to capture every potential event that could impact the strategy's performance. The backtesting process typically involves running the algorithm through a historical data series to observe how it would have performed under past market conditions.

To enhance the robustness of testing, strategies should be evaluated across different market environments. For instance, a strategy should be tested in periods of high volatility, low volatility, bull markets, and bear markets. This breadth of testing helps in understanding how the strategy might perform in various future scenarios.

When conducting backtests, several key performance metrics need to be analyzed, including:

- **Profit and Loss (P&L):** Evaluate the overall profitability of the strategy. This includes considering the net profit or loss that would have been realized.

- **Sharpe Ratio:** Measure the strategy's risk-adjusted return. A higher Sharpe ratio indicates better performance on a risk-adjusted basis.

- **Drawdown:** Assess the maximum peak-to-trough decline experienced by the strategy. Lower drawdowns are typically preferable, indicating less risk of substantial losses.

- **Win Rate:** Calculate the percentage of winning trades versus losing trades. A higher win rate is indicative of the strategy's ability to predict correct market moves.

- **Execution Speed and Slippage:** Account for the time taken to execute trades and any differences between expected and actual trade prices.

Emphasis should also be placed on stress testing the strategy under extreme market conditions—such as flash crashes or sudden market surges. This can help uncover vulnerabilities that may not be apparent in normal market conditions.

A critical part of the testing phase is validating the strategy's performance through out-of-sample testing. This involves using a dataset that was not part of the initial backtest to ensure that the strategy has not been overfitted to the historical data. Overfitting occurs when a strategy is too closely tailored to past data and fails to perform in varying future conditions. A successful out-of-sample test indicates a higher likelihood of real-world applicability.

Furthermore, it's essential to conduct a walk-forward analysis, a more advanced method where the strategy is periodically re-optimized and re-tested on new data. This process helps to maintain the relevance of the strategy as market conditions evolve over time.

Testing HFT strategies is an iterative process. Based on test results, strategies may need to be refined or adjusted to improve performance. This iterative refinement continues until the strategy demonstrates consistent profitability and robustness across different market conditions and datasets.

Ultimately, the goal of testing HFT strategies is to ensure that they can deliver consistent and reliable performance in live trading scenarios. Rigorous testing helps in mitigating risks, optimizing trades, and maximizing returns, providing a solid foundation for successful high-frequency trading operations.

10.7 Analyzing Backtest Results

Analyzing backtest results is a pivotal step in high-frequency trading strategy development. It provides valuable insights into the performance, robustness, and potential profitability of a trading strategy before deploying it in live markets. To ensure a thorough and effective analysis, it is essential to focus on a set of key metrics and methodologies that allow for a comprehensive evaluation.

1. Performance Metrics

A critical aspect of analyzing backtest results involves scrutinizing various performance metrics that provide an overview of the strategy's effectiveness. Some of the most important performance metrics include:

- **Cumulative Returns**: The total return generated by the strategy over the backtesting period. This metric helps in understanding the overall profitability.

- **Annualized Return**: The geometric average amount of money earned by an investment each year over a given time period. Calculated as:

$$\text{Annualized Return} = \left(\frac{P_{\text{end}}}{P_{\text{start}}}\right)^{\frac{1}{T}} - 1$$

where P_{end} and P_{start} are the portfolio values at the end and start of the period, and T is the number of years.

- **Sharpe Ratio**: This measures the risk-adjusted return of the strategy. It is calculated by:

$$\text{Sharpe Ratio} = \frac{R_p - R_f}{\sigma_p}$$

where R_p is the return of the portfolio, R_f is the risk-free rate, and σ_p is the standard deviation of the portfolio returns.

- **Max Drawdown**: This indicates the maximum observed loss from a peak to a trough during the backtesting period and is defined as:

$$\text{Max Drawdown} = \frac{\text{Peak Value} - \text{Trough Value}}{\text{Peak Value}}$$

- **Sortino Ratio**: Similar to the Sharpe Ratio, but it only considers downside volatility, which can provide a more accurate risk-adjusted return. Calculated as:

$$\text{Sortino Ratio} = \frac{R_p - R_f}{\sigma_d}$$

where σ_d is the standard deviation of the negative asset returns.

- **Alpha and Beta**: Alpha measures the strategy's performance relative to a benchmark, while Beta measures the strategy's volatility compared to the market. They are given by:

$$\text{Alpha} = R_p - (R_f + \beta(R_m - R_f))$$

$$\beta = \frac{\text{Cov}(R_p, R_m)}{\sigma_m^2}$$

where R_m is the return of the market, and σ_m is the standard deviation of the market return.

2. Analyzing Trade Details

An in-depth analysis of individual trades executed by the strategy can uncover critical patterns and anomalies that might not be evident from aggregate performance metrics alone. Key points of analysis include:

- **Win Rate**: The percentage of trades that were profitable. High-frequency strategies often rely on a high win rate to ensure profitability.
- **Average Profit and Loss (P&L)**: The average gain or loss per trade. This helps in understanding the trade-off between win rate and the size of profits or losses.
- **Trade Duration**: The average holding period of trades helps in assessing the strategy's responsiveness to market changes.
- **Slippage and Transaction Costs**: Calculating the impact of slippage (the difference between the expected and actual trade prices) and transaction costs is crucial as they can significantly affect net returns.

3. Distribution Analysis

Analyzing the distribution of returns provides insight into the strategy's risk profile and stability. Metrics to consider include:

- **Return Distribution**: Assessing the frequency of returns within different ranges can indicate the presence of fat tails or skewness in the return distribution.
- **Risk of Ruin**: Estimating the probability that the strategy will lead to significant losses, potentially depleting the portfolio. This is particularly important for high-frequency strategies to ensure sustainability.

4. Sensitivity Analysis

Conducting a sensitivity analysis can help in understanding how changes in assumptions or input parameters affect the strategy's performance. This involves varying key parameters such as:

- **Entry and Exit Criteria**: Altering the conditions under which trades are entered or exited and observing the impact on performance.
- **Execution Latency**: Simulating different levels of latency to see how execution speed affects profitability.
- **Market Impact**: Considering different scenarios for market impact costs, which occur when large orders affect the market price.

5. Visualizing Results

Graphical representations can make it easier to interpret complex backtest results. Common visualizations include:

- **Equity Curve**: A graph of the strategy's equity value over time, typically a cumulative P&L chart.
- **Drawdown Curve**: Charts the drawdowns over time, helping to visualize periods of significant loss.
- **Scatter Plot of Trades**: Displays individual trades on a risk-return matrix, helping to identify outliers or clusters of winning or losing trades.

By combining these methodologies and metrics, traders can gain a robust understanding of their high-frequency trading strategy's potential effectiveness and inherent risks. A meticulous analysis of backtest results ensures that only strategies with a high probability of success, reasonable risk levels, and realistic assumptions are considered for live trading. This comprehensive approach to result analysis builds confidence in the robustness of the developed strategies, ultimately paving the way for optimization and real-world application.

10.8 Pitfalls and Limitations of Backtesting

While backtesting is an essential tool for evaluating and refining trading strategies, it is not without its pitfalls and limitations. Overlooking these limitations can lead to overly optimistic expectations and significant financial losses. Understanding these pitfalls not only prepares traders to handle the challenges but also helps in designing more robust strategies.

One major pitfall in backtesting is the problem of overfitting. Overfitting occurs when a strategy is excessively tailored to the historical data, capturing noise rather than genuine market signals. This can result in a strategy that performs remarkably well in backtesting but fails in real-time trading. Overfitting can be detected by using techniques such as cross-validation, where the data is split into training and test sets to evaluate the strategy's performance on out-of-sample data. However, even with cross-validation, there is a risk of subtle overfitting, especially when multiple strategies are tested on the same dataset.

Another limitation is survivorship bias, which occurs when the dataset used for backtesting only includes assets that have survived until the end of the dataset period. This can create an unrealistic picture of performance, as it ignores assets that may have been delisted or gone bankrupt. To mitigate survivorship bias, it is important to use data that includes delisted securities and to understand the historical context of the assets in the dataset.

Data snooping or look-ahead bias is also a common issue in backtesting. This occurs when future information is inadvertently used to make decisions at earlier points in the backtest. For instance, if a strategy makes trading decisions based on end-of-day prices that were not available at the time the trade was supposed to be executed, this can artificially inflate performance. Ensuring proper alignment of data and using only information that would have been available at the time of the trade can help avoid look-ahead bias.

Market impact and transaction costs are often underestimated or ignored in backtesting. In real trading, executing large orders can impact the market price of the asset, a factor that is usually not accounted for in a backtest. Additionally, transaction costs, including commissions, slippage, and bid-ask spreads, can significantly erode the profitability of a strategy. Accurate modeling of these factors is crucial for a realistic assessment of a strategy's performance. This can involve incorporating historical transaction cost data and estimating market impact based on the order size relative to market liquidity.

The historical data itself can also pose limitations. Data quality is paramount, as inaccurate or incomplete data can lead to unreliable backtest results. Missing data, bad ticks, and incorrect corporate actions adjustments can all distort the backtest. High-quality data from reputable providers, along with thorough preprocessing and data cleaning, are essential for reliable backtesting.

Changing market conditions present another challenge. A strategy that performed well in historical periods characterized by specific market behaviors may not perform well in future periods with different dynamics. Market regimes can shift due to macroeconomic changes, regulatory developments, or technological advancements. Therefore, it's important to test strategies across different market cycles and to be cautious about extrapolating past performance into the future.

Moreover, the psychological aspect of trading is not captured in backtests. Real trading involves emotional responses to market movements, which can affect decision-making. Strategies that seem sound during backtesting may not be executed with the same precision in live trading due to human factors.

Backtesting also does not account for the operational and technological risks associated with live trading. Issues such as latency, system failures, and order execution problems can arise in real-time trading but are not typically simulated in backtests.

Despite these limitations, backtesting remains a valuable tool when used appropriately. By being aware of these pitfalls and taking steps to mitigate them, traders can develop more realistic expectations and build more robust trading strategies. The integration of robust statistical techniques, careful data handling, and thorough validation procedures are critical for effective backtesting practices.

10.9 Enhancing Simulation Accuracy

In the domain of high-frequency trading (HFT), simulation accuracy is paramount to the development and refinement of successful trading strategies. The precision of a simulation can directly impact the reliability of the backtesting results and, consequently, the performance of the trading strategy in live market conditions. To this end, enhancing simulation accuracy involves addressing several key components: data fidelity, latency modeling, order book dynamics, and execution quality.

First and foremost, the cornerstone of any accurate simulation is high-quality historical data. Reliable high-fidelity tick data for every asset traded is essential. This data should include all trades and quotes, time-stamped at the finest resolution available (typically in nanoseconds). Tick data provides granular insights into market behavior, allowing traders to accurately replicate past market conditions. The fidelity of this data must extend to include information on market microstructure elements such as bid-ask spreads, trading volumes, and market participant behaviors. Therefore, using comprehensive datasets from reputable sources can substantially enhance the reliability of your simulations.

> **Example:** Suppose you are backtesting a strategy for trading the S&P 500 E-mini futures. Ensure that your tick data includes all bid and ask prices and sizes, as well as trade prices and volumes, for each trade that took place during your backtest period. This level of detail will help ensure

that your simulations accurately reproduce the historical trading environment.

Another critical aspect of enhancing simulation accuracy is the precise modeling of latency. Latency refers to the delay between the initiation of a trade order and its execution in the market. Within the hyper-competitive realm of HFT, even microsecond discrepancies can lead to significant trade execution differences. To this end, simulating network latencies, order processing delays, and communications lags with high precision is essential. These can be modeled using statistical distributions derived from empirical measurements of network performance between trading systems and exchanges.

Order book dynamics are another critical factor. The order book represents the available buy and sell orders at various price levels and significantly influences execution and price movements in the market. Accurate simulation thus requires a dynamic order book model that adjusts in real-time based on market events and trading activities. This could involve simulating other market participants' behaviors, liquidity availability, and the impact of large orders. Advanced modeling techniques such as agent-based modeling or econometric modeling can further refine order book simulations.

Moreover, the execution quality within the simulation is equally vital. This involves modeling slippage—the difference between the expected price of a trade and the price at which it is executed. Slippage can substantially affect the performance of a trading strategy, especially in high-frequency domains where large volumes of trades are executed within short time frames. Ensuring that your simulation environment accurately accounts for slippage and market impact will lead to more reliable backtesting results. For instance, placing market orders within your backtesting framework should reflect the real-world impact on the order book and subsequent price adjustments.

> **Tip:** Enhance execution modeling by incorporating realistic market impact models. These models predict how your trades will affect market prices, accounting for factors such as trade size and market liquidity. Integrating these models into your simulations can provide a more accurate representation of trading performance.

In addition to these technical enhancements, rigorous validation practices play a crucial role in simulation accuracy. Continuously validate your simulation outputs against real market behavior. This involves comparing simulated trading outcomes with actual historical trades to identify and rectify discrepancies. Subjecting your simulations to extensive stress testing under various market conditions, including periods of high volatility and low liquidity, can uncover potential flaws and further refine your models.

Ultimately, enhancing simulation accuracy is a continuous and iterative process that necessitates meticulous attention to detail and constant refinement. By leveraging high-quality data, precise latency models, dynamic order book simulations, and accurate execution modeling, traders can develop more reliable HFT strategies. Such rigorous simulation practices not only improve the robustness of trading strategies but also instill greater confidence in their deployment in live market environments.

10.10 Case Studies: Successful Backtesting in HFT

In the world of High-Frequency Trading (HFT), the rigorous testing and validation of trading strategies through backtesting are paramount. This section delves into several case studies of successful backtesting endeavors, shedding light on how robust frameworks and meticulous analysis lead to effective HFT strategies. These real-world examples highlight the practical application of backtesting concepts and provide insights into how traders can harness historical data to predict future performance.

One notable case study involves a proprietary trading firm that specializes in statistical arbitrage. The firm's strategy was based on exploiting pricing inefficiencies between correlated financial instruments. The traders identified a spread trading opportunity between two exchange-traded funds (ETFs) that tracked closely related indices. To ensure the strategy's viability, the firm embarked on a comprehensive backtesting exercise.

The backtesting framework was designed to replicate the firm's trading environment as accurately as possible. They collected minute-by-minute historical data for both ETFs over a five-year period. This granularity of data was crucial to capturing the high-frequency nature of their trades. The backtest not only included the primary price data but also incorporated detailed transaction costs, slippage, and latency effects.

Using Python and a well-optimized backtesting engine, the firm ran simulations to evaluate the historical performance of their strategy. The initial results were promising, showing a consistent alpha over the test period. However, the traders noticed occasional periods of significant drawdowns, prompting further investigation.

To address these issues, the firm adjusted its strategy parameters and incorporated more refined risk management rules. They implemented stop-loss levels and diversified the trade initiation times to reduce the likelihood of correlated market stress affecting their positions. After these adjustments, the enhanced backtesting results exhibited reduced drawdowns and an improved Sharpe ratio.

Another intriguing example comes from a quantitative hedge fund focusing on market making in the foreign exchange (Forex) markets. Their strategy revolved around providing liquidity by quoting bid and ask prices, benefiting from the bid-ask spread. For backtesting, the fund utilized a highly sophisticated simulation environment that mimicked the market microstructure intricately.

The firm's approach to backtesting required massive computing power, given the need to process vast amounts of tick data. They leveraged distributed computing resources and parallel processing to expedite the simulations. The backtests considered various trading scenarios, incorporating random market shocks and varying liquidity conditions to stress-test the strategy's robustness.

The outcome of this meticulous backtesting was a market-making algorithm that showed resilience across different market conditions. The fund's strategy consistently generated profits while maintaining tight spreads and low inventory risk. Furthermore, the backtesting enabled the identification of specific times of day when the strategy performed suboptimally, allowing the traders to fine-tune their trading schedules accordingly.

A final case study explores the development of a momentum-based HFT strategy by an academic research group. The strategy capitalized on short-term price movements driven by investor reactions to news events. The researchers gathered a vast dataset of historical price and volume information, alongside a comprehensive repository of news headlines and sentiment analysis scores.

The backtesting process involved integrating the sentiment scores with their trading signals. By analyzing the sentiment data in conjunction with price movements, the researchers aimed to predict short-term trends more accurately. Their backtesting framework was built in R, with custom scripts to parse news data and align it with the corresponding price action.

Through iterative testing and refinement, the researchers discovered that positive sentiment correlated strongly with upward price momentum in the short term. They adjusted their trading strategy to act on these signals with a high degree of responsiveness. The backtest results demonstrated a high hit rate for profitable trades, although the researchers remained cautious of overfitting their model to historical data.

These case studies illustrate the critical role of thorough backtesting in the success of HFT strategies. By leveraging detailed historical data, sophisticated simulation environments, and iterative analysis, traders can develop and validate strategies that stand the test of time. The real-world applications showcased here provide invaluable lessons for aspiring HFT practitioners, emphasizing the importance of meticulous preparation and continuous improvement.

Chapter 11

Ethical Considerations in High-Frequency Trading

This chapter examines the ethical considerations inherent to High-Frequency Trading (HFT). It discusses the ethical implications of market manipulation and the importance of fairness and market integrity. The chapter addresses issues of transparency, disclosure, and potential conflicts of interest. It explores the impact of HFT on small investors and the regulatory and ethical standards designed to ensure market fairness. Case studies of ethical dilemmas in HFT provide practical context, and the chapter concludes with the development of an ethical framework for guiding HFT practices and future industry directions.

11.1 Overview of Ethical Considerations in HFT

High-Frequency Trading (HFT) represents a paradigm shift in financial markets, driven by sophisticated algorithms and advanced technology. These developments facilitate trading at speeds and volumes unimaginable a few decades ago. As HFT rapidly evolves, it prompts a re-examination of ethical considerations within the financial markets. Ethical considerations in HFT are multi-faceted, encompassing fairness, market integrity, transparency, disclosure, and potential conflicts of interest. This section provides a comprehensive overview, setting the stage for more detailed analyses in subsequent sections.

HFT's foundation lies in using complex computer algorithms to execute orders at exceptionally high speeds. This lightning-fast execution can provide HFT firms with a competitive edge, but it also raises questions about fairness. The ethical debate centers on whether HFT creates an uneven playing field where those with access to cutting-edge technology can consistently outmaneuver traditional investors, leading to a system of haves and have-nots.

Fairness in HFT also extends to market integrity. Market integrity is premised on the idea that markets should operate in a manner that is fair and equitable to all participants. The activities of HFT firms, such as exploiting milliseconds of latency, may erode this integrity by allowing some traders to influence prices to their advantage, often unbeknownst to other market participants. This is particularly problematic given the sheer volume of trades executed by HFT systems, potentially leading to significant price distortions.

Transparency and disclosure are crucial ethical tenets that underpin trust in financial markets. HFT strategies are often opaque, with firms guarding their algorithms and strategies closely. This lack of transparency can prevent regulators and the general trading public from fully understanding the impact of HFT on market dynamics. Ethical practice in HFT would call for greater transparency to ensure that the actions of HFT firms do not undermine market confidence.

Conflicts of interest are another significant ethical consideration. HFT firms often rely on complex relationships with exchanges and other market participants. These relationships can occasionally lead to situations where an HFT firm's duty to its clients may conflict with its proprietary trading activities. Ethical trading necessitates robust mechanisms to identify and mitigate these conflicts, ensuring that the interests of all parties are fairly represented.

The impact of HFT on small investors cannot be understated. Small investors often lack the technological resources to compete with HFT firms, potentially placing them at a disadvantage. The ethical question here revolves around whether the benefits that HFT brings to market liquidity and efficiency outweigh the potential harm to less technologically sophisticated investors.

Regulators play a pivotal role in enforcing ethical standards in HFT. Existing regulatory frameworks strive to balance the innovation and efficiency gains brought by HFT with the need to protect market participants from unethical practices. This often involves scrutinizing the conduct of HFT firms, ensuring compliance with regulations designed to uphold market fairness and integrity.

Case studies provide tangible examples of the ethical dilemmas faced within the HFT landscape. These real-world scenarios highlight the complexities and consequences of ethical lapses, illustrating how actions taken by HFT firms can ripple through the market ecosystem, affecting various stakeholders.

As we proceed to develop an ethical framework for guiding HFT practices, it is essential to integrate these diverse considerations into a cohesive strategy. This framework will seek to balance the innovation and efficiency of HFT with the imperatives of fairness, transparency, and market integrity. It will also provide a roadmap for future industry practices, promoting an ethical culture that can sustainably support the continued evolution of high-frequency trading.

Without explicitly concluding, it becomes clear that a thorough understanding of these multifaceted ethical issues is vital for anyone participating in or regulating the HFT arena. The ongoing advancement of trading technologies necessitates a continuous re-evaluation of ethical standards to ensure that the markets function in a manner that is equitable for all participants.

11.2 Ethical Implications of Market Manipulation

The evolution of High-Frequency Trading (HFT) has significantly transformed financial markets, introducing unprecedented velocity and precision to trade execution. However, with these advancements arise pressing ethical concerns, particularly around market manipulation. Market manipulation refers to strategies or actions that deliberately interfere with the free and fair operation of the market, often to the detriment of other participants. In the context of HFT, such practices can undermine market integrity, erode investor trust, and lead to unequal playing fields.

One primary form of market manipulation in HFT is *quote stuffing*, where traders rapidly place and cancel large volumes of orders to congest the order books and create latency. This deliberate cluttering can deceive other market participants into forming misled perceptions of market demand and supply, often forcing them to react based on false information. While quote stuffing can be highly profitable for the initiators, it engenders an environment of distrust and inefficiency, contravening the ethical principles of transparency and fairness.

Another manipulative tactic is *layering* or *spoofing*. Spoofing involves placing orders with no intention of executing them; the goal is to create a misleading appearance of market depth or momentum. For instance, a high-frequency trader might place a large buy order to inflate the perceived demand, encouraging others to raise their bid prices. Subsequently, the trader cancels their buy order and sells at the artificially elevated price. This practice exploits slower traders who fall prey to the artificial signals, raising critical ethical and regulatory questions regarding market fairness and true price discovery.

$$\text{Market Manipulation}_{\text{net effect}} = \frac{\text{Artificial volume impact}}{\text{Genuine market activity}}$$

This formula, albeit simple, illustrates the detrimental ratio of artificial volume to true trades, highlighting the erosion of genuine liquidity when manipulative practices prevail.

The ethical implications of these HFT strategies extend beyond individual transactions. They impact the broader market ecosystem, leading to increased volatility and unpredictability, which disproportionately affects small investors. These investors, often lacking the sophisticated tools and sub-millisecond reaction times of HFT firms, are disadvantaged, exacerbating the divide between institutional and retail investors. As a result, market manipulation through HFT can perpetuate a cycle wherein confidence in market fairness is eroded, deterring broader participation.

Consider the role of regulatory bodies such as the Securities and Exchange Commission (SEC) in mitigating market manipulation. While regulations exist to curb such practices, enforcing them in the high-speed, data-rich environment of HFT poses a significant challenge. The ethical responsibility thus falls on HFT practitioners to adhere to a moral code that respects market fairness over deceptive profits.

Apropos the principle of *utilitarianism*, which emphasizes the greatest good for the greatest number, market manipulation by a few undermines the collective welfare of the market participants. It is essential to recognize that while certain HFT tactics may not always breach legal boundaries, they nonetheless cross ethical ones. The distinction between legality and ethicality must be appreciated and rigorously maintained by traders and firms that prioritize long-term market sustainability over short-term gains.

Ultimately, tackling the ethical implications of market manipulation demands a multifaceted approach. It includes stringent regulatory oversight, robust internal compliance cultures within HFT firms, and the cultivation of ethical awareness among practitioners. By actively discouraging manipulative tactics and fostering a commitment to ethical trading, the integrity and fairness of financial markets can be preserved for all participants.

11.3 Fairness and Market Integrity

The concept of fairness and market integrity lies at the very heart of financial markets, embodying the principles that ensure all participants operate on a level playing field. In the context of High-Frequency Trading (HFT), fairness pertains to ensuring that no trader or institution can gain an undue advantage over others through unethical practices or exploitation of technological disparities. Market integrity, meanwhile, refers to the trustworthiness and reliability of the market structure, ensuring that it operates efficiently and transparently, reflecting genuine supply and demand without distortions.

High-Frequency Trading, characterized by its reliance on advanced algorithms and low-latency infrastructure, raises several pivotal questions concerning fairness. One critical issue is the latency advantage that HFT firms possess over traditional or retail investors. These firms invest significant resources into technology that allows them to execute trades in microseconds, capitalizing on minute price differentials that are imperceptible to slower participants. This creates a scenario where the playing field is ostensibly tilted in favor of those who can afford such advancements.

To elucidate this, consider the following simplified model illustrating the temporal advantage of HFT firms:

$$T_{\text{execution}} = T_{\text{decision}} + T_{\text{communication}} + T_{\text{processing}}$$

In this equation, $T_{\text{execution}}$ represents the total time taken for a trade to be executed. For High-Frequency Traders:

$$T_{\text{execution, HFT}} \approx \text{microseconds}$$

For traditional traders:

$$T_{\text{execution, traditional}} \approx \text{milliseconds}$$

Even a disparity measured in milliseconds can lead to significant differences in trading outcomes, as HFT firms can exploit market inefficiencies before traditional traders even receive the same information. This introduces an element of asymmetry, potentially undermining the foundational notion of market fairness.

Another facet of fairness in the realm of HFT is the practice of "quote stuffing," where traders place a flurry of orders at various price levels to create congestion and temporarily slow down the processing speed of competitors' systems. This tactic not only impacts the transparency and smooth operation of the market but also skews the price discovery process. Regulatory bodies have increasingly scrutinized such practices, as they can be deemed manipulative and contrary to fair trading principles.

Consider the formulaic representation of the order placement and cancellation strategy in quote stuffing:

$$N(t) = N_0 \cdot e^{-\lambda t}$$

Here, $N(t)$ is the number of orders remaining after time t, N_0 is the initial number of orders placed, and λ is the rate at which these orders are canceled. The rapid placement and subsequent cancellation of a large volume of orders can create artificial volatility and confuse market participants, again challenging the integrity of the marketplace.

To mitigate these concerns, exchanges and regulatory bodies have implemented measures aimed at leveling the playing field. For instance, some exchanges have introduced speed bumps or random delays, designed to reduce the latency advantage that HFT firms exploit. The inclusion of "minimum resting times" for orders — wherein an order must remain open for a set period before it can be canceled — helps curb quote stuffing and ensures that the market reflects genuine trading interest.

Market integrity hinges not only on technological fairness but also on the assurance that market outcomes are representative of true economic conditions and investor intentions. This necessitates robust regulatory frameworks that can adapt to the evolving landscape of HFT. Regular audits, surveillance mechanisms, and stringent penalties for malpractices are vital components of such frameworks.

One effective regulatory measure involves the mandatory reporting and transparent disclosure of trading algorithms and strategies. By understanding the mechanisms that drive HFT activities, regulators can more effectively detect and curb manipulative practices. Additionally, promoting transparency in order execution quality and transaction costs encourages fairness, as it enables market participants to make more informed decisions.

The role of self-regulatory organizations (SROs) also cannot be understated. These bodies, comprising market participants themselves, can establish and enforce ethical standards that enhance both fairness and integrity. Through peer-review processes and adherence to a code of conduct, SROs can foster a more equitable trading environment.

Ultimately, the pursuit of fairness and market integrity in HFT is a multifaceted endeavor, requiring the alignment of technological, regulatory, and ethical considerations. By addressing the inherent disparities introduced by high-frequency strategies and ensuring that all market participants can operate under fair conditions, we uphold the trust and stability integral to the functioning of financial markets. As the trading landscape continues to evolve, ongoing vigilance and adaptive regulatory practices will be essential to sustaining these core principles.

11.4 Transparency and Disclosure

Transparency and disclosure are critical components in maintaining the integrity and trustworthiness of financial markets, especially in the context of High-Frequency Trading (HFT). The rapid pace and complex algorithms that characterize HFT can obscure trading strategies and intentions, making it imperative to enhance visibility into these operations to protect market participants.

At its core, transparency in HFT involves the clear and open reporting of trading activities, algorithms, and the logic underpinning trading decisions. This openness helps mitigate the perception of an uneven playing field where only those with access to advanced technology and proprietary knowledge can thrive. It is crucial for regulators, market participants, and the public to comprehend the workings of HFT to ensure a fair and equitable trading environment.

Transparency measures can be broadly categorized into pre-trade and post-trade transparency. Pre-trade transparency involves providing information on the orders present in the market before they are executed. This may include the volumes and prices of orders submitted to the market. Implementing pre-trade transparency in HFT can be challenging due to the sheer volume and speed of order submissions, but it is essential to ensure fair price discovery and market integrity.

Post-trade transparency, on the other hand, involves the disclosure of details about executed trades. This includes information such as the price, volume, and time of trades, published in real-time or near-real-time. Post-trade transparency helps in providing a clear picture of the market's supply and demand dynamics, which is indispensable for both market participants and regulators in monitoring trading behavior and market trends.

Trade ID	Execution Time	Trade Volume (Shares)
123456	09:30:01	10,000
123457	09:30:02	15,000
...	...	...

Table 11.1: Sample Trade Data

Transparency must also extend to the algorithms used in HFT. Regulators often face a considerable challenge in requiring firms to disclose proprietary algorithms without risking the exposure of intellectual property. To strike a balance, firms might be required to submit detailed documentation of their algorithmic strategies under confidentiality agreements, ensuring that regulators can assess the fairness and potential market impact without making sensitive information public.

Disclosure involves the onus on HFT firms to proactively release information regarding their trading activities and strategies. This includes the rationale behind specific algorithms, the sources of data used, and any material changes to their trading systems. Adequately disclosing such details aids in understanding and monitoring the risks associated with HFT strategies, thereby fostering a safer trading environment.

Further complications in the landscape of HFT transparency and disclosure arise due to dark pools—private exchanges where trading volumes are not displayed publicly. HFT in dark pools can significantly impact price discovery and market liquidity, posing substantial transparency challenges. Ensuring appropriate disclosure from these private venues is critical to maintaining overall market transparency.

Transparency and disclosure are also pivotal in addressing potential conflicts of interest that may arise within HFT firms or between HFT firms and other market participants. For example, clear disclosures can illuminate instances where an HFT firm may have a dual role, such as a market maker and a proprietary trader, which could lead to preferential treatment or market manipulation. Ensuring these activities are transparent allows for greater scrutiny and holds firms accountable to ethical standards.

The benefits of enhancing transparency and disclosure in HFT can be considerable. Firstly, they promote a more level playing field, allowing investors—regardless of their technological capability—to access and understand market conditions more equitably. Secondly, transparency deters unethical behavior by exposing malpractices to public and regulatory scrutiny, thus fostering a culture of ethical trading.

Practical steps toward enhanced transparency might include the implementation of standardized reporting requirements for HFT activities, mandating real-time trade reporting, and developing robust mechanisms for the continuous monitoring and auditing of HFT algorithms. Policymakers and regulators must work in conjunction with market participants to develop these standards, ensuring they are technologically feasible and do not stifle innovation within the industry.

As the landscape of HFT continues to evolve, the principles of transparency and disclosure will remain foundational to maintaining market integrity and investor confidence. By fostering an environment where trading activities are visible and comprehensible, the market can function more efficiently, equitably, and ethically.

Transparency and disclosure are thus not merely regulatory requirements but fundamental tenets that sustain the trust and smooth operation of financial markets in the high-speed era of HFT. Properly implemented, these measures will support a healthier market ecosystem where all participants can thrive and compete on a fair and informed basis.

11.5 Conflicts of Interest

Conflicts of interest are a pivotal concern in the realm of High-Frequency Trading (HFT) and warrant careful examination to ensure that trading practices adhere to ethical standards and promote market integrity. Such conflicts can arise when the professional responsibilities of individuals or firms overlap with their personal interests, potentially leading to decisions that benefit themselves at the expense of clients or the broader market. Understanding the various dimensions of these conflicts is essential for developing robust strategies to mitigate their impact.

In the context of HFT, conflicts of interest can manifest in several ways. One prevalent issue is the dual role of market makers who also engage in proprietary trading. Market makers are responsible for providing liquidity to the market by continuously quoting buy and sell prices for securities. However, when these same entities engage in proprietary trading, where they trade on their own account, a conflict arises. The concern is that proprietary trading activities could be prioritized over market-making obligations, leading to a deterioration in market quality and disadvantaging other market participants.

Consider the scenario where a firm operates both as a market maker and a proprietary trader. The firm could, in theory, execute trades based on superior market information gained through its market-making activities, thereby securing an unjust advantage. This practice, often referred to as front-running, is ethically questionable and undermines fairness. Front-running can erode trust in the financial markets, as other investors may feel they are trading on an uneven playing field.

Another conflict of interest in HFT is related to the use of dark pools. Dark pools are private trading venues where large orders can be executed without exposing the trade intentions to the public market. While they provide benefits such as reduced market impact, dark pools can also harbor conflicts of interest, especially when operated by firms that also participate in the public markets. There is a potential for these firms to use the information gleaned from dark pool trades to inform their HFT strategies, thus generating profits at the expense of the clients using the dark pools.

Furthermore, latency arbitrage presents another significant conflict of interest in HFT. Latency arbitrage involves exploiting small time differences in the release of market data. HFT firms with superior technology and faster data feeds can detect and act on price changes more quickly than their slower counterparts, capturing profits from these latency discrepancies. The ethical issue arises when these firms possess better data or infrastructure not due to fairness of competition but because they have preferential access. This situation questions the fairness of the market, as it privileges those with better resources over ordinary investors.

To illustrate, imagine an HFT firm with privileged access to market data through contractual agreements with exchanges. This firm can react to market-moving news milliseconds before the broader market becomes aware. While not illegal, this practice raises ethical concerns about equal access to information. It also exacerbates inequality among market participants, creating an environment where small investors are structurally disadvantaged.

Addressing these conflicts of interest requires a multi-faceted approach. Regulatory frameworks play a crucial role in establishing standards for fair conduct. For instance, regulations might mandate the separation of market-making and proprietary trading activities to prevent conflicts in dual-role firms. Enhanced transparency in reporting activities and order execution can also mitigate conflicts. By requiring detailed disclosure of trading activities, regulators can monitor for potential abuses and hold firms accountable.

Ethical training and robust internal governance are equally important. Firms must foster a culture of integrity where the interests of clients and market integrity supersede personal or corporate gains. Conflicts of interest should be managed through clear policies and enforced through regular audits to ensure compliance. For example, implementing Chinese walls can guard against improper information flow within a firm, maintaining the separation between market-making and proprietary trading desks.

To conclude, conflicts of interest in High-Frequency Trading present significant ethical challenges that must be diligently addressed to promote fairness and market integrity. Through stringent regulatory oversight, enhanced transparency, and a steadfast commitment to ethical practices, the industry can navigate these conflicts, ensuring that the interests of all market participants are safeguarded. This holistic approach not only fosters trust in financial markets but also underpins their long-term sustainability and growth.

11.6 The Impact of HFT on Small Investors

High-Frequency Trading (HFT) has profoundly transformed market dynamics, and its influence on small investors warrants an in-depth examination. Small investors, often retail traders, can experience both positive and negative impacts due to the velocity and methodology of HFT. This section explores these multifaceted effects, providing a thorough understanding of the interaction between HFT and small investors.

One of the primary benefits that HFT brings to small investors is enhanced liquidity. Due to the rapid buying and selling of securities, HFT firms contribute significantly to the overall trading volume. This liquidity often results in narrower bid-ask spreads, which can be advantageous for small investors by enabling them to transact at more favorable prices. A narrower spread reduces the cost of trading, enhancing the ability of small investors to enter and exit positions with minimal price slippage. The liquidity provided by HFT can also facilitate the swift execution of trades, crucial for implementing various investment strategies effectively.

However, the high-speed environment fostered by HFT poses substantial challenges for small investors. The technological prowess of HFT firms enables them to execute trades in microseconds, placing retail traders at a disadvantage. This discrepancy in speed can lead to issues of adverse selection, where small investors often find themselves executing trades at less favorable prices due to the lag between placing and filling an order. HFT algorithms can detect momentum and price trends, adjusting their strategies swiftly. As a result, small investors might face increased price volatility and difficulty in achieving their desired trade outcomes.

The phenomenon of market fragmentation further complicates the landscape for small investors. HFT firms capitalize on differences in prices across various trading venues, quickly arbitraging inefficiencies. This arbitrage can result in disparate prices for the same security across different platforms, adding complexity to the trading environment for small investors who may not have access to sophisticated tools and real-time data required to navigate these discrepancies effectively. Consequently, the increased complexity and the requirement for advanced trading technologies can act as barriers to entry for small investors, widening the gap between institutional and retail participants.

There are also concerns regarding the potential for HFT to exacerbate market volatility. While HFT contributes to liquidity under normal conditions, its algorithms can also trigger rapid market movements during periods of stress. Flash crashes, although rare, exemplify the abrupt and severe market dislocations caused by HFT activity. Small investors, who typically rely on more stable market environments, might find such episodes particularly detrimental. The swift and significant price swings during flash crashes can lead to unanticipated losses, eroding the confidence of small investors in market stability.

Another aspect to consider is the information asymmetry created by HFT. Due to their advanced technology and access to real-time data, HFT firms often possess superior knowledge about market conditions compared to retail investors. This disparity can result in an uneven playing field where small investors are disadvantaged. For instance, HFT algorithms can analyze order flow and predict near-term price movements, trading ahead of other market participants. This practice, known as front-running, can disadvantage small investors who might end up paying higher prices for their trades.

Despite these challenges, regulatory efforts are underway to level the playing field and protect the interests of small investors. Enhanced transparency measures, such as the implementation of consolidated audit trails, aim to provide regulators and market participants with a comprehensive view of market activity. These measures are designed to detect and deter manipulative practices, ensuring that small investors can transact in a fair and orderly market.

Additionally, the development of better educational resources and trading tools for small investors can mitigate some of the disadvantages they face due to HFT. By improving access to real-time data and executing strategies with greater efficacy, retail investors can enhance their market participation and make more informed decisions. Financial literacy programs are essential in this regard, empowering small investors to comprehend the complexities of modern trading environments and adapt their strategies accordingly.

Ultimately, while HFT presents both opportunities and challenges for small investors, a balanced perspective acknowledges the nuanced interplay of various factors. Enhancing market liquidity, improving trading costs, and fostering rapid execution are undeniable benefits. However, addressing the disadvantages posed by speed disparities, market fragmentation, volatility, and information asymmetry is crucial to ensuring an equitable market for all participants. Continuous regulatory oversight and investment in educational resources will serve as vital components in aligning the interests of HFT firms with those of the broader investor community, particularly small investors who form the backbone of the market ecosystem.

11.7 Regulatory and Ethical Standards

As High-Frequency Trading (HFT) continues to evolve and integrate deeply into global markets, regulatory and ethical standards play a pivotal role in shaping its landscape. These standards ensure that HFT practices promote market integrity, protect investors, and foster a fair trading environment. The regulatory frameworks governing HFT vary by jurisdiction yet share common objectives: transparency, accountability, and prevention of market abuse.

One of the primary goals of regulatory standards in HFT is to enhance transparency. Regulations often require HFT firms to disclose their trading algorithms and strategies to regulatory bodies. This transparency enables regulators to monitor for potential market abuses such as spoofing or layering—practices where traders place large orders with the intent to cancel them to manipulate prices.

Spoofing and *layering* are manipulative tactics that undermine market integrity. Regulatory bodies like the U.S. Securities and Exchange Commission (SEC) and the European Securities and Markets Authority (ESMA) have imposed stringent rules to detect and penalize such activities. For instance, under the Dodd-Frank Act, the Commodity Futures Trading Commission (CFTC) has enhanced its surveillance capabilities to identify and address spoofing.

Accountability mechanisms are integral to maintaining ethical standards in HFT. Regulatory frameworks often mandate the registration of HFT firms and their key personnel. This registry ensures that firms adhere to specific codes of conduct and operational standards. In the U.S., the SEC's Market Access Rule (Rule 15c3-5) requires broker-dealers to implement risk management controls before providing market access to HFT firms. This ensures that trading activities are pre-checked for compliance with regulatory requirements, minimizing the risk of erroneous or manipulative trades.

Moreover, HFT firms must adhere to best execution policies, which aim to achieve the best possible trading results for clients. The European Union's Markets in Financial Instruments Directive II (MiFID II) requires firms to take all sufficient steps to ensure the best execution of trades. This involves considering various factors such as price, costs, speed, and likelihood of execution. By mandating best execution policies, regulators ensure that HFT firms prioritize their clients' interests, thereby contributing to market fairness.

Ethical standards extend beyond mere compliance with regulatory requirements. They encompass a broader commitment to corporate social responsibility and ethical decision-making. HFT firms are encouraged to establish internal codes of conduct that emphasize ethical trading practices, integrity, and professionalism. These codes often include guidelines for responsible innovation, such as ensuring that algorithmic trading strategies do not exploit market inefficiencies to the detriment of other market participants.

Educational initiatives are also a key component of ethical standards. Regulators and industry bodies frequently conduct training programs to raise awareness about ethical trading practices and regulatory compliance. These programs aim to cultivate a culture of integrity within the HFT industry, helping traders and firms internalize ethical principles and apply them in their daily operations.

A robust regulatory and ethical framework not only protects market participants but also enhances overall market confidence. By adhering to stringent standards, HFT firms can mitigate the risks associated with high-speed trading and contribute to a more stable and trustworthy market environment. Market confidence is further reinforced through collaboration between regulators and HFT firms in developing and refining these standards.

In conclusion, regulatory and ethical standards are indispensable in navigating the complex and rapidly evolving world of High-Frequency Trading. These standards ensure that HFT practices are transparent, accountable, and aligned with the broader objectives of market integrity and fairness. As HFT continues to advance, ongoing dialogue between regulators, industry participants, and stakeholders will be crucial in adapting these standards to new challenges and innovations.

11.8 Case Studies in Ethical Dilemmas

Throughout the history of high-frequency trading (HFT), there have been numerous instances where ethical dilemmas have surfaced, challenging the integrity of financial markets. Examining these case studies helps illuminate the complexities inherent in HFT practices and provides valuable insights into the moral and ethical landscape of modern trading. Here, we explore some pivotal case studies that highlight key ethical concerns within HFT.

The first notable case involves the notorious Flash Crash of May 6,

2010. On this day, the U.S. stock market experienced an unprecedented, rapid decline and rebound of around 1,000 points within minutes. Investigations revealed that the event was exacerbated by high-frequency trading algorithms that executed trades at lightning speed, outpacing human traders and traditional institutional investors. The ethical dilemma here revolves around the responsibility of HFT firms to ensure that their algorithms do not inadvertently destabilize the market. While the primary intent of these algorithms is often to identify and exploit momentary price inefficiencies, the potential for unintended consequences that disrupt market operations raises significant ethical questions about the preparedness and robustness of HFT algorithms in volatile conditions.

Another insightful case is the manipulation scandal involving Navinder Singh Sarao, a London-based trader who employed algorithmic trading strategies to spoof the market. Spoofing involves placing large orders with the intent of canceling them before execution to create a false sense of market demand or supply. Sarao's manipulative tactics contributed to the conditions that triggered the Flash Crash and highlighted the thin line between aggressive trading strategies and outright market manipulation. The ethical implications of this case lie in the intent behind trading actions and the broader impact on market fairness and integrity. While aggressive strategies may be legally permissible, manipulations that mislead other market participants violate ethical standards and regulations designed to promote transparent and fair trading environments.

One cannot overlook the ethical quandaries presented by the practices of Renaissance Technologies' Medallion Fund. Known for its extraordinary returns, the fund employs sophisticated HFT strategies and operates with a high degree of secrecy. The ethical considerations here pertain to the fairness of information access and market competition. While the fund's success is attributed to advanced mathematical models and technological supremacy, there are concerns about the potential creation of an uneven playing field. When certain market participants benefit from unparalleled technological resources and data access, it raises questions about equal opportunities in trading and the systemic advantages enjoyed by a select few.

Moreover, the case of the 2014 incident where Virtu Financial disclosed that it had only one trading day loss in six years encapsulates another ethical dimension. This disclosure raised concerns about the inherent risks posed by HFT to market stability and the principles of fair competition. Virtu's near-perfect trading record was achieved through the use of ultra-fast algorithms that could adapt instantly to market changes. Critics argue that such dominance can erode trust in the financial markets, suggesting that the playing field is heavily skewed in favor of firms with superior technology and resources. This scenario underscores the ethical responsibility of HFT firms to consider the broader implications of their practices on market confidence and the principle of fair competition.

Further illustrating ethical dilemmas is the case of Barclays' LX dark pool scandal. Barclays was accused of misleading its customers about the nature of its dark pool and favoring HFT firms within its trading platform. Dark pools are private exchanges where trades are executed away from the public eye, often attracting institutional investors seeking to minimize the market impact of large trades. The ethical breach in this case stemmed from the deceptive practices and lack of transparency towards clients, coupled with conflicts of interest that prioritized certain high-frequency traders. This case highlighted the critical need for disclosure, transparency, and the ethical obligation of financial institutions to uphold the integrity of their representations to all market participants.

Finally, we consider the ethical implications of co-location services offered by stock exchanges. These services allow HFT firms to place their servers physically close to the exchange's servers, reducing latency and giving them significant speed advantages over other traders. The ethical dilemma revolves around the fairness of offering such preferential treatment, which may inherently favor well-resourced HFT firms over smaller investors. Debates continue about whether these practices contribute to market efficiency or skew the market dynamics in favor of wealthier participants, raising important questions about the equitable treatment of all market participants.

Each of these case studies provides a window into the intricate ethical challenges faced by high-frequency traders and regulators alike. By carefully examining these scenarios, we can better understand the moral considerations that must guide HFT practices to ensure a fair, transparent, and equitable financial marketplace. '''

This section delves deeply into various historical and contemporary case studies, illustrating the nuanced ethical dilemmas that come with high-frequency trading. By presenting these cases, it aims to foster a deeper understanding of the ethical landscape and the responsibilities of HFT practitioners to uphold market integrity and fairness.

11.9 Developing an Ethical Framework for HFT

Implementing an effective ethical framework for High-Frequency Trading (HFT) is crucial in ensuring market integrity, fairness, and transparency. Traders, financial institutions, and regulatory bodies must collaboratively establish and enforce guidelines that promote ethical behavior within the rapidly evolving landscape of HFT. This section will outline the fundamental components required to develop a comprehensive ethical framework, emphasizing key principles and actionable strategies.

Ensuring ethical practices in HFT starts with a commitment to transparency. Transparency not only builds trust among market participants but also helps mitigate misconceptions about HFT activities. Financial institutions must provide clear and accessible disclosures regarding their trading algorithms, strategies, and the potential impact on the market. Educating market participants about the nuances of HFT can reduce suspicions and foster a more informed trading environment.

Another cornerstone of the ethical framework is the principle of fairness. Fairness in HFT implies creating an even playing field where no participant can unduly exploit latency advantages or asymmetrical information. This requires stringent monitoring and the implementation of systems that can detect and prevent market manipulation tactics, such as quote stuffing or layering. Employing advanced surveillance technologies can aid in identifying unethical behaviors and ensuring prompt corrective actions.

Conflict of interest is a pressing concern in HFT, where proprietary trading desks and market-making operations may have competing priorities. Establishing clear organizational policies that segregate these functions can prevent potential conflicts. Additionally, rigorous internal audits and compliance checks should be mandated to ensure adherence to ethical guidelines.

The ethical framework must also address the impact of HFT on small investors. High-frequency traders often hold a latency advantage that can potentially disadvantage retail investors. To mitigate this, regulators can explore measures such as implementing speed bumps or adjusted tick sizes, which level the playing field. Moreover, fostering an ecosystem that supports diverse market participants, including retail investors, enhances overall market robustness.

Regulatory compliance is another pivotal aspect of the ethical framework. Adhering to established regulatory standards and proactively engaging with regulatory developments ensure that HFT practices remain within legal boundaries. Continuous dialogue between regulators and industry players can lead to the refinement of rules that are both practical and effective. Firms should also invest in compliance training programs to instill a culture of ethical awareness among employees.

Case studies of ethical breaches in HFT have highlighted the need for effective whistleblowing mechanisms. Implementing secure and confidential channels for reporting unethical behavior without fear of retribution encourages accountability. Protection for whistleblowers underpins a culture of transparency and ethical vigilance.

Establishing an ethical framework is not a one-time effort but an ongoing process that evolves with market dynamics. Regular evaluation and updates of the ethical policies ensure they remain relevant and effective. Encouraging feedback from diverse market participants can provide critical insights for continuous improvement.

Finally, fostering an ethical culture within HFT firms begins with leadership. Senior management must lead by example, emphasizing the importance of ethics and accountability. Establishing a code of ethics that clearly defines expected behaviors and ethical standards sets a foundation for all employees. Incorporating these values into performance evaluations reinforces the significance of ethical conduct.

By integrating these principles into the operations and strategies of HFT firms, the industry can enhance market integrity and maintain public trust. As the market continually adapts to new technologies and methodologies, a robust ethical framework ensures that HFT contributions are aligned with the broader goal of a fair and transparent financial system. This commitment to ethics not only safeguards market participants but also supports the sustainable development of the financial markets.

11.10 Future Directions in Ethical HFT Practices

As we look ahead to the future of High-Frequency Trading (HFT), the evolution of ethical practices within this domain will play a critical role in shaping a fair and robust financial market. Ethical HFT practices are not merely reactive measures; they require forward-thinking strategies and concerted efforts from regulators, trading firms, and market participants to foster a sustainable trading environment. In this section, we delve into prospective directions that could redefine ethical standards in HFT and ensure long-term market integrity.

Firstly, advancements in technology will continue to push the envelope for what is possible in HFT, challenging existing ethical frameworks. It is essential to anticipate these changes and develop proactive measures to ensure that new technologies are integrated ethically. For instance, the rise of Artificial Intelligence (AI) and Machine Learning (ML) in trading algorithms demands strict oversight to prevent unintended market distortions. Implementing rigorous testing environments and ethical AI guidelines could mitigate risks associated with these powerful tools.

Another significant focus area is the transparency of algorithms and trading strategies. While the proprietary nature of algorithms is a competitive necessity, striking a balance between transparency and intellectual property rights is paramount. Regulators could adopt a tiered disclosure system where critical algorithmic parameters are shared in a controlled and secure manner with regulatory bodies, ensuring that these algorithms operate within ethical bounds without exposing sensitive competitive intelligence.

Market fairness can be further enhanced by leveling the playing field for all market participants. One prospective measure is the introduction of speed bumps or latency floors—deliberate delays in trade execution that reduce the advantage of faster traders and enhance market liquidity. These mechanisms not only promote fairness but also prioritize the quality of trades over sheer speed, potentially stabilizing market dynamics.

Regarding oversight, independent monitoring bodies specifically focused on HFT have the potential to revolutionize ethical standards in the industry. These bodies, armed with comprehensive market data and advanced monitoring tools, could provide real-time surveillance and offer immediate corrective interventions if unethical practices are detected. Integrating advanced data analytics and real-time monitoring would significantly enhance the capability to detect and respond to market manipulations swiftly.

Education and ethical training within HFT firms will likely play a crucial role in maintaining ethical practices moving forward. Creating an industry-wide culture of ethics through mandatory training programs, certifications, and continuous professional development initiatives would solidify the understanding and importance of ethical considerations among traders and developers alike. These programs could be standardized across the industry and supported by industry associations and regulatory bodies.

Moreover, the development of universal ethical standards tailored specifically for HFT practices would provide a vital roadmap for future compliance. While current regulations address broader market conduct, specific guidelines developed in collaboration with global financial regulators, industry leaders, and academic experts would be instrumental in addressing the nuances of HFT. These standards should be dynamic, evolving with technological advancements and market developments.

Regulatory sandboxes could serve as incubators for testing new HFT strategies under close supervision, allowing for innovation while ensuring adherence to ethical principles. These controlled environments would provide invaluable insights into the practical implications of new trading technologies and strategies before their broader market implementation, reducing the risk of ethical breaches.

From an international perspective, greater cooperation and harmonization of ethical standards across different jurisdictions are necessary. With HFT being a global phenomenon, inconsistencies in regulations across markets can create loopholes that unethical traders might exploit. International regulatory bodies, such as the International Organization of Securities Commissions (IOSCO), should spearhead efforts to align ethical standards, fostering a more cohesive global trading environment.

In summary, the future of ethical HFT practices hinges on embracing technological advancements, enhancing transparency, ensuring market fairness, and fostering a culture of ethics within the industry. Proactive regulation, advanced monitoring, robust education, and international cooperation will be the pillars upon which these ethical frameworks rest, guiding HFT towards a future that upholds market integrity and investor trust. As we move forward, these considerations will be instrumental in crafting a high-frequency trading landscape that is both ethically sound and economically efficient.

Chapter 12

Case Studies and Real-World Applications

This chapter presents a series of case studies and real-world applications of High-Frequency Trading (HFT). It examines the strategies of early HFT pioneers and their successes and failures. The chapter analyzes significant events like the Flash Crash of 2010 and regulatory responses to such incidents. It covers the role of HFT in various markets, including equities, foreign exchange, commodities, and futures. The impact of technological innovations on HFT is also explored, providing lessons learned and best practices from these real-world scenarios to offer a comprehensive understanding of HFT's practical applications.

12.1 Introduction to Case Studies in HFT

High-Frequency Trading (HFT) has been a transformative force in modern financial markets. This section aims to introduce readers to the critical role that real-world case studies play in understanding HFT's multifaceted landscape. By delving into specific instances of HFT applications, we can extract valuable insights that illustrate the practical, strategic, and ethical considerations inherent to this advanced trading approach.

What is High-Frequency Trading? Before exploring the case studies, it is essential to reestablish a foundational understanding of HFT. High-Frequency Trading involves the use of algorithms and sophisticated technological infrastructure to execute large volumes of trades at exceptionally high speeds. These trades are often initiated and completed in fractions of a second, exploiting minute market inefficiencies and price discrepancies that are imperceptible to traditional traders.

The importance of case studies in elucidating HFT practices cannot be overstated. Real-world examples provide tangible evidence of how theoretical principles and strategies are applied in practice. Through these narratives, readers can observe the dynamism and complexity of HFT, gaining a deeper appreciation for the factors that drive both success and failure in this domain.

Identifying Key Themes In this chapter, we will explore a variety of themes through different case studies. These themes include the evolution of HFT strategies, the technological arms race, regulatory challenges, and the ethical implications of ultra-fast trading. By compartmentalizing these themes, we aim to provide a structured and comprehensive analysis.

The first case studies will focus on the *early pioneers of HFT*, examining how initial innovations set the stage for future developments. These pioneers employed rudimentary algorithms and hardware, laying the groundwork for the sophisticated systems we see today. We will uncover their strategic decisions, examining both their successes and the limitations they faced.

Following this, we will delve into high-profile events such as the *Flash Crash of 2010*. This incident serves as a pivotal case study for understanding the systemic risks and potential consequences of HFT. By analyzing the causes and effects of the Flash Crash, we gain insight into the volatile nature of high-speed trading and the need for regulatory oversight.

In addition, we will look at *successful HFT firms* that have managed to thrive in the competitive environment of modern markets. By scrutinizing their strategies, technological innovations, and market adaptations, we can extract best practices and lessons learned. Contrarily, examining cases of HFT firms that faced significant setbacks will provide a balanced perspective, highlighting the pitfalls and challenges that traders must navigate.

The Role of Technology Given the inherent reliance on technology in HFT, our case studies will also examine the impact of technological advancements. From the adoption of cutting-edge hardware to the development of sophisticated algorithms, technology is the backbone of HFT. Understanding the technological evolution within these case studies will shed light on the continuous innovation required to maintain a competitive edge in the market.

Regulatory frameworks play a crucial role in shaping the HFT landscape. Case studies detailing *regulatory responses* to various HFT incidents will provide an understanding of how legal and ethical considerations affect trading behavior. These accounts will illustrate the delicate balance regulators must maintain between fostering innovation and protecting market integrity.

Lastly, we will consider the *practical applications of HFT across different markets*, including equities, foreign exchange, commodities, and futures. Each market presents unique opportunities and challenges for HFT, and examining these specific contexts will broaden our understanding of the adaptability and diversity of high-frequency trading strategies.

By the end of this section, readers will be equipped with a detailed understanding of the significance of case studies in HFT. They will see how practical experiences and historical events inform current practices and guide future developments. Through these narratives, the intricate tapestry of HFT will come to life, providing a richer, more nuanced perspective of this high-stakes arena.

12.2 Early HFT Pioneers and Their Strategies

The origins of High-Frequency Trading (HFT) can be traced back to the early 1990s when technological advancements began significantly reducing the time it took to execute trades. The pioneers of HFT identified the potential to exploit these technological improvements in ways that traditional trading methods could not match. This section delves into the strategies employed by these early adopters, who laid the groundwork for what would become a rapidly evolving industry.

Early HFT pioneers such as Jane Street, Renaissance Technologies, and Getco (now part of Virtu Financial) were among the first to realize the advantages of rapid trade execution. Their strategies often revolved around arbitrage opportunities, market-making, and exploiting inefficiencies through advanced algorithms. Each of these strategies leveraged technological infrastructures to achieve speeds unattainable by human traders.

One of the fundamental strategies was statistical arbitrage, which involves the identification of price anomalies between correlated assets. An example can be seen with equity pairs trading, where an HFT firm would simultaneously buy a temporarily undervalued stock while short selling an overvalued one. These positions are usually held for very short periods, with the trades executed in milliseconds. The mathematical models used often included mean reversion methodologies and other quantitative analysis techniques.

Another essential strategy was electronic market-making, which provided liquidity to the markets while earning the bid-ask spread. HFT market makers constantly submit buy and sell limit orders for various securities. By providing liquidity, they could capitalize on the transaction spread. This not only required the ability to process large volumes of data but also to update prices in real-time based on market movements and order book changes. The strategy was beneficial for both the traders and the market, as it improved liquidity and reduced spreads.

The pioneers also utilized low-latency arbitrage, which is the practice of exploiting price discrepancies between different exchanges or markets. To achieve this, firms constructed low-latency networks that connected different trading venues as quickly as possible. This sometimes involved laying down proprietary fiber optic lines or taking advantage of the latest microwave communication technology, drastically cutting down the time it took for trade signals to travel. By arbitraging these very short-lived discrepancies, firms could achieve consistent profitability.

Algorithmic execution strategies were designed to minimize market impact and reduce the cost of trading by breaking large orders into smaller fragments that were then executed over time or across multiple exchanges. These algorithms are often driven by complex statistical models that determine how to best execute trades without causing significant price movement. For instance, a volume-weighted average price (VWAP) strategy aims to execute orders in a manner that matches the volume profile of the market, thus achieving an execution price close to the market's average price over a specific time horizon.

The early pioneers faced numerous challenges, including market data latency, execution risks, and the continuous need for technological upgrades. However, their relentless focus on speed, technology, and strategy refinement allowed them to remain profitable and sustain a competitive advantage. These firms often reinvested profits back into technology, thereby fueling a cycle of continuous improvement and innovation.

Implementing a successful HFT strategy also required profound expertise in both quantitative finance and computer science. The development teams comprised mathematicians, statisticians, physicists, and computer scientists who collaborated to create sophisticated trading algorithms. Such interdisciplinary collaboration was pivotal to addressing the multifaceted challenges posed by HFT.

The trailblazing efforts of these early pioneers set the stage for the evolution of HFT. Their innovative approaches not only demonstrated how technology could transform trading but also established the foundational principles upon which modern HFT strategies are built. By understanding these early strategies, we gain insights into the principles of speed, data processing, and risk management that continue to drive high-frequency trading today.

12.3 The Flash Crash of 2010

On May 6, 2010, an unprecedented and highly significant event shook the foundations of the global financial markets: the Flash Crash. During a brief 36-minute period, the Dow Jones Industrial Average (DJIA) plummeted nearly 1,000 points, roughly 9%, only to rebound rapidly. This sudden and severe market disruption highlighted critical vulnerabilities within the market's structure and raised questions about the role of High-Frequency Trading (HFT) in exacerbating such situations.

The events leading up to the Flash Crash were multifaceted, involving a confluence of market conditions and technological mechanisms. In the weeks prior, concerns about the European sovereign debt crisis had instilled a heightened level of market anxiety. On the day of the crash, the market was already volatile, experiencing significant fluctuations.

The initial trigger for the crash was identified as a large sell order initiated by a mutual fund company using an algorithm designed to protect against market movements by executing trades based on volume rather than price. This sell order, totaling approximately $4.1 billion in E-mini S&P 500 futures contracts, was executed in an algorithmic manner that massively contributed to liquidity disruptions.

Algorithmic Strategies and Their Impact

To fully appreciate the dynamics of the Flash Crash, it is essential to delve into the mechanics of the algorithmic strategies at play. HFT firms use complex algorithms to capitalize on minuscule price discrepancies by rapidly buying and selling shares, oftentimes executing thousands of trades per second. In normal circumstances, these strategies provide liquidity and enhance market efficiency. However, during the Flash Crash, they inadvertently contributed to a liquidity vacuum.

As the large sell order from the mutual fund company was executed, it quickly absorbed available liquidity. HFT algorithms detected the liquidity stress and sought to mitigate risk by retracting bids or selling off positions, resulting in an exacerbation of downward price pressure. This automated withdrawal of liquidity was magnified by the fact that many HFT strategies also incorporate momentum-based algorithms, which amplify trends by further selling into a declining market.

Regulatory and Market Responses

The extraordinary nature of the Flash Crash prompted immediate scrutiny from regulatory bodies, including the Securities and Exchange Commission (SEC) and the Commodity Futures Trading Commission (CFTC). The joint report released by these agencies detailed the intricate interplay between various market participants and provided a comprehensive account of the incident.

One of the critical findings of the report was the identification of the so-called "hot-potato" effect, where HFT firms rapidly traded the same positions back and forth among themselves, drastically amplifying volume without contributing meaningful liquidity. This phenomenon led regulators to reconsider existing safeguards and market structure.

In response to the Flash Crash, several regulatory measures were instituted to prevent recurrence. Among these were the introduction of circuit breakers and the implementation of the Limit Up-Limit Down (LULD) mechanism. Circuit breakers provide a temporary halt to trading when significant price movements occur within a short timeframe, allowing markets to stabilize. The LULD mechanism prevents trades from occurring outside of a specified price band, thus reducing the impact of sudden and extreme price swings.

Technological and Structural Considerations

The Flash Crash underscored the importance of robustness in market infrastructure and the potential pitfalls of technological advancements in trading. The event highlighted that while HFT can enhance liquidity under normal conditions, it can also precipitate severe dislocations when market equilibrium is disrupted.

Technological innovations, such as co-location services and direct market access, were scrutinized for their role in facilitating the rapid execution of trades, which may amplify market instability. Co-location allows HFT firms to place their servers in close proximity to the exchange's servers, thereby reducing latency and gaining a competitive edge. While advantageous in terms of execution speed, this practice was criticized for potentially contributing to systemic risks.

Moreover, the event drew attention to the need for more effective oversight of algorithmic trading strategies. The interplay between various algorithms, especially in a fragmented market where multiple trading venues exist, necessitated a reevaluation of coordination mechanisms among different market centers.

Educational Takeaways

The Flash Crash of 2010 serves as a pivotal case study in understanding the complex dynamics and risks associated with high-frequency trading. It exemplifies the unintended consequences of advanced trading technologies and algorithms, as well as the critical need for robust regulatory frameworks.

For both novice and experienced investors, the Flash Crash provides invaluable lessons on the importance of market liquidity, the interplay of various market participants, and the potential for technological innovations to both benefit and disrupt market stability. By studying such real-world incidents, traders and investors can better appreciate the intricacies of modern market mechanics and the paramount importance of risk management in an increasingly automated trading landscape.

As we discuss HFT's role in different markets and explore further case studies, the insights from the Flash Crash continue to inform our understanding and drive ongoing improvements in market structure and oversight. This event remains a cornerstone in the discourse on safeguarding financial markets in the age of algorithmic trading.

12.4 High-Profile HFT Firms: Successes and Failures

High-frequency trading (HFT) has evolved significantly since its inception, with various firms emerging as both exemplars of success and cautionary tales of failure. These firms leveraged cutting-edge technology and advanced mathematical models to execute trades within microseconds. Their journey through the peaks and troughs of the financial markets offers invaluable insights into the dynamics of HFT. This section delves into the narratives of some of the most prominent HFT firms, highlighting the factors behind their triumphs and tribulations.

At the pinnacle of HFT's rise were firms like Virtu Financial, a paragon of consistency and profitability. Founded in 2008, Virtu Financial rapidly became renowned for its impressive track record of profitability, boasting a nearly perfect record of daily trading gains. One of Virtu's significant advantages lay in its technological infrastructure, which minimized latency and capitalized on arbitrage opportunities across different markets. Their ability to process vast amounts of market data in real-time allowed them to make instantaneous trading decisions, affording them a competitive edge. Virtu's success underscores the importance of state-of-the-art technology, risk management, and a robust strategy focused on liquidity provision and market-making rather than speculative trading.

Another exemplar of HFT success is Citadel Securities, a subsidiary of the hedge fund behemoth Citadel LLC. Citadel Securities distinguished itself through its diversified approach, integrating HFT with traditional asset management and execution services. Their multifaceted strategy allowed them to weather the volatility of financial markets better. The firm's top-notch team of quants, software engineers, and risk managers played a crucial role in developing sophisticated algorithms that adapt to changing market conditions swiftly. Citadel's ability to continuously innovate, adapt and manage risk effectively highlights the core attributes required for sustained success in the HFT domain.

On the other end of the spectrum, Knight Capital's story serves as a stark reminder of the potential pitfalls within HFT. Once a leading market maker, Knight Capital's ordeal in August 2012 illustrated how technological mishaps could lead to catastrophic losses. A software glitch in the firm's trading platform resulted in errant trades that inflated its positions by over $7 billion within forty-five minutes, culminating in losses exceeding $440 million. This incident starkly exposed the vulnerabilities associated with intricate and automated trading systems. Despite subsequent recovery and eventual acquisition by Getco LLC, Knight Capital's experience emphasized the critical need for rigorous system checks, comprehensive risk management protocols, and the importance of maintaining a failsafe mechanism to avert such debacles.

A contrasting narrative can be seen with the rise and fall of Tradeworx, once a burgeoning HFT firm founded by Manoj Narang. Tradeworx aimed to democratize HFT by making high-frequency trading technology available to a broader array of market participants. Initially successful, the firm struggled as the HFT landscape became increasingly competitive and regulatory scrutiny intensified. Tradeworx's eventual retreat from the HFT scene underlines the evolving nature of regulatory responses and market competition, which may disrupt even the most innovative business models. This underscores the necessity for firms to not only maintain technological prowess but also be adaptable to regulatory shifts and competitive dynamics.

Conversely, DRW Trading, an HFT and proprietary trading firm, managed to sustain its position by maintaining a diversified set of trading strategies and a focus on future-oriented markets such as cryptocurrencies. Led by Don Wilson, DRW's perseverance and strategic foresight allowed it to transition successfully through various market phases and technological advancements. DRW's experience underscores the importance of diversification, strategic foresight, and the integration of emerging market trends into their trading paradigms to remain competitive.

Analyzing the trajectories of these high-profile HFT firms reveals several common threads that delineate the boundary between success and failure in high-frequency trading. Foremost is the paramount importance of technology and infrastructure; firms that invest substantially in enhancing their technological capabilities consistently outperform their peers. Equally crucial is a comprehensive and dynamic approach to risk management, enabling firms to mitigate potential pitfalls associated with rapid and automated trading. Furthermore, the ability to innovate continually and adapt to regulatory changes plays a decisive role in sustaining long-term success. Finally, maintaining a diversified approach and the flexibility to pivot according to emerging trends can safeguard firms against market and regulatory upheavals.

The stories of these firms provide a detailed tapestry of lessons learned within the high-stakes arena of high-frequency trading, underscoring success factors and failure triggers in equal measure.

12.5 Regulatory Responses to HFT Incidents

The rapid growth and complexity of High-Frequency Trading (HFT) have presented unique challenges to financial regulators globally. In response to notable market disruptions and the increasing influence of HFT on market dynamics, regulatory bodies have undertaken several measures aiming to mitigate potential risks. This section examines the various regulatory responses to HFT incidents, highlighting key initiatives and their implications for markets and traders.

The financial markets witnessed a paradigm shift with the emergence of HFT, leading regulators to adapt their oversight mechanisms. One of the most significant regulatory responses followed the Flash Crash of May 6, 2010, an event that underscored the vulnerabilities introduced by high-speed trading. During the Flash Crash, major U.S. stock indices plummeted and recovered within minutes, causing widespread market turmoil.

Following this event, the U.S. Securities and Exchange Commission (SEC) and the Commodity Futures Trading Commission (CFTC) conducted a thorough investigation. Their joint report identified that a significant sell algorithm, executed by a mutual fund company, had triggered a sequence of automated trading responses, exacerbated by the lack of liquidity from market makers and HFT firms. As a direct consequence, the SEC implemented several regulatory changes.

One such change was the introduction of circuit breakers, also known as the "Limit Up-Limit Down" (LULD) mechanism, effective June 2013. This mechanism aims to prevent erroneous trades by halting trading when prices move too rapidly beyond predefined thresholds. LULD provides a crucial buffer ensuring that trading pauses temporarily, giving market participants the chance to assess and respond to rapid price movements.

In addition to circuit breakers, the SEC introduced Rule 15c3-5, commonly referred to as the Market Access Rule. This rule, effective in late 2010, requires brokers and dealers to implement risk management controls before providing clients with market access. The goal was to ensure that all orders are subject to automated pre-trade risk checks, preventing erroneous or manipulative orders from disrupting the market.

Another notable regulatory response was the enhancement of the Consolidated Audit Trail (CAT). Implemented in 2016, CAT aims to collect comprehensive data on all orders, quotes, and trades across U.S. equity and options markets. By enabling regulators to track and analyze the entire lifecycle of trades, CAT provides invaluable insight into market behavior, facilitating the identification and mitigation of misconduct or systemic risks.

Beyond the U.S., European regulatory initiatives have also sought to address the challenges posed by HFT. The European Union's Markets in Financial Instruments Directive II (MiFID II), which took effect in January 2018, introduced stringent regulations for HFT firms. MiFID II mandates that HFT firms must be authorized and must adhere to high standards of systems and controls, including maintaining accurate records of trading algorithms and ensuring effective risk management protocols are in place.

Additionally, MiFID II requires firms engaging in algorithmic trading to ensure their algorithms are robustly tested, monitored, and cannot contribute to disorderly trading conditions. This regulation emphasizes the obligation of HFT firms to prevent market abuse and maintain market integrity.

In Asia, countries such as Japan and Australia have also been proactive in their regulatory approach towards HFT. Japan's Financial Services Agency (FSA) has implemented measures requiring HFT firms to register and subject themselves to supervisory controls. These measures include mandatory provisioning of order data and system resilience reports, aimed at enhancing transparency and stability in markets.

Australia's Securities and Investments Commission (ASIC) introduced guidelines to monitor and regulate the impact of HFT activities. These guidelines include minimum resting times for orders and stringent requirements for algorithm testing and certification before deployment.

Collectively, these regulatory responses have shaped the landscape of HFT, striving to balance innovation with market stability. By implementing mechanisms to curb excessive volatility and ensuring rigorous oversight of trading algorithms, regulatory bodies intend to cultivate a fair and orderly market environment.

The diverse range of regulatory initiatives highlights the global effort to harness the benefits of HFT while mitigating potential disruptions. For traders and firms operating within these frameworks, understanding and adhering to these regulations is imperative, not only for compliance but also for maintaining a sustainable and resilient trading environment.

12.6 HFT in Equity Markets

High-Frequency Trading (HFT) in equity markets represents one of the most prominent and scrutinized aspects of modern financial trading. By leveraging cutting-edge technology and algorithmic strategies, HFT firms aim to capitalize on minute price discrepancies at unprecedented speeds, often completing trades in microseconds. This section delves deeply into how HFT operates within equity markets, the strategies employed, and the broader implications for market dynamics and participants.

The primary objective for HFT firms in equity markets is to exploit fleeting arbitrage opportunities that arise due to price differences across exchanges or temporal inefficiencies. This necessitates the deployment of sophisticated systems capable of processing large sets of data, performing complex calculations, and executing trades almost instantaneously. One common strategy is statistical arbitrage, which involves constructing mathematical models to predict price movements based on historical data, correlations, and patterns. To ensure success, HFT firms must maintain and continuously update their models to accurately reflect ever-changing market conditions.

Another prevalent strategy is market making, where HFT firms provide liquidity by offering to buy and sell securities at publicly quoted prices. These firms profit from the bid-ask spread, which, although typically minuscule, becomes substantial when multiplied by the enormous volumes traded. Market makers also enhance market efficiency by narrowing spreads and facilitating smoother transaction flows. However, the practice requires sophisticated risk management techniques to mitigate potential losses from adverse price movements and quote fading, where the displayed price rapidly changes before a trade can be executed.

Latent arbitrage is another notable strategy utilized by HFT firms in equity markets. This approach involves the tactical placement of orders across multiple exchanges to benefit from slight delays (latency) in information dissemination. By having a fraction-of-a-second advantage, HFT firms can act on new information before it is fully reflected in all market prices, thereby profiting from the temporary mispricing.

The implementation of HFT in equity markets is not without controversy. Critics argue that HFT can exacerbate market volatility, particularly during periods of uncertainty or stress. The Flash Crash of 2010 serves as a poignant example, where the sudden withdrawal of liquidity by HFT firms, amidst a cascade of rapid-fire trades, contributed to a precipitous and erratic decline in stock prices. Such incidents have prompted regulators to scrutinize HFT practices and implement measures aimed at mitigating systemic risks and ensuring market stability.

To understand the impact of HFT on traditional market participants, it is essential to consider the role of order types and routing. HFT firms often employ a variety of order types, including limit orders, market orders, and immediate-or-cancel orders, to tactically navigate the market landscape. The ability to route orders to different trading venues allows HFT firms to minimize execution costs, avoid detection by other market participants, and capitalize on the most favorable conditions available.

In recent years, the emergence of dark pools—private exchanges where trade details are not publicly disclosed—has introduced new dimensions to HFT in equity markets. HFT firms actively participate in these venues to execute sizeable trades with reduced market impact and decreased likelihood of detection by competitors. While dark pools contribute to overall market liquidity, they also raise concerns about transparency and fairness, prompting ongoing regulatory scrutiny and the enactment of new rules.

Technological advancements have been a driving force behind the proliferation and evolution of HFT. From co-location services, where HFT firms place their servers in close proximity to exchange data centers to minimize latency, to the development of ultra-low latency networks and optimized algorithms, the relentless pursuit of speed and efficiency defines the HFT landscape. Investments in proprietary trading platforms, exchange connectivity, and real-time data analytics enable HFT firms to maintain a competitive edge.

Despite the complexities and controversies, HFT's presence in equity markets has yielded several benefits. The increased liquidity provided by HFT firms can lead to tighter spreads and reduced transaction costs for investors. Additionally, the speed and efficiency of HFT have contributed to more precise and timely price discovery, reflecting market conditions with greater accuracy.

As the landscape of HFT continues to evolve, both opportunities and challenges persist. The ever-advancing technological frontier presents ongoing potential for innovation and enhanced trading strategies. However, market participants and regulators must remain vigilant to address the risks associated with high-speed trading and to ensure that equity markets operate in a fair, orderly, and resilient manner.

Ultimately, understanding HFT in equity markets requires a nuanced appreciation of its multi-faceted nature. From the intricate algorithms and sophisticated technologies driving its execution to the regulatory frameworks and market conditions shaping its practice, HFT remains a dynamic and critical component of contemporary equity market structure. By examining both the benefits and potential pitfalls, one can gain a comprehensive perspective on the significant role HFT plays in the modern financial ecosystem.

12.7 HFT in Foreign Exchange Markets

High-frequency trading (HFT) has exerted a profound influence on the foreign exchange (FX) markets, transforming the way currency pairs are traded. Unlike equities which trade on centralized exchanges, the FX market operates as an over-the-counter (OTC) market, meaning trades occur directly between parties and not through a centralized exchange. This unique structure has both facilitated and complicated the integration of HFT strategies within the FX domain.

High-frequency traders in FX markets rely upon ultra-fast execution speeds to exploit minute differences in currency prices across different venues. This process, known as arbitrage, involves simultaneous buying and selling of equivalent assets to profit from price discrepancies. Let's delve deeper into how HFT manifests itself in FX trading, the instruments commonly used, and the specific strategies employed by high-frequency traders.

The primary instruments in FX HFT are currency pairs, which include major pairs like EUR/USD, GBP/USD, and USD/JPY. The choice of currency pairs depends on factors such as liquidity, volatility, and the spread between the bid and ask prices. Major pairs are preferred due to their higher liquidity, which is crucial for the rapid trading required in HFT.

One prevalent strategy in FX HFT is statistical arbitrage, which leverages sophisticated algorithms to identify and exploit statistical inefficiencies between currency pairs. These algorithms analyze vast amounts of market data, including past price movements, order book information, and macroeconomic indicators, to generate trading signals. The algorithms are designed to execute trades in milliseconds, often leveraging colocation services to minimize latency.

Consider the example of triangular arbitrage, a specific type of statistical arbitrage unique to FX markets. Triangular arbitrage takes advantage of discrepancies in the exchange rates between three different currencies. If the rate at which one currency can be exchanged for a second, and the second for a third, exceeds the direct rate between the first and third currencies, a risk-free profit opportunity arises. For instance, if the exchange rates between USD to EUR, EUR to GBP, and GBP to USD allow for a higher return when converting through intermediaries than direct conversion, an HFT algorithm would rapidly execute the needed trades to capitalize on this spread.

Another key strategy in FX HFT is market making, where traders provide liquidity to the market by continuously quoting buy and sell prices of a particular currency pair. By doing so, they earn the spread between the bid and ask prices. The success of market making hinges on the ability to maintain a net-neutral position, thereby avoiding excessive exposure to market risk. Market makers must also manage their inventory efficiently to prevent excessive holding costs or adverse price movements against their positions.

Additionally, HFT firms in FX markets often engage in event-driven strategies, which revolve around trading on economic news releases and geopolitical events. Given the global nature of FX markets, events such as central bank announcements, employment reports, and political instability can cause significant price swings. HFT systems detect these events through high-speed news feeds and parse the information using natural language processing algorithms. In reaction to these discoveries, the algorithms execute trades within fractions of a second to capitalize on the resulting volatility before slower traders can react.

Despite the advantages of HFT in FX markets, this trading style faces several challenges. The decentralized nature of FX trading results in disparities in price feeds from different liquidity providers, complicating the process of identifying true arbitrage opportunities. Regulators across various jurisdictions have also sought to impose measures to prevent potential market manipulation and ensure fair trading practices. For example, the European Securities and Markets Authority (ESMA) has introduced regulations such as MiFID II, aiming to enhance the transparency and stability of financial markets, including FX trading.

The technological arms race in HFT demands constant innovation. High-frequency traders are continually investing in cutting-edge technology such as machine learning algorithms, hardware acceleration, and quantum computing to stay ahead of their competitors. Machine learning models particularly enhance the predictive power of trading algorithms by identifying complex patterns in historical trade data, thus improving the accuracy of trade signals.

While HFT brings undeniable liquidity and efficiency benefits to FX markets, its presence also raises concerns regarding market stability. The rapid buying and selling activity inherent to HFT could potentially exacerbate market shocks or lead to currency flash crashes, as witnessed in the 2016 GBP/USD flash crash.

As we reflect on the integration of HFT within the FX markets, it becomes apparent that the benefits must be weighed against the risks. Balancing innovation with regulatory oversight remains crucial to harnessing the full potential of HFT while safeguarding market integrity.

12.8 HFT in Commodity and Futures Markets

High-Frequency Trading (HFT) has made a significant impact in commodity and futures markets, transforming the landscape with its need for speed and precision. This section delves into the intricate mechanisms through which HFT operates within these markets, examines the various strategies employed, analyzes the implications on market liquidity, volatility, and price discovery, and discusses regulatory considerations specific to commodities and futures.

In commodity markets, HFT strategies often exploit price discrepancies between related commodities or between commodities and their derivative contracts. These strategies, commonly referred to as arbitrage strategies, capitalize on inefficiencies to generate profits with minimal risk. For example, a trader might simultaneously buy and sell wheat futures on different exchanges to profit from slight differences in prices. The speed at which HFT can execute these trades is key, enabling traders to capture opportunities that may only exist for fractions of a second.

The futures market, characterized by contracts to buy or sell an asset at a predetermined future date and price, is particularly conducive to

HFT. Futures contracts are standardized and traded on centralized exchanges, providing the liquidity and transparency conducive to high-frequency strategies. Common techniques include market-making, where HFT firms provide liquidity by continuously bidding and offering at different price levels. In doing so, they earn the spread between the buy and sell prices while assuming the risk of holding positions for short periods.

Consider the following mathematical model often employed in HFT within futures markets:

$$P_{\text{profit}} = \sum_{i=1}^{N} (P_{\text{sell},i} - P_{\text{buy},i}) - C_{\text{transaction},i}$$

where P_{profit} is the total profit from N trades, $P_{\text{sell},i}$ and $P_{\text{buy},i}$ are the sell and buy prices of each individual trade, and $C_{\text{transaction},i}$ represents the associated transaction costs. The objective is to maximize P_{profit} by executing trades with tight spreads and low costs.

HFT's impact on liquidity in commodity and futures markets has been notable. By providing continuous buy and sell orders, HFT firms increase the volume of available trading activity, often reducing bid-ask spreads and making it cheaper for other market participants to trade. However, the benefits are nuanced and come with the potential for increased short-term volatility. The massive volume of HFT orders can overwhelm markets, particularly during stress periods, leading to sudden and sharp price movements.

An intriguing aspect of HFT in these markets is the role of co-location, where firms place their servers physically close to exchange servers to minimize latency. The proximity—potentially mere meters—ensures that orders are executed milliseconds faster than competitors' orders. This setup requires significant capital investment but can immensely improve the chances of capturing profitable trades.

Regulatory frameworks have responded in various ways to the rise of HFT in the commodity and futures markets. The Commodity Futures Trading Commission (CFTC) in the United States, for instance, has implemented rules to increase market transparency and stability. These include requirements for HFT firms to register as swap dealers or major swap participants, depending on their activity levels, and to adhere to new risk management standards that mitigate the chances of disruptive trading.

A real-world example of HFT influence is the 2011 Silver Futures flash crash. For a brief period, the price of silver futures plummeted by almost 12% within minutes before recovering. An investigation revealed that HFT algorithms had exacerbated this dramatic price swing, reacting to a sell-order spike and amplifying the downward spiral through microsecond-level trades.

As we explore the implications and outcomes of HFT in commodity and futures markets, it is crucial to remember the lessons learned. Effective risk management, the importance of robust regulatory frameworks, and continual technological advancements remain central themes. Firms engaging in HFT must continuously refine their algorithms and strategies, adapting to evolving market conditions while maintaining a keen awareness of the broader impact their activities may have on market stability.

High-Frequency Trading has undoubtedly revolutionized commodity and futures markets. The balance of speed, strategy, and regulation continues to shape its contribution to modern financial markets, propelling not only the profitability of active firms but also challenging the stability and fairness of trading ecosystems.

12.9 Technological Innovations and Their Impact

Technological innovations have fundamentally reshaped the landscape of High-Frequency Trading (HFT), propelling it into an era where milliseconds and even microseconds can mean the difference between profit and loss. The emergence and rapid evolution of sophisticated technologies have enabled HFT firms to execute orders at unprecedented speeds, manage vast volumes of data, and implement complex algorithms with remarkable precision. This section delves into the key technological advancements that have driven the progress of HFT and examines their profound impact on the trading ecosystem.

At the heart of HFT lies the continuous pursuit of reducing latency — the delay between the initiation and execution of a trading order. To achieve zero latency, or as close to it as possible, HFT firms have leveraged a multitude of cutting-edge technologies. One significant advancement is the deployment of co-location services. By placing their trading servers physically close to exchange servers, HFT firms have significantly reduced the time required for order transmission. Co-location reduces the physical distance that data packets must travel, thereby minimizing latency. Exchanges like the New York Stock Exchange (NYSE) and NASDAQ offer co-location services, providing HFT firms with the proximity advantage necessary for ultra-fast trading.

Another pivotal innovation is the development of custom hardware, particularly Field-Programmable Gate Arrays (FPGAs) and Application-Specific Integrated Circuits (ASICs). These technologies allow for the direct execution of trading algorithms at the hardware level, bypassing the relatively slower software-based processing. FPGAs can be programmed to perform specific trading tasks with extreme efficiency, enabling nanosecond-level order execution. ASICs, on the other hand, are designed for specific applications such as market data analysis and order matching, providing customized solutions that further reduce latency and enhance performance.

In addition to hardware advancements, the optimization of network infrastructure has played a crucial role in the evolution of HFT. The use of microwave and millimeter-wave networks has garnered significant attention due to their ability to transmit data faster than traditional fiber optic cables. These wireless technologies can establish direct line-of-sight communication between major financial centers, such as New York and Chicago, reducing signal latency by leveraging the curvature of the Earth. The implementation of such networks represents a significant step towards achieving near-zero latency communication.

The rise of algorithmic trading has also been bolstered by advancements in machine learning and artificial intelligence (AI). Machine learning algorithms can analyze historical and real-time market data to identify patterns and predict price movements with greater accuracy. AI-driven strategies enable HFT firms to adapt to changing market conditions dynamically, optimizing their trading decisions based on complex data interactions that would be impossible to process manually. These intelligent systems continuously learn and improve, offering a competitive edge in the fast-paced world of HFT.

High-speed data feeds and advanced market data analytics tools are another cornerstone of technological innovation in HFT. Access to low-latency data feeds from multiple exchanges allows HFT firms to monitor market conditions in real-time and respond instantaneously. This requires robust data analytics platforms capable of processing vast quantities of data within microseconds. Such platforms employ sophisticated techniques, including time-series analysis and high-frequency signal processing, to derive actionable insights from raw market data.

Parallel processing and the use of distributed computing architectures further enhance the computational capabilities of HFT firms. By distributing the computational load across multiple processors and servers, HFT systems can handle complex calculations and large datasets more efficiently. Technologies such as Graphics Processing Units (GPUs) and cloud computing resources offer scalable and flexible solutions, enabling HFT systems to maximize throughput and minimize latency.

Technological innovation has not only enhanced the capabilities of HFT firms but has also had a significant impact on market dynamics and structure. The increased speed and volume of trading facilitated by these technologies have led to heightened market liquidity and tighter bid-ask spreads. However, this has also introduced new challenges, such as the potential for market fragmentation and the increased risk of market manipulation through techniques like spoofing and layering.

Moreover, the rapid pace of technological advancement has necessitated ongoing regulatory scrutiny and adaptation. Regulators must continuously monitor and address the implications of new technologies to ensure market integrity and protect investors. Efforts to implement circuit breakers, enhance transparency, and establish fair access to market data are crucial in maintaining a balanced trading environment.

In essence, the technological innovations driving HFT have revolutionized the financial markets, enabling unprecedented levels of speed, efficiency, and complexity in trading. These advancements have equipped HFT firms with the tools to capitalize on even the smallest market inefficiencies, fundamentally altering the competitive landscape. As technology continues to evolve, so too will the strategies and capabilities of HFT, making it imperative for market participants and regulators alike to stay abreast of these developments and their far-reaching implications.

The implications of these technological innovations reach beyond the financial markets themselves, influencing the broader economy and the way businesses operate. Enhanced market efficiency can lead to more accurate pricing of financial instruments, which in turn impacts investment decisions, corporate financing, and the allocation of resources. The continuous feedback loop between technology and market practices drives the evolution of financial systems, underscoring the importance of innovation in fostering economic growth and stability.

12.10 Lessons Learned and Best Practices from Real-World Scenarios

The exploration of High-Frequency Trading (HFT) in real-world scenarios reveals not only the profound impact of technological advancements on market dynamics but also the essential lessons that can guide future endeavors in the domain. The lessons learned from various historical events and practical applications can serve as a foundation for developing more robust and sophisticated trading strategies. This section delves into key takeaways and best practices that have emerged from the evaluation of HFT activities.

One of the pivotal lessons from the case studies is the indispensable role of speed in HFT. The consistent drive towards minimizing latency has underscored the importance of cutting-edge technology in executing trades. For instance, the Flash Crash of 2010 demonstrated that milliseconds could be the difference between profit and significant loss. It has become evident that HFT firms must invest continuously in state-of-the-art infrastructure, including low-latency networks and high-performance computing systems. By leveraging the fastest possible connections, traders can exploit fleeting market inefficiencies more effectively.

Another crucial aspect is the importance of risk management. The volatile nature of HFT demands that firms implement sophisticated risk management frameworks. The Flash Crash further highlighted that automated trading systems need robust fail-safes and contingency plans to prevent cascading failures. Real-time monitoring systems should be in place to detect any anomalies that could potentially lead to substantial financial repercussions. By integrating comprehensive risk assessment models and real-time oversight mechanisms, HFT players can mitigate the risks associated with rapid trading activities.

The case studies also underscore the importance of regulatory compliance. The ever-evolving landscape of financial regulations necessitates that HFT firms remain vigilant and adaptive. Regulatory bodies have introduced various measures post-Flash Crash to curb the potential for market disruptions caused by HFT. This has included mandating circuit breakers, imposing latency floors, and enhancing transparency requirements. Firms must develop proactive compliance strategies, regularly updating their algorithms and trading practices to align with the latest regulatory standards. This adaptation not only ensures legality but also fosters market stability and integrity.

Furthermore, the competitive nature of HFT has emphasized the significance of innovative trading strategies. Historical analysis of successful HFT firms reveals that innovation, rather than mere replication of existing strategies, creates sustainable competitive advantages. The ability to devise unique algorithms that can identify and capitalize on novel trading opportunities is paramount. Firms should encourage research and development, fostering an environment where creativity and technological ingenuity are paramount.

Technology's role in HFT extends beyond speed and innovation to include data analysis and machine learning. The vast amounts of data processed by HFT firms can be harnessed to refine trading models and improve predictive accuracy. Machine learning algorithms, for instance, can optimize parameter settings in trading strategies dynamically, based on historical data and real-time market conditions. The effective use of data analytics tools helps in uncovering patterns and trends that are not immediately visible, allowing for a more informed decision-making process.

Collaboration and knowledge sharing within the HFT community are also best practices that should not be overlooked. By participating in industry forums and engaging in dialogue with other market participants, firms can stay abreast of the latest trends, technological advancements, and regulatory developments. This collective wisdom provides a deeper understanding of market intricacies and helps in refining individual strategies.

Lastly, ethical considerations and market impact awareness are essential components of responsible HFT. The cases examined underline that HFT should not merely focus on profitability but also on contributing to market efficiency and liquidity. Ethical trading practices and a thorough consideration of the broader market impact can enhance the reputation and sustainability of HFT operations. Engaging in practices that distort the market or exploit vulnerabilities could lead to stricter regulations and erode public trust.

Reflecting on these lessons, HFT firms are encouraged to adopt a holistic approach that integrates technological prowess, risk management, regulatory compliance, innovation, data analytics, community collaboration, and ethical trading. By internalizing these practices, firms can not only enhance their profitability but also contribute positively to the financial markets' overall health and stability, ensuring a more resilient and fair trading environment for all participants.